Poverty in Nigeria

Causes, Manifestations and Alleviation Strategies

Published by
Adonis & Abbey Publishers Ltd
P.O. Box 43418
London
SE11 4XZ
http://www.adonis-abbey.com
Email: editor@adonis-abbey.com

Nigerian office:
35A Bode Thomas,
Surulere, Lagos
Tel: +234 1 8950040

First Edition, May 2008

British Library Cataloguing-in-Publication Data
A catalogue record for this book is available from the British Library

ISBN: 9781906704018(HB)

Printed and bound in Great Britain

Poverty in Nigeria

Causes, Manifestations and Alleviation Strategies

Edited by

Mustapha C. Duze, Habu Mohammed & Ibrahim A. Kiyawa

Adonis & Abbey
Publishers Ltd

Table of Contents

Foreword

Poverty is the most serious global problem which adversely affects sustainable development in the developing world. As far back as 1944, the International Labour Organization (ILO) in its Philadelphia Declaration stated that "poverty constitutes a danger to prosperity everywhere". Indeed, the world summit on sustainable development in Rio de Janeiro in 1992 identified poverty as the most important factor militating against sustainable development and, therefore, called for its eradication/reduction.

Poverty and diseases are today the causes of many social, economic, political and environmental ills of the world, particularly in the developing economies, and most particularly in the Sub-Saharan Africa. Reports from international organizations show that the proportion of poor people in total population is widening with over half of the people in the developing countries living below the poverty line. For example, a World Bank report around 1999 indicated that the Nigerian Human Development Index (HDI) was 0.416 and that about 70% of the populace lived below the bread line, often considered to be below US$1.00 a day. It is believed that the proportion of the Nigerian population living below this poverty line in the Northern parts of the country is higher than this national average; more so in the North-west geo-political zone of the country.

As Faculty in a University located in the North-western Nigeria, the Faculty of Social and Management Sciences, Bayero University, Kano, took it as a challenge to conduct studies whose results could show the way out of the poverty bondage the Northwest geo-political zone, the North and the country as a whole are suffering from. It is a book project that is aimed at rooting out the causes and manifestations of poverty in Nigeria and beyond, with a view to finding concrete and practicable solutions in line with the targets set in the United Nations' Millennium Development Goals (MDGs).Chapter contributors have been studying issues on poverty at different levels for many years and, for this reason, they are well qualified to, theoretically and empirically, do justice to their chosen topics for the achievement of the overall objectives of the book project.

This book entitled *Poverty in Nigeria: Causes, Manifestations and Alleviation Strategies* is the fourth in the series of books project embarked upon by the Faculty, comprising of five pace-setting scholarly books. The book covers seventeen chapters, addressing the nature, causes, manifestations, and the alleviation/eradication strategies to be put in place by policy makers at all levels. Each of the 17 chapters covers conceptual explanation, discussion of the causes of poverty and its characteristics and manifestations as well as strategies to be used for poverty eradication/alleviation in Nigeria and other developing economies. The book would be of immense benefit to government agencies responsible for poverty eradication/alleviation, policy makers, Non-Governmental Organizations

(NGOs) waging war against poverty and students of political economy, history, sociology, and development economics, among others, at all levels. This collection being volume one, it is hoped that volume two of the book would cover other serious issues on poverty and its eradication/alleviation.

I would like to thank the contributors of chapters to this book for their input to the Nigerian version of the global fight against poverty. I also appreciate the commitment and dedication of the three editors of the book, especially Dr. Habu Mohammed who served as a co-editor and coordinator of the project. My colleagues in the Deanery, the administrative staff of the Faculty and the generality of the Faculty membership deserve commendation for their support in seeing to the success of this pace-setting book project.

On behalf of the Faculty members, I would want to express our propound gratitude to the Vice Chancellor, Professor Attahiru M. Jega, and his management team for the moral and financial support the Faculty enjoys from the university management. In fact the idea behind the publication of this book was initiated by the Vice Chancellor when he encouraged the Faculty to make an entry for the UK/British Council research grant on the "Global Fight against Poverty". While we await the outcome of the assessment conducted on the entries for the grant, it is to the credit of the Vice Chancellor that his proud Faculty has taken the challenge of publishing this book on the same subject matter.

Kabiru Isa Dandago, PhD, ACA, ACTI, MNES, MNIM, MBEN
Dean, Faculty of Social and Management Sciences (FSMS),
Bayero University, Kano- Nigeria
18th January, 2008.

Preface

The increasing rate of poverty in the Third World countries in general and Africa in particular is a source of concern not only to policy makers, scholars (local and international), state and non state actors, including NGOs and social groups, but also among the poor themselves. This concern is most prevalent particularly in countries like Nigeria where immense wealth exists side-by-side with excruciating poverty. The country's tremendous wealth in human and natural resources has not been optimally utilized, in most cases it is squandered and appropriated by a handful of public officials and their close associates. By 1990s and 2000s, Nigeria is one of the countries in the world that provides an example of the paradox of wealth in the midst of plenty resources because it has been ranked as one of the poorest countries of the world whose average income is less than $1 per day.

Over the years, successive governments in Nigeria have introduced an avalanche of policies and programmes aimed at addressing the scourge of poverty. Either because of the absence of an affirmative action backed by a strong political will, or politicization of policy design and implementation, corruption and misplacement of the priority needs of the poor, policies on poverty alleviation are not successful in reducing the increasing rate of poverty in the country. To crown it all, the policy framework of poverty alleviation programmes in Nigeria lacks the much needed local content and grassroots participation and, at best, it exemplifies the rhetoric of the political class. This explains why there have been contradictions between policy objectives and implementation on poverty alleviation programmes in the country.

This book, *Poverty in Nigeria: Causes, Manifestations and Alleviation Strategies*, provides illuminating insights into the central issues of poverty in Nigeria and the role of the state, society and economy in overcoming the persistent increase in the number of the poor population in the country. It provides multidisciplinary perspectives on the theories, causes, dimensions and consequences of poverty in Nigeria, with practical recommendations on how best to alleviate poverty in the country.

The book opens with a chapter by Sani Lawal Malumfashi on the concept of poverty and its various dimensions. It provides a conceptual definition of key terms and their various theoretical conceptions. While arguing that poverty is a relative term, the chapter also posits that it is also a social problem which must be addressed by any government in its search for a better society.

In chapter two, Dr. Shehu A. U. Rano reviews the classical and modern literature on poverty and examines its causes, nature and measurement indices. His review of the empirical studies on poverty across different regions of the world shades light on the situation of poverty in developing countries, particularly Nigeria, which according to him, could be blamed for her failure to meet the basic needs of the people. This, he further notes, is an irony because the country is blessed with enormous resources that could have made it a prosperous nation.

In chapter three, Professor Mohammed Sanni Abdulkadir looks at the history of policies on poverty alleviation in Northern Nigeria from 1900 to 1960. His historical account of the dynamics of poverty begins with the colonial period. Adopting the structural poverty thesis, Sanni advances the argument that structural poverty had been very pervasive in the period of colonial rule because of the colonial policy on agriculture, which neglected the sector and emasculated the indigenous structures in favor of the British commercial interests, thereby generated famine, unemployment and poverty in the country. The chapter also brings to light the inadequacies of the colonial and postcolonial states' policies to address the problem of poverty which had been compounded by famine and food insufficiency in the 1970s. In sum, Sanni concludes that for most of the period covered in the chapter "the 'faces' of poverty have been demonstrated, but poverty alleviation and development strategies have failed to provide remedies".

Chapter four is contributed by Dr. Kabiru Isa Dandago in which he examines the poverty alleviation strategies in Nigeria, with specific focus on the Local Empowerment and Environmental Management Project (LEEMP). As a community driven development initiative designed to, among other things, alleviate poverty via the empowerment of the local communities, LEEMP, according to Dandago, is a laudable project on poverty in Nigeria. His central argument is that the success of the project depends significantly on the political will of the state actors involved and the ability of policy makers to carryout the implementation of the project without deviation from its major objectives. When this goal is realized, Dandago argues that LEEMP will serve as the long awaited solution to Nigeria's problem of industrialization and a remedy to poverty. Hence, the chapter concludes by advocating for the speedy introduction of LEEMP in all the Local Government areas in the country.

In chapter five, Dr. Murtala Sabo Sagagi examines the various efforts made by the federal government in Nigeria to alleviate poverty from 1999-2007. He submits that despite government's unequivocal declaration of war against poverty since 1999, a lot of efforts need to be made towards the achievement of poverty eradication goal. Using international and local statistical facts, he provides a comparative analysis of the extent of poverty across Nigeria. Accordingly, Sagagi supports the argument that poverty is pervasive in Nigeria, but it is more pronounced in the North than in the South.

Chapter six is Dr. Dandago and Maiyaki's contribution in which the authors highlight the role the state governments can play in the war against poverty in Nigeria. It is the view of the authors that the 36 states in the federation are not inherently poor, but their failure to tap the resources they are endowed with is a major cause of the prevailing condition of poverty in their respective areas. Central to Dandago and Maiyaki's argument is that local governments in Nigeria alone have natural resources which could be tapped and utilized to support the local councils in their bid to alleviate poverty at the grassroots level.

In chapter seven, Dr. Shehu Dalhatu's contribution goes further by examining the central role the local governments can play in the eradication of poverty in Nigeria. In what he calls "repositioning" the local government for poverty eradication, the author is very emphatic about the need to foster collaborative initiatives at the grassroots level which would form the basis of grassroots mass mobilization towards self-sufficiency and employment generation in local governments.

In chapter eight, Dr. Garba Bala Bello looks at the role of the business community in the war against poverty in Nigeria. His contribution brings to the fore some of the silent practices of corporate organizations which, according to him, supplement government's efforts in tackling the problem of poverty in Nigeria. Citing the specific case of the Nigerian business community, Bello examines at length the role of corporate multinational organizations such as the Zenith Bank, the British American Tobacco Company, UAC, Mobil, Unilever, etc, in the provision of infrastructural facilities and in giving out educational supports to local communities in Nigeria, especially in the Niger Delta region, as a sign of a better beginning in poverty alleviation efforts of the corporate organizations.

In chapter nine, the role of mass media in the fight against poverty in Nigeria is contributed by Balarabe Maikaba. He argues that the extent to which media portrays and projects poverty issues is related to development. Therefore, media's intervention in the fight against poverty is aimed at not only reporting the news, but also in influencing the opinion of citizens to accept policies on poverty eradication, thereby contributing its share in setting the agenda for government action on poverty. Thus, Maikaba argues that the media is not doing enough towards fighting poverty in Nigeria, hence, it should rise up to this challenge and avoid neglecting issues of poverty in news coverage.

A relationship between poverty and ethno-religious conflicts in Nigeria is established by Fatima Oyine Ibrahim in chapter ten on ethno-religious conflicts in Kano state. Her major argument is that although poverty is widespread in the country, its manifestations take various forms in Kano, the dynamics of the excruciating poverty is an explanatory to the persistent ethno-religious conflicts in the state. Sampling the opinion of the victims of ethno-religious conflict in the state and the general public on the issue, she finds out that the failure of the Obasanjo regime to resolve the socio-economic crises on assumption of office since 1999 has worsened the already debilitating condition of the poor in Nigeria. As a result, unemployed youths and aggrieved hungry people find religious conflicts as a stepping stone for expressing their anger and untold hardship which manifested in the looting of the property of innocent victims.

Mahmoud Mohammed Lawan's contribution is presented in chapter eleven. His chapter delves at length on the phenomenon of military rule and the extent to which it exacerbated poverty in Nigeria. Specifically, Lawal's critical examination of the nature, style and dynamics of military rule between 1984 and 1999, exposes the military regimes as poor managers of the economy, and destroyers of the socio-economic well being of the Nigerian people. According to him, despite the introduction of various policies purportedly targeted at poverty alleviation, such as MAMSER, Better life for Rural Women, and Family Economic Advancement Programme (FEAP), the condition of the poor has remain deplorable. The main reason for the deplorable condition of the poor in the period covered was, among other things, corrupt practices in the conception and implementation of poverty alleviation policies of the military regimes.

In chapter twelve, Dr. Adamu I. Tanko provides an illuminating examination on poverty in the Niger Delta region of Nigeria. Thus, his contribution shades light on the relationship between poverty among the people of the Niger Delta, being the region in which the country's oil resources are tapped. Having posits that environmental hazards and ecological problems that are caused by oil exploration and exploitation in the region are the major threats, he goes further to state that the neglect of the poor by multinational oil companies and the poor state responses to the plight of the people of the Nigeria Delta have made the condition of the poor people in the region more precarious by the day. Therefore, he calls on the Nigerian government, which he refers to as the "collaborator of major oil companies" and the oil MNCs to observe international laws and conventions against environmental damages of oil operations.

In a related contribution, Prof. Kabiru Ahmad's chapter (chapter thirteen) examines the nexus between environment, conflict and poverty in the Niger Delta Region of Nigeria. He begins by examining the various reasons for the region's agitation for resource control and goes further to state that the aggressive or adversarial responses of the people to oil exploration activities in the region which take the form of kidnapping, pipelines vandalisation and the resurgence of communal conflicts are the direct consequences of the failure of the state to meet the basic needs of the people in the region. As such, it is the view of the author that as far as the Niger Delta is concerned the Nigerian government is capable of controlling the situation of conflict in the region through dialogue and, by controlling the corrupt activities of state actors as well as reducing poor condition of the people to the barest minimum.

In his critical examination of the International Monetary Fund (IMF)/World Bank Structural Adjustment programme in chapter fourteen, Dr. Habu Mohammed's contribution looks at the public sector workers in Nigeria and the extent to which the Bank and the Fund contribute profoundly in the deepening of poverty in Nigeria. Using a variant of radical political economy, Mohammed argues that the ideological underpinnings of SAP are biased in favor of the wholesale importation of capitalist mode of production and social relations. This, according to him, generated a lot of contradictions in the way the state and society relates and in the manner in which the Nigerian economy was plundered by profit seekers through the process of primitive capitalist accumulation. On the whole, the author argues that SAP pauperized and eliminated the middle class, which is mostly found in the public sector, and expanded the accumulation process through the devaluation of Naira, withdrawal of subsidy on various goods and services, privatization and commercialization of public institutions, among other measures.

In chapter fifteen, Dr. Sadiq Isa Radda's contribution looks at the much celebrated world programme on Millennium Development Goals (MDGs) and poverty in Nigeria. In his appraisal of the programme, Radda clearly points out that MDGs is one of the major obstacles to the nation's goal of sustainable development. Rather than alleviating the plight of the poor in Nigeria, the author opines that MDGs is a "business-as-usual encapsulated in verbal official rhetoric by politicians", and, therefore, have nothing to add new in poverty alleviation crusade in the country. Instead, it is another opportunity for politicians and corrupt public officials to accumulate donor's financial 'support' to Nigeria and widen the income gap between the rich and poor people.

In the sixteenth chapter, Mustapha Mukhtar looks at policies on poverty alleviation in the past and present, unveil their lapses and recommends the way forward in Nigeria's continuing search for better poverty alleviation strategies. Using a time-series analysis, the author presents poverty reduction strategies in the pre-SAP and post-SAP periods and concludes that lack of sustainability of policies is the major hitch that destroys whatever is introduced to address the problem of the poor in Nigeria. He, therefore, calls for involvement of the local people in the identification and design of projects on poverty alleviation instead of the existing tradition of top-down policy making and implementation which effectively sidelines the poor and, in some cases, relegated them to the background.

Chapter seventeen is the final chapter and the contribution is by Professor Emmanuel Ajayi Olofin who, after a synoptic looks at the past poverty alleviation programmes in Nigeria, recommends what should be done by the Nigerian government in order to attain a poverty free society by the year 2015. His major argument is that a lot of efforts need to be made to overcome the escalating rate of poverty in the country, particularly among the restless youths who are mainly the frustrated jobless social groups and, therefore, have nothing to add to the society other than constituting social nuisance. He also calls for the private sector involvement in the implementation of NAPEP and NEEDS and for the government to provide the enabling environment for the participation of different social groups in the war against poverty in Nigeria.

Taken together, this book presents an X-ray on poverty in Nigeria from different perspectives. Contributors combine their theoretical knowledge, empirical facts, as well as experience gained from their involvement in practical field studies on poverty in Nigeria and answer bewildering questions such as: *what* are the causes of poverty in Nigeria and *how* does it manifest in the country, and *why* should it be eradicated? By reading the book, either in part or in whole, social scientists, students and policy makers will learn how to enrich their knowledge in the area and overcome poverty at different levels of government. I, therefore, recommend the book for wider readership.

Habu Mohammed, PhD.
(Book project coordinator & co-editor)
22nd January, 2008.

CHAPTER ONE

THE CONCEPT OF POVERTY AND ITS VARIOUS DIMENSIONS

Sani Lawal Malumfashi

Introduction

Poverty is a naked reality. It can be assessed objectively and felt subjectively. It is the oldest and yet unresolved social problem. Historically, the problem of poverty started with the early formation of human society. Societies of the past and present are either stratified between the slaves and slave owners, feudal lords and serfs, or the capitalists and working class. These different forms of social division are simply translated into division between the 'haves' and 'have not' or 'rich' and 'poor'. The rich are of course the better opportune, privileged, educated, and sheltered, the healthier and secured social groups, while the poor are the complete opposite - deprived, depressed and diseased.

There are two contrasting explanations as regards the social and economic positions of the poor. The first explanation hinges on the fact that the poor are virtually responsible for their status. The reason is simply that poor are in poverty because they are lazy and unintelligent.

The second explanation stressed on the socio-economic structure of the society. According to this argument, poverty is determined by unequal distribution of economic resources and social opportunities between members of society. Thus, poverty is a product of weak and corrupt governmental institutions, bad leadership, limited access to opportunities (land, capital, education, employment etc); lack of investment, lack of market for both agrarian and industrial products; ill health and disease and so on. Each of these views is relevant to the understanding of the focus of governmental decisions on any poverty alleviation policy that might be proposed.

Defining the Concept of Poverty

The popular notion of poverty in the pre-industrial era was that it was, as Giddens (1981) argued, 'God given' part of divine order of things. Later on poverty was viewed as product of individuals' inaction, laziness, lack of intelligence and ingenuity; it is in a way a personal problem. The present understanding of poverty, however, is that it is a social problem; its effects do not reside with the person alone but permeate through the society. To this extent higher than usual and acceptable level of poverty affects social, economic, and political security and stability of society. Problems of infant and maternal mortality, illiteracy, social and political conflicts, migration and immigration are to a large extent related to poverty.

There is general agreement that poverty means lack of basic needs and services such as food, clothing, bedding, shelter, basic healthcare and education. This is what Lendenfeld (1973), Haralambos (1980) and Giddens (1981) referred to as lack of minimum standards of living. In addition, poverty is translated to mean powerlessness, indicating lack of ability to express ones view locally and nationally. In a more diverse fashion Haralambos (1980) defined poverty in 'absolute' 'relative' and 'subjective' terms. In absolute term, the definition of poverty is concerned with drawing a 'poverty line' below which poverty begins and above which it ends. This simply refers to minimum requirement for a healthy, efficient, and quality living. Absolute poverty is sometimes referred to as subsistence poverty since it is based on evaluation of minimum subsistence requirement for desirable living. For instance, when a population is living below one dollar a day, that population is regarded as living in absolute poverty. Other measures used to determine 'minimum requirement' include, among others, nutrition which can be measured by the amount of protein and calorie intake; shelter measured by the quality of housing, residential location and degree of sanitation; and health measured by such factors as infant mortality and access to a quality medical care and safe water. In Nigeria and other developing countries, additional index like educational facility (private or public) is also considered.

The problem with this definition, however, is that as societies differ in culture and structure so is the definition of 'minimum requirement'. *Relative poverty*, on the other hand, is measured by what members of society considered desirable and acceptable standards of living within the context of their situations, circumstances, environment and culture. Relative definition of poverty is here justified to the extent that standards and needs are dynamics. What was considered as a luxury yesterday may be a necessity today and of no relevance tomorrow. Yet the problem with relative conception of poverty is that there is hardly uniform conception of 'desirable' or 'acceptable standards' amongst members of society. For example, while obesity in our society is considered a sign of comfort, in most western societies, including U.S., obesity is associated with poverty. In rural agrarian society, wealth is associated with number of wives and children while in urban industrialized and monetized society large family is identical to the poor.

Thus in a diverse society with different ethnic, religious, and income groups, conception of poverty may differ according to those divides. At the international level, a division on the basis of economic development is relatively made between rich and poor countries. Comparatively and in line with such division, poverty is peculiarly African identity. Some Asian and Latin American countries are also desperately poor. Those third world countries are economically and socially characterized by low G.D.P and per capita income, low investment, low industrial and technological breakthrough, low rate of employment, high rate of infant and maternal mortality, high dependency culture, and rapid rural – urban migration. The people's living standards in most third world countries are far below what is obtainable in the developed regions of the world. For instance, while in western societies, products and services such as hot and cold running water, refrigerators, and washing machines, medical and dental care, quality education and motor cars are according to Haralambos and Holborn (2004) necessities of life, in Africa and the rest of third world countries they are luxuries.

The last conception is *subjective poverty*. This refers to individuals' or groups' subjective feelings of being poor. Under subjective definition, poverty is not measured by the level of income or living standards but by individual's intrinsic feeling of contentment and sense of fulfillment or otherwise in life. The concern here is not of being rich or wealthy but being able to live a quality and improved life within the limited amount of resources. It is about feeling satisfied, enriched and enhanced.

In addition to the three conceptions of poverty discussed above, we can still make a distinction between *moral and material poverty*. Moral poverty is also not within the confinement of income or minimum requirement for living but measured by the normative way of life defined by society. While developing societies of Africa and Asia face the problem of material poverty, the developed societies of the West face the problem of moral poverty. Even though morality itself is socially defined, there is what is referred to as 'moral universals' i.e. behavior or practice which all societies accept as moral. Moral poverty manifests itself in such behavior and practices as same sex marriage, sex changes and gender crossing, incest, abortion, single parenthood, drug culture, child abuse and exploitation and other practices universally conceived as morally inadequate and questionable.

Landenfeld (1973) also identified two additional components of what he referred to as 'new poverty': *Case and Insular poverty. Case poverty* is mostly attributed to physical and mental deformities as a result of which the affected persons are excluded from economically productive and income generating activities. People suffering from mental melt down and chronic physical disabilities are likely to be poor because they are less likely to be employed, admitted into colleges, enjoy credit facilities and open businesses.

Insular poverty on the contrary exists when a particular section of a population becomes "economically obsolete". Insular poverty is ironically the result of technological advancement. It is true that scientific and technological achievements improve social and material conditions of life whereby, people have more opportunities, more skills, and are healthier. Yet the same technological breakthrough subjects more and more people to poverty and economic invisibility.

The automation of industries, for instance, make unskilled manual laborers economically unviable, computerization of knowledge and activities reduces the need for typists in most organizations, and mechanization of agriculture and massive importation of agricultural products further pauperized peasants, especially in Nigeria. The peasants are economically displaced as they can't afford fertilizer and other inputs and their locally produced products cannot compete with those imported from other parts of the world. This implies pushing them into poverty cage.

Theories of Poverty

Culture of Poverty Thesis

The 'culture of poverty' thesis is of the idea that the poor are poor because they have values and ways of life different from the rest of society, i.e. a culture of their own which is instrumental to their being poor and prevent them from achieving success and material progress. One of the proponents of this thesis is of course Lewis (1966, cited in Giddens, 1981). Lewis identified such way of life which is identical to the poor as: mother centered families, a males' obsession of masculinity, fatalism, inability to defer gratification, and a narrow conception of the world, fixation to immediate environment and conditions. These features according to Lewis comprise a unique culture of poverty, preventing the poor from aspiring to a better position in society.

The *culture of poverty* thesis is criticized for being too narrow and inadequate. Some of the features constituting the 'culture of poverty' are also found among non poor working class. Again, the 'culture of poverty' is not a chosen way of life but a subjected reality for being poor.

The Neo –Marxist Explanation of Poverty

According to neo –Marxists, poverty results from the economic arrangements and relationships of society which shape the distribution of material resources and power; in a society relationships are not based on equal equanimity nor on functional complementarities; where employers low wages for overloaded and inhuman work; where political decision further socially excluded the disadvantage group, poverty will inevitably be a perpetual fact of life.

Dimensions of Poverty

Poverty has multiple dimensions. The dimensions themselves are relative to culture, environment, and socio economic and political conditions faced by people. The economic dimension of poverty refers to poverty as a situation of inadequate income or low consumption. According to Osunubi (2003) people are referred to as poor when their estimated standard of living in terms of income or consumption is below poverty line. In terms of living standard, Nigerians are becoming increasingly poor. In 1980, for example, an estimated 27% of the population lived in poverty. By 1999 about 70% of the population had income of less than one dollar a day (NEEDS 2005). Basically, by contemporary standards predominant population of Nigeria has less than enough income to keep it adequately fed, clothed and sheltered. The poor are socially visible on streets either as beggars, hawkers or militia. By contrast, as Landenfeld (1973) observed, American poor are socially invisibles; blacks are segregated in the city ghettos hardly noticed by the white middle class. Old persons are hidden away in their rooms and because they are out of sight the rest of American poor are therefore out of mind.

In urban areas poverty manifests itself in to hunger, unemployment, under employment and poor wages for those employed. Urban poverty and poor environmental conditions are mutually connected. The urban poor do not have access to municipal waste collection service and therefore live in endangered, marginal and environmentally unfit areas such as congested slums and contaminated sites.

In rural areas poverty is associated with lack of factors of production (e.g. land). Whether or not a rural person is rich depends on the number of his lands, wives and children. Wives and children are usually the instruments of production. Standards of living in terms of differential access to medical facility, education, and quality of nutrition are of little concern with reference to rural poverty.

Politically the poor are invisible. This is a universal phenomenon. The dispossessed that are at the bottom of society are unable to speak for them. Because they are unemployed and mostly uneducated the poor are excluded from union membership, fraternal organizations, political parties or corporate bodies. As they are socially marginal, the poor are also politically powerless.

Health wise the poor are still the disadvantaged groups. According to Nettleton (1995), Senior (1998) and Taylor (2003), material conditions of a person impact considerably on his health status and entire quality of his life. Patterns of health and illness are related to economic condition because the main determinants of health are social and environmental in origin. Improved health is more attributable to improved nutrition and wealth than with development in medical science. Given this assertion it is safe to hypothesize that poor people die earlier than the rich; they are more likely to suffer from most of the major 'killer' diseases; and they are more likely to suffer from chronic life time illnesses.

Race and Gender Dimensions of Poverty

Race and gender dimension of poverty is also a growing concern. In such multi- racial societies as in the U.S and South Africa wealth and opportunities are unevenly distributed. More blacks in those societies are poor than whites; they are less educated, opportune, privileged than their white counterparts. Like wise, in most patriarchal societies more women are in abject poverty than men. The sex role segregation is such that women play the culturally prescribed role of 'taking care of', 'looking after the', attending to' and 'comforting the' husband and children. Their role is basically domestic and economically obscured. Men, on the other hand, do the most economically engaging activities such as farming, trading and commerce, and wage employment. They are also more opportune to go to school than women and to be highly educated and also freer than women to take life time private and public sector employment. Women are undoubtedly the vulnerable group in relation to poverty because they are less free than men to own properties. On the contrary they are in some societies part of the properties to be possessed, inherited, disposed and discarded without much cultural sanction. This explains why of the 70% Nigerian poor majority are women.

Conclusion

Poverty is a social problem. Its effects are not limited to the poor alone but permeate through the entire society. It connotes lack of minimum requirements for acceptable and desirable living. Majority Nigerians are poor by contemporary standards; this is in spite of the fact that the country is resourcefully rich. Many Nigerians have less than enough income to feed themselves well, educate their children, and enhance their physical and mental well being.

Poverty can take economic, social, political and environmental dimensions. Each dimension is mutually linked to the other. Lack of enough income to feed, shelter and educate oneself may translate into such social ailment as deprivation, frustration, discrimination, illness and illiteracy. The political implication of all these is political powerlessness and invisibility. The poor do not belong to any organized group and cannot advance their course politically or influence governmental decision. They are partly responsible for their social status for being lazy and unskillful. The unjust socio –economic structure of the society is again partly to blame.

By way of policy recommendation it is imperative that women economic and social empowerment featured prominently in the design and implementation of poverty alleviation policy. Other vulnerable groups to be taken into consideration are: youths, the elderly, orphans, refugees and disabled.

Conducive investment climate must be created and this may mean revitalization of rail transportation, improvement of road transportation, sustainable electricity supply, rural agricultural development and massive vocational skill acquisition program for unemployed and under employed youth. The problem of begging in northern Nigeria and other initiative killing culture must be aggressively tackled and addressed.

References

Giddens, A. (1981), *Introductory Sociology*, London: Macmillan Press Limited.

Haralambos, M. and Holborn, (2004), *Sociology; Themes and Perspectives*; HarperCollins Publishers Limited.

Landenfeld, S. (1973), Radical *Perspectives on Social Problem*, London: Collier Macmillan Ltd.

Nettleton, S. (1995), Sociology *of Health and Illness*, Oxford: Polity Press Ltd.

NEEDS, (2005), *National Economic Empowerment and Development Strategy*, Abuja: Central Bank of Nigeria CBN).

Senior, M, & Vivesh, B (1998), *Health and Illness*, Oxford: Ashford Color Press Ltd.

Taylor, S & Field, D. (2003), *Sociology of Health and Health Care*, UK: Blackwell Publishing Ltd.

Osunubi, T.S (2003), *Urban Poverty in Nigeria: A Case of Agege Area of Lagos State*, Nigeria, Unpublished field Work

CHAPTER TWO

POVERTY: CAUSES, NATURE AND MEASUREMENT

Shehu Usman Rano Aliyu

Introduction

Attempts at identification, conceptualization and measurement of poverty have been the major preoccupation of economists and policy makers alike. In the seventeenth century, Robert Malthus (1798) first raised the alarm that 'population explosion' would lead to mass starvation and famines in his geometric and arithmetic analyses of population and food production growth rates. Although this view was seen by many as a pessimist or alarmist position most suited to the pre-industrial revolution era, the same argument was reawakened by Ehrlich (1968) who predicted that "The battle...is over; hundreds of millions of people are going to starve to death in the 1970s."

In another development, the Global monitoring report (2004) on attainment of Millennium Development Goals (MDGs), confronts us with mixed scenarios; on one hand, the report observes that the world at large will likely meet the first goal of halving income related poverty between 1990 and 2015, while on the other hand, Low-Income Countries Under Stress (LICUS), about half of which are in Africa, are especially at the risk of falling far short. The report further adds that the trends are broadly similar with respect to the target of halving the proportion of people who suffer from hunger. Reasons are not farfetched; low economic growth performance, macroeconomic policy shocks and failure, demographic factors, low level of human and capital development, corruption and mismanagement of resources, crime and collapse of law and order, etc. Sala-i-Martin (2002) and Dollar and Kraay (2002) for example, present evidence which suggest that differences in economic growth have been largely responsible for the differences in poverty alleviation across regions. They argue that initiatives that boost national economic growth rates are, therefore, likely to be helpful in the fight against poverty, *ceteris paribus*. Recently, Nissanke and Thorbecke (2007) opine that globalization affects poverty through many different channels: growth, inequality, international capital movements and labor migration, technology, and information vulnerability.

Although poverty is never ever hard to comprehend, yet it is seen and defined differently by people. Acknowledging this difficulty, Aboyade (1975) observes that like an elephant, poverty is more easily recognized than defined. Different criteria have, therefore, been used to conceptualize poverty. Rein (1970:46) identified three broad concepts of poverty that seem to encompass most of the difficulties associated with poverty analysis: subsistence, inequality, and externality. Subsistence is concerned with "minimum of provisions needed to maintain health and working capacity" (capabilities). Inequality is concerned with the "relative position of income groups to each other." Externality is concerned with the

> "social consequences of poverty for the rest of society rather than in terms of the needs of the poor. In other words, it is not so much the misery and plight of the poor but the discomfort and cost to the non-poor part of the community which is crucial to this view of poverty."

Blackwood and Lynch (1994) identify the poor using the criteria of the level of consumption expenditure. Streeten and Burki (1978), Irfan Ul Haq (1996) and the World Bank (1996) define the concept in terms of the basic needs. It implies a state whereby resources at the disposal of an individual are insufficient to meet his basic needs; food, clothing, shelter etc. Sen (1977) and Adeyeye (1987) define poverty in terms of denial of access to economic resources.

Similarly, measurement of poverty is plagued with as much controversy as in the definition of the term. Yet some times, it is highly complex and varied. More often than not, one is faced with the choice between objective and subjective poverty line measures. Psychologist, sociologist and normative economist often rely on 'subject-qualitative' measure, while empiricist economists talk of 'objective-quantitative' measure. Regardless of whichever measure of poverty one uses, the objective, however, is to be able to, at the end, arrive at a poverty cut-off line, which separates the poor from the non-poor.

Against this background this chapter aims at exploring the theoretical debates surrounding the nature, sources, dimensions and measurement of poverty in Nigeria. The chapter is, therefore, divided into five sections. Section one is the introduction, while section two presents the literature review and theoretical issues. Section three explores the causes of poverty and characteristics of poor, while section four reviews some of the instruments of measuring poverty. Section five takes care of the summary and recommendations of the chapter.

Literature Review and Theoretical Issues

From a pure economic stand point, otherwise christened 'traditional view of poverty' by the World Bank (1990), poverty is based on the assumption that the welfare of an individual household depends primarily on the number of baskets of goods and services he consumes. The more he consumes, therefore, the less the level of poverty. However, since income constrains consumption, the definition of poverty should hence incorporate the definition of a threshold income that could mark household below such threshold income level as poor. Town-send (1974) criticized this definition saying that it is devoid of such dimensions of social welfare as health, life expectancy, literacy and access to public goods. More broadly, therefore, World Bank (2000/01:15) incorporates low achievement in education, health and vulnerability and exposure risk – voicelesssness and powerlessness, in the characterization of poverty. Even in the classical economic literature, Adam Smith (1776) emphasizes the fact that man's necessities of life go beyond the basket of commodities he needs for his physical survival.

Consequently, the broader definition of poverty such as being unable to meet the basic necessities encompassing food water, clothing shelter, education, health as well as basic non material needs including participation, identity, dignity, etc., is now recognized (Streeten, 1979; Blackwood and Lynch, 1994). Sen (1981) de-scribes these as the 'capabilities that a person has, that is, the substantive free-doms he or she enjoys to lead the kind of life he or she values.

Theoretically, poverty is seen in either relative or absolute terms; World Bank (1977) defines relative poverty as a condition when households have a per capita income of less than one-third (_) of the average per capita income of the country. The Bank further defines absolute poverty in terms of household's command over resources, which are sufficient to obtain a basket of goods and services required to guarantee a minimum decent living standard. Townsend (1973) defines relative poverty as a situation where individuals or families are in command of resources which, over time, fall seriously short of the resources commanded by the average persons or families in the community in which they live.

Broadly, Paudel (2004) conceptualizes poverty in four ways; these are: lack of access to basic needs/goods; lack of or impaired access to productive resources; outcome of inefficient use of common resources; and result of "exclusive mecha-nisms". Poverty as lack of access to basic needs/goods is essentially economic or consumption oriented. It explains poverty in material terms and specifically em-ploys consumption-based categories to explain the extent and depth of poverty, and establish who is and who is not poor. Although there were several attempts at conceptualizing poverty in Nigeria; see: Ogwumike (1991), Ogwumike and Ekpenyong (1996), Onah (1996), World Bank (1995 and 1996, Odusola (1997), etc.; yet the sources poverty in Nigeria are unending, lack of access to basic infra-structural services, loss of job through inappropriate government policies such as deregulation of the economy, insecurity due to increasing wave of crime and armed robbery, communal and religious crises, corruption, lack of good govern-ance, etc. These factors and more tend to expose the poor to greater risk and weaken his access to income earning opportunities or consumption goods. Using Paudel's conceptualization, therefore, Nigeria's pattern of poverty can be con-ceptualized, but not limited to lack of basic needs largely due to the decaying state of social and economic infrastructures in the country.

On the link between poverty and other socioeconomic indicators; economic growth, globalization, demographic factors such as population, birth control, disease, etc.; direct and indirect effect are expected to occur. According to the Economist (2000) Growth really does help the poor: in fact it raises their incomes by about as much as it raises the incomes of everybody else. In short, globalization raises incomes, and the poor participate fully. World Bank (2000) discovers that while on the average economic growth benefits the poor, there are a number of countries, however, where this has not happened. Yet, there is no clear recipe for translating growth into poverty reduction for all country cases. Human Development Report (2003) posits that sustained economic growth helps break the shackles of poverty in two ways. First, it directly increases average household incomes and indirectly, reduces non-income poverty by raising government revenues and enabling increased public investments in education, basic infrastructure, disease control and health. In congruence to this, the UN WIDER policy brief (2007) opines that globalization–poverty nexus captures the combined net effect of growth and a change in income inequality on poverty. According to the report, higher aggregate growth rate of GDP is good for poverty reduction, while increased inequality acting as a filter dampens the positive effects of growth on poverty reduction.

Furthermore, World Bank (2001) examines the globalization-growth-inequality-poverty chain and discovers that globalization positively affects growth via openness of the economy. This manifests through trade and capital movement liberalization, which in turn is presumed to affect growth directly through the following:

- Trade liberalization policies encourage exports, which benefit export industries and contribute directly to GDP growth.
- Switching from import substitution to opening up the domestic economy to imports leads, over time, to more efficient resource allocation and a higher growth path.
- Foreign direct investment (FDI) raises the productive capacity of the receiving countries, and is often the conveyer belt for transferring technology and know-how, and this exerts positive impact on growth.

Borenzstein, De Gregoria and Lee (1998) argue that the potential for domestic diffusion of best practice through FDI depends on the absorption capacity of the host economy, which adequate levels of education and infrastructure as well as competition in domestic markets (Bromstrom and Kokko, 1996). However, Rodrik (1998) argues that there are trade-offs between growth, distribution and poverty as illustrated by economic modeling that include political factors in their specifications. Ali and Elbadawi (1999) for instance used a simple dynamic model of poverty, growth, and distribution to explain the observed experience of selected developing countries. Forsyth (2000) argues that there is plenty of evidence that current patterns of growth and globalization are widening income disparities and hence acting as a brake on poverty reduction. Shane and Roe (2004) lament that although less than 1 percent of world's GDP could eliminate this insecurity if it could be translated into food in the hands of the poorest populations, almost 1 billion people continue to live in a state of food insecurity with less than $2 per day to spend on food and all other necessities of life.

Empirical Literature

Employing different conceptualization of poverty, a number of empirical studies have identified and assessed the link between poverty and macroeconomic and social indicators. Family size and high fertility level is more often associated with high incidence of poverty, especially among rural dwellers. Eastwood and Lipton (2001) and Merrick (2001) evaluated the relationship between demographics and poverty. Their studies revealed modest correlations between high fertility and poverty both at the national and household level. In addition, Eastwood and Lipton (2001) discover in a sample of 45 developing countries that high fertility is associated with higher levels of absolute poverty, and that a 5 per thousand reductions in the average country's birthrate would have reduced the incidence of poverty from 18.9 percent in the mid-80s to 12.6 percent in the early 1990s. Merrick (2001) claims that "There is little debate about whether poverty and household size are correlated." Anand and Morduch (1996) earlier argued that such correlation between household size and poverty should not be taken for granted because even with modest economies to scale according to them, household well-being is a positive rather than negative function of family size. These notwithstanding, Birdsall and Sindig (2001) point out that high fertility in poor households, which is a prelude to large family, may simply reflect a conscious decision by households to tolerate high child costs today in return for increased old age security in the far off future when these children are working and can support their parents. Thus an observed correlation between household size and poverty is not a causal effect of the former on the latter, but rather they are both the simultaneous outcome of some deeper decision making process.

According to the United Nations (2006), the total fertility for the world was 2.65 children per woman in 2000 - 2005; Africa's 4.97 children per woman was the highest among all continents, followed by that of Latin America and the Caribbean (2.55), with Europe recording the lowest fertility. In contrast the report reveals that life expectancy at birth averaged 65.4 years at the level of the world for the period 2000 - 2005. All continents achieved a life expectancy in excess of 60 years except for Africa with only 49.1 years, declining from 51.5 years for the period 1985 - 1990.

Furthermore, the 2007 World Bank report "*Global Economic Prospects*" predicts that although by the year 2030 the number of people living on less than the equivalent of $1 a day will fall by half to about 550 million. The report, however, warns that Africa in 2030 will be home to a larger proportion of the world's poorest people than it is today.

Progress on poverty reduction has also been uneven. According to Sala-i-Martin (2007) that although poverty lessens in the world as a whole, it, however, continues to pose an enormous problem:

- One third of deaths - some 18 million people a year or 50,000 per day - are due to poverty-related causes. That's 270 million people since 1990, the majority women and children, roughly equal to the population of the US,
- In every year nearly 11 million children die before their fifth birthday;
- In 2001, 1.1 billion people had consumption levels below $1 a day and 2.7 billion lived on less than $2 a day;
- 800 million people go to bed hungry every day.

Empirical evidences point to the fact that Nigeria is a poor country judging from its $260 per capita in 1996 and during the nineties. The nation shows no appreciable growth in the growth of per capita GDP. Consequently, the incidence of poverty increased from 27.2 percent of the population in 1980 to 65.6 percent in 1996, and it is estimated the incidence increases by 10 percent every three years. The implication of this incidence of poverty for Nigeria is that about 67 million Nigerians are languishing in poverty out of an estimated population of over 100 million. Locationally, a report by the FOS (1999) observes that Nigeria's poverty is generally more pronounced in the rural areas and majority of the poor in the country are located there. Reasons for this include; over population in some rural areas and heavy reliance on declining natural resources (NRs) for livelihoods (World Bank Group, 2002). As a result of the high incidence of poverty, Nigeria was ranked 151 among 174 poor countries by the year 2000 (Sofo et al, 2003). In an empirical study on the role of household endowment in determining poverty in Nigeria, Olaniyan (2000) discovers the importance of both human and physical capital endowments in determining poverty and the importance of education, according to him, cannot be overemphasized as it represents an important policy tool that can be used to escape poverty by households.

Aliyu (2001) observes that among other indicators of poverty, the per capita income at current prices between 1997 and 2001 stood at and average of N1047.5, while life expectancy at birth remain 53 years. The average number of patients per physician and hospital bed for the five years are as high as 4699 and 1734 persons respectively. The infant mortality per 1000 live birth stood at an alarming level of 21.7 percent. The incidence of poverty at state levels shows mixed results. Evidence from the Federal office of statistics (FOS) on percentage distribution of poor and non-poor in the 1996/1997 reveals that while the average for all States in the federation stood at 56.6 percent, few States recorded less than 50 percent of their population that are poor. However, up to five (5) States, largely from northern part of the country, of the total twenty two (22) States had over 60 percent of their population that are poor. Thus, according to Soludo (2006) poverty in Nigeria is largely a northern States' affair. It is sad to note that although huge sum of money is committed to poverty alleviation measure at States and Federal levels, assessment of these measures reveal very disappointing results. See: CASSAD (undated), FGN (2001 & 2001), Maduagwu (undated) and Nwaobi (undated).

Causes of Poverty

There is no one cause or determinant of poverty. On the contrary, combinations of several complex factors contribute to poverty. They include low or negative economic growth, inappropriate macroeconomic policies, deficiencies in the labor market resulting in limited job growth, low productivity and low wages in the informal sector, and lag in human resource development. Beside, our characterization of poverty above embodies some of the causes of poverty. Notwithstanding, some other possible factors include:

- Natural factors such as the climate or environment;
- Geographic factors, for example access to fertile land, fresh water, minerals, energy, and other natural resources, etc.;
- Natural resource curse such as crude oil, gold reserve, uranium, etc. The presence of these resources creates opportunity for quick wealth from exports and this tends to have less long-term prosperity than countries with less of these natural resources.

- Inadequate nutrition in childhood may lead to physical and mental stunting that may lead to economic problems. It is estimated that 2 billion people (one-third of the total global population) are affected by iodine deficiency, including 285 million 6 to 12 year-old children. In developing countries, it is estimated that 40% of children aged 4 and under suffer from anaemia because of insufficient iron in their diets;
- Disease specifically AIDS, malaria, and tuberculosis, cholera, and others
- Poverty according to Aboyade (1975) like Biblical sin begets poverty. Poverty prevents, for example, various forms of investment;
- Globalization, too much or too little. Joseph E. Stiglitz, a *Nobel Laureate Economist,* (2002) challenged econometric studies on globalization, growth and poverty as being misleading and distracting; shifting the debate away from where it should be, that is, on the appropriateness of particular policy for particular country, on how globalization can be shaped (including the rules of the game) and on international economic institutions, to better promote growth and reduce poverty in the developing world;
- Lacking rule of law, democracy, infrastructure, health care, education and corruption;

- Tax havens, which tax their own citizens and companies but not those from other nations and refuse to disclose information necessary for foreign taxation. This enables large scale political corruption;
- Economic system such as Capitalism, Socialism, Communism, Monarchy, Fascism and Totalitarianism have all been named as causes by scholars writing from different perspectives.
- Lacking free trade and protectionism, in particular, the very high subsidies to and protective tariffs for agriculture in the developed world. For example, almost half of the budget of the European Union goes to agricultural subsidies, mainly to large farmers and agribusinesses, which form a powerful lobby. Japan gave 47 billion dollars in 2005 in subsidies to its agricultural sector. The US government gives 3.9 billion dollars each year in subsidies to its cotton sector, including 25,000 growers, three times more in subsidies than the entire USAID budget for Africa's 500 million people.
- War, including civil war, genocide, and democide, etc.;
- Brain drain and lack of economic and social skills;
- Exploitation of the poor by the rich through unfretted access to knowledge, economic and political power;
- Overpopulation and lack of access to birth control methods and access to medical care;
- Historical factors, for example imperialism and colonialism, dictatorship, etc.;
- *Matthew effect:* the phenomenon, widely observed across advanced welfare states, that the middle classes tend to be the main beneficiaries of social benefits and services, even if these are primarily targeted at the poor.
- Cultural/religious causes, which attribute poverty to common patterns of life, learned or shared within a community. Traditional leadership – rulership followership or the argument among some religious groups, where poverty is considered a necessary or desirable condition, which must be embraced in order to reach certain spiritual, moral, or intellectual states. Poverty is often understood to be an essential element of renunciation among Buddhists and Jains, whilst in Roman Catholicism

Characteristics of Poor

The words "poverty" and "poor" came from Latin *pauper* - "poor", which originally came from *pau-* and the root of *pario*, that is, "giving birth to not much". If poverty connotes a condition in which a person or community is deprived of, and or lacks the essentials for a minimum standard of well-being and life; then to be poor means to be hungry, to lack shelter and clothing, to be sick and not cared for, to be illiterate and not schooled, to be deprived access to common resources, etc. Thus, the poor are conceived as those individuals or households in a particular society, incapable of purchasing a specified basket of basic goods and services. Basic goods are nutrition, shelter/housing, water, health care, access to productive resources including education, working skills and tools and political and civil rights to participate in decisions concerning socio-economic conditions

(Streeten and Burki, 1978). According to World development report (2000/01) poor people are particularly vulnerable to adverse events outside their control.

In a survey conducted by Narayan *et al* (2000) entitled *'Poverty in the Voices of Poor'*, a Kenya man says: "don't ask me what poverty is because you have met it outside my house. Look at the house and count the number of holes. Look at my utensils and the clothes I am wearing. Look at everything and write what you see. What you see is poverty". In a very lucid presentation of the living condition of the poor, the survey further reports Somalis as saying "We are skinny; we are deprived and pale and speak of the life that makes you older than your age". In addition, the survey identifies the following elements most of which are social rather than material issues:

- Precarious livelihoods
- Excluded locations
- Gender relationships
- Problems in social relationships
- Lack of security
- Abuse by those in power
- Disempowering institutions
- Limited capabilities, and
- Weak community organizations.

Poverty Measurement/Indicators

In a classic study first published in 1901, Seebohm Rowntree calculated that 10 percent of the population of the English city of York in 1899 was living in poverty. His definition of poor is any household whose total income is insufficient to obtain the minimum necessities for the maintenance of 'merely physical efficiency', including food, rent, and other items. World Bank and other documented empirical studies have been using this income measure of poverty at global, country or sub-country level. Broadly, poverty may be measured in absolute or relative sense. *Absolute poverty* refers to a set standard which is consistent over time and between countries. An example of an absolute measurement would be the percentage of the population eating less food than is required to sustain the human body (approximately 2000-2500 calories day for an adult male) or percentage of people living below a certain income threshold. Relative poverty views poverty as socially defined and dependent on social context. In this case, the number of people counted as poor could increase even as their income rise. A relative measurement would be a comparison of the total wealth of the poorest one-third of the population with the total wealth of richest 1% of the population. There are several different income inequality metrics that could be used under this measure. One example is the Gini coefficient.

According to Paudel (2004) poverty measurement is undertaken to:

- Determine a yardstick for measuring standard of living;
- Choose a cut-off poverty line, which separates the poor from the non-poor;
- Take account of the distribution of standard of living among the poor;
- Comparison of poverty overt time, among individuals, group or nations;
- Guide policy on poverty alleviation.

He further observes that poverty analysis has become polarized between the "objective-quantitative" schools and "subjective-qualitative" schools. Quantitative poverty line measure relies on the use of statistics to anchor the reference utility level necessary to attain basic capabilities for a healthy and active living. Sen (1985 &1987) identifies two methods of measuring objective poverty line and these are the food energy intake (TEI), which involves finding the consumption expenditure or income level at which food energy intake is just sufficient to meet pre-determined food energy requirements and cost of basic needs (CBN), which stipulates a consumption bundle adequate for basic consumption needs. Subjective poverty lines on the other hand are based on subjective answers to the "minimum income question" (MIQ), which according to Kapteyn *et al.* (1988) include questions like: "What income level do you personally consider to be absolutely minimal? That is to say that with less you could not make ends meet". One defines as poor everyone whose actual income is less than the amount the sample respondents give as an answer to this question.

In another context, *extreme* poverty according to the World Bank (2007) using purchasing power parity approach (PPP) is when people live on less than US$1 per day, and *moderate* poverty when they live on less than $2 a day. For example, on the basis of these criteria, the report discovers that in 2001, 1.1 billion people had consumption levels below $1 a day and 2.7 billion lived on less than $2 a day. For more elegant and sophisticated models on various dimensions of poverty, see: Sen (1981), Foster, *et al* (1984), Lipton and Ravallion (1995), Mujeri and Khandaker (1998), Jung and Thorbecke (2001), Khan (1999 & 2004).

Non-income poverty indicators, popularly called *'Conventional indicators'* of poverty are the social indicators such as health and education status; the most common being life expectancy, illiteracy rate, number of patients per physician and per hospital bed, and a lot more. The usual child-specific indicators are infant and child mortality (a key measure of ill being), and school enrolments. For example, Cornia and Danziger (1997) recognize the need to move beyond income, but such things like physical health and education. Furthermore, UNICEF studies typically report infant and under-5 mortality rates and primary and secondary school net enrolment ratios in addition to income-poverty, while UNESCO (1995) proposes a set of measures for the well-being of children grouped into: three areas: (1) family - male and female literacy, age, total fertility; (2) community - Gross National Product per capita, access to health care services, access to safe water; and (3) education - age group enrolled in pre-primary education, pre-primary enrolment ratio.

Information on these is largely from secondary sources and their veracity and accuracy could hardly be established. However, whichever approach or indices one uses, measuring poverty permits an overview of poverty that permeates beyond individual experiences. It aids formulation and testing of hypotheses on the causes and dimensions of poverty in an empirical study. It equally serve as a yardstick or beacon for policy on poverty for governments and other institutions.

Conclusion

This chapter entitled poverty: nature, causes and measurement attempts to explore the nature and various dimensions of poverty both from theoretical and empirical standpoints. It also seeks to identify and appraise the causes of poverty and explore the various tools/instruments of its measurement. Poverty has different forms; income poverty in terms of what we earn or the bundles of goods our income commands, relative poverty in terms of our position in the income or consumption bracket vis-à-vis that of others. Other things like where we live, the type of food we eat and the cloth we wear, our sex, demographic and geographical or locational factors all counts in the identification and characterization of poverty. Review of literature on Nigeria show the precarious poverty situation in the country, which largely could be blamed on lack of basic needs. Nigerians generally are being pauperized in spite of enormous resources in the country and at State and regional levels; the incidence of poverty is as high as over 70 percent. Measurement of poverty like its definition is plagued with a lot of approaches from both quantitative objective method and subjective-qualitative method. Yet they all seek to achieve the same objective, which is, to be able to, at the end, arrive at a poverty cut-off line, which separates the poor from the non-poor.

The chapter hereby recommends the following:

- Government should heavily invest in the revitalization of basic infrastructure in the country because they are the bedrock of small and medium scale informal sector economic activities and are anti-poverty;
- Rural poverty could be tackled by investment in agriculture through improved access to capital inputs, credits, markets and better farming practices. Evidences have shown that there is no country in Europe or the United States that do not give support to agricultural production through subsidies and other market incentives. The Nigerian government should, therefore, go back to the drawing board and develop a sumptuous package of subsidies and other agricultural support programmes to fight rural poverty;
- Finally, as White, et al. (2003) observe different dimensions of poverty reinforce one another; poor health or education restrict income earning, and lack of political voice can result in alienation from common property resources. Government ex-

penditure should be devoted to provision of sound medical care, education and the promotion of civil liberties

References

Aboyade, O. (1975), *On the Need for an Operational Definition of Poverty in the Nigerian Economy*, in *Conference Proceedings,* Organized by the Nigerian Economic Society (NES).

Adeyeye, V.A (1987) "Rural Crisis in Nigeria: Increase in Food Deficits, Decline in Real Income and widespread Rural Poverty" paper presented at the second 1987 NISER Seminar series.

Aliyu, S. U. R. (2001), "Fiscal Policy, Economic Growth and the Eradication of Poverty: Comparative Approach between the Capitalist and Islamic Economic Positions", Being a *Paper Presented at the Islamic Political Class* Organized by the Muslim Students' Society, Bayero University Chapter.

Anand, S. and R. Kanbur, (1993), "The Kuznets Process and the Inequality- Development Relationship"; *Journal of Development Economics*, no. 40.

Anand, S. & R. Kanbur, (1993), "Inequality and Development: A Critique"; *Journal of Development Economics*, No. 41.

Blackwood, D.L. and Lynch, R.G. (1994), "The Measurement of Inequality and Poverty: A Policymaker's Guide to the Literature", *World Development*, 2 (5).

Blomstrom, Magnus, and Ari Kokko (1996) "The Impact of Foreign Investment on Host Countries: A Review of the Empirical Evidence." *Policy Research Working Paper 1745.* Washington DC: World Bank.

Borenzstein, E. De Gregorio, J. and Lee. J. (1998) "How Does ForeignDirect Investment Affect Economic Growth?"*Journal of International Economics*. 4.:

Centre for African Settlement Studies and Development (CASSAD, (undated), "Poverty Eradication Programmes in Nigeria", Being A Conference paper Presented at The Third Conference of the International Forum on Urban PovertyYamoussoukro, Cote D'Ivoire Cassad@infoweb.abs.net

Christiaensen, L, L. Demery, and S. Paternostro (2003), "Macro and Micro Perspectives of Growth and Poverty in Africa", *World Bank Economic Review*, 17.Cornia, G. and Danziger, S. (1997a) *Child Poverty and Deprivation in the IndustrializedCountries, 1945–1995,* Clarendon Press, Oxford.

Dollar, D. and A. Kraay, (2002), "Growth is Good for the Poor"; *Journal of Economic Growth*, Vol. 7,

Ehrlich, P. (1968), *The Population Bomb*, New York: Ballantine.

FGN (2000), *Draft National Policy on Poverty Eradication,* ABUJA: Federal Government of Nigeria.FGN (2001), *National Poverty Eradication Programme (NAPEP)* ABUJA: Federal Government of Nigeria (FGN).

Forsyth, J. (2000), *Letter to 'The Economist',* Oxfam Policy Director, June 20,

Global Monitoring Report (2004) Policies and Actions for Achieving the Millennium Development Goals (MDGs) and Related Outcomes, World Bank

FOS (1999), Poverty Profile for Nigeria 1986-1999, FOS, Lagos

Foster, J. J. Greer and E. Thorbecke (1984), "A Class of Decomposable Poverty Measures", *Econometrica*, 52(3).

Gini, C. (1955) "Variabilitá e mutabilita" 1912 Reprinted in Memorie di Metodologica Statistica (Ed. Pizetti E, Salvemini, T). Rome: Libreria Eredi Virgilio Veschi.

Howard, W. H, Jennifer, L. and Andrew, M. (2003),"Comparative Perspectives on Child Poverty: A Review of Poverty Measures", *Journal of Human Development*, Vol. 4, No. 3, November.

Jung, H. and Thorbecke, E. (2001), The Impact of Public Education Expenditure on Human Capital, Growth, and Poverty in Tanzania and Zambia: A General Equilibrium Approach. Working Paper No. 01/106, International Monetary Fund (September).

Kanbur, R. (2003), *Q-squared: Qualitative and Quantitative Methods of Poverty Appraisal.* New Delhi: Permanent Black

Kapteyn, A., Kooreman, P. and Willemse, R. (1988), "Some Methodological Issues in the Implementation of Subjective Poverty Definitions." *Journal of Human Resources,*

Khan, H. A. (1999), "Sectoral Growth and Poverty: a multiplier decomposition analysis for South Africa, *World Development*, March.

Khan, H. A. (2004, "Using Macroeconomic Computable General Equilibrium Models for Assessing Poverty Impact of Structural Adjustment Policies", ADB Institute Discussion, July, Paper No.12

Maduagwu, A. (Undated), "Alleviating Poverty in Nigeria", in Anthony Maduagwu's Forthcoming book: *Growing Up in Oguta: The Economics of Rural Poverty in Nigeria* Please send comments to amaduagwu@hotmail.com

Malthus, T. R. (1798), Essay on the Principle of Population, As It Affects the Future Improvement of Society with Remarks on the Speculation of Mr. Godwin, M. Condorcet, and Other Writers, Penguin Classics ed. (Harmondsworth, 1982).

Mujeri, M. K. and Khandaker, B.H.(1998), "Impact of Macroeconomic Policy Reforms in Bangladesh: A General Equilibrium Framework for Analysis". Paper presented at the Micro Impacts of Macroeconomic and Adjustment Policies (MIMAP), Third Annual Meeting, November 2-6, Kathmandu, Nepal.

Nissanke, L. and Thorbecke , E. (2007), "Linking Globalization to Poverty", *Policy Brief,* United Nations University-World Institute for Development Economic Research No.2,

Nwaobi , G. C. (undated), "Solving the Poverty Crisis in Nigeria: An Applied General Equilibrium Approach", Department Of Economics, University of Abuja, Nigeria.

Odusola, F. A. (1997) Poverty in Nigeria, An Eclectic Appraisal, in National *Conference Proceedings* Organized by the Nigerian Economic Society (NES) on Poverty Alleviation in Nigeria, Chapter 7.

Ogwumike, F. O. (1991), "A Basic Needs Oriented Approach to the Measurement of Poverty in Nigeria", *Nigerian Journal of Social and Economic Studies (NJESS)*, Vol. 33 No. 2.

Ogwumike, F. O. and Ekpenyong, D. B. (1996), "Impact of Structural Adjustment Programme on Policies on Poverty in Nigeria", *Research Report* Submitted to Africa Economic Research Consortium (AERC), Nairobi.

Olaniyan, O. (2000), *The Role of Household Endowments in Determining Poverty in Nigeria, Department of Economics,* University of Ibadan, Nigeria

Onah, F. E. (1996) Post Adjustment Policies Towards Poverty Alleviation in Nigeria, *Nigerian Journal of Social and Economic Studies (NJESS)*, Vol. 38 No. 1, 2, 3.

Ravallion, M. (1994), "Poverty Comparisons in Chur, Switzerland", in *Fundamentals of Pure and Applied Economic*, Hardwood Academic Press. Volume 56

Rein, M. (1970), "Problems in the Definition and Measurement of Poverty", in Romer, P. (ed.) *Advanced Macroeconomics.*, New York: McGraw-Hill.

Rodrik, D. (1998), "Where did all the Growth Go? External Shocks, Social Conflict, and Growth Collapse." John F. Kennedy School of Government, Harvard University(Memo).

Rowntree, P. B. S. (1901), *Poverty-A Study of Town Life*. London: Macmillan.

Paudel, L. (2004), "Analysis of the Relationship between Poverty and Income Inequality", An Unpublished M. Sc. Thesis Submitted in partial fulfillment of the requirements for the Degree of Master of Science in the Department of Agribusiness, School of Graduate Studies Alabama A & M University.

Perotti, R. (1993), "Political Equilibrium, Income Distribution and Growth." *Review of Economic Studies*, 60,

Sala-i-Martin, X. (2001), The Disturbing "Rise" of Global Income Inequality, Retrieved from http://www.columbia.edu/

Sala-i-Martin, X. (2002), "The World Distribution of Income (Estimated from IndividualCountry Distributions)", NBER Working Paper 8933. Cambridge MA (May).

Sala-i-Martin, X. (2007), "Global Inequality Fades as the Global Economy Growths", *Index of Economic Freedom*.

Scitovsky, T. (1978), *The Joyless Economy*. Oxford: Oxford University Press.

Shane, M. and T. Roe (2004), *Overcoming Food Insecurity: A CGE Analysis* Economic Research Service and University of Minnesota, Washington, DC and St. Paul, Minnesota

Sirageldin, I. (2000), *Elimination of Poverty: Challenges and Islamic Strategies,* The Johns Hopkins University

Sen, A. (1985), *Commodities and Capabilities* Amsterdam: North-Holland.

Sen, A. (1987), *The Standard of Living*. Cambridge University Press.

Sen, A. (1990), "More than 100 Million Women are Missing", *New York Review of Books,* December 20, 1990. vol. 37, number 20.

Sen, A. (1992), Missing Women. *British Medical Journal,* Vol. 304.

Sen, A. (2003), Missing Women-Revisited, *British Medical Journal,* Vol. 327.

Steeten, P. and S.J. Burki. (1978). "Basic Needs: Some Issues", in *World Development Report* 6(3).

Sofo C. A. et al. (2003), *Measuring Poverty in Nigeria, Oxfam Programme Team,* Abuja, Nigeria.

Townsend, P. (ed.) (1974), *The Concept of Poverty*, London: Heinemann Educational Books.

UN Population Division, (2006) World Population Prospects: The 2004 Revision: Volume III: *Analytical Report;* www.un.org

UNESCO (1995), *Basic Indicators on Young Children* [www.unesco.org/education/educprog/ecf/html/chart/stats.htm].

UNICEF (1999), *The State of the World's Children 1999* [www.unicef.orf/sowc99].

UNICEF (2000), *The State of the World's Children 2000* [www.unicef.orf/sowc00].

World Bank (1990), *World Development Report 1990: Poverty.* New York: Oxford University Press.

World Bank (1993), Poverty Reduction Handbook, WB, Washington, D. C.

World Bank (1996), Nigeria: Poverty in the Midst of Plenty, The Challenge of Growth With Inclusion, WB, Washington, D. C.

World Bank (2000/01). *World Development Report,* Washington, D.C.: World Bank.Worldbank.org reference (2007).

The Economist (2007) May 27

The Moral Doctrine of Poverty (2007), Retrieved on 2007-01-17.

CHAPTER THREE

POVERTY ALLEVIATION IN NORTHERN NIGERIA: C.1900-1960

Mohammed Sanni Abdulkadir

Introduction

Poverty can be looked at from the perspectives of lack of access to basic needs and basic goods and services like employment, nutrition, housing, water, shelter as well as to productive resources such as education and political and civil rights. In conceptualizing poverty, low income or low consumption has frequently been targeted as the key symptom. This is used to construct poverty income necessary to purchase the minimum necessities of life. Income, consumption, knowledge, skill, social support system or family, lack of power to be truly human, lack of the moral foundations of abundant life and material based indicators constitute indicators for defining poverty. Typology and periodization are very important in our understanding of poverty. Poverty can be absolute (lack of physical requirements for a person/household) or relative (person whose available goods and services are lower than other people) or structural (chronic) or transient (transitory/temporary) (Abdulkadir, 2004:13; Abubakar, 2003:103; Kalu, 2003:433).

In this chapter the structural poverty thesis is advanced because it was more pronounced in the colonial period when indigenous structures came under pressure as a result of colonial policies. Structural poverty goes deep into the fabrics and roots of community life and threatens the food security of the people. During this period, the changing nature of the economy and society involving cash economy, new consumption habits, new forms of needs, social obligation and vulnerability, employment collectively changed the face of poverty. In this chapter, the discussion is rooted on poverty alleviation by the British as it affected the common man during their time on watch. This is because the measurement of the development of an economy and the measure of poverty and its alleviation should be determined by the standard of economic life achieved/enjoyed/obtained by the people in that economy.

Statement of the Problem

The harshness and scourge of poverty spur scholars to reflect on the problem. Social and political history during this period was dominated by legitimating and glorifying the activities of the rulers, elites and policies of the British to the neglect of the ordinary people. Even during the 1930s economic depression when poverty alleviation was needed due to the devastating effects of the economic crises on the ordinary Nigerians, scholars avoided the period because of its complexity. Some who attempted viewed the era only in terms of export prices, decreased income terms of trade, decline in government revenue and volume of exports without reference to the ordinary people (Bauer, 1954/1969:308-310, 410-424; Crowder, 1968:320-326; Helleiner, 1976:19-21; Ekundare, 1973:163-174). There is the need to look at the connection between colonialism and poverty because the impact of colonial rule tended to have reshaped the socio-economic, political, moral and even religious foundations of communities. Most studies regarding poverty Nigeria frequently began from the 1980s with the introduction of the Structural Adjustment Program (SAP) with the neglect of the preceding periods. For example, the discussion of incidence, indicators, measures, distribution and major causes of poverty in Nigeria by Abubakar began with the SAP period (Abubakar, 2002:103-111). Also, Ajakaiye's statistical analysis of Occupational Incidence of Poverty in Nigeria started from 1980 (Ajakaiye, 2002:13). Furthermore, studies of poverty and the meaning of poverty lack consensus because of the varied cultural perceptions and the spatial factor differentiating between rural and urban poor. Equally, globalization and global processes meant that the definition of poverty and its alleviation strategies are provided by external donors operating from differing world-views. Indeed, the force of global or external processes needs to be balanced with an understanding of internal factors in discussing poverty and proffering solutions to it (Kalu, 2003:423-6). Worst still, during the colonial period, poverty was misconceived only in terms of the disabled: sick, deaf, blind, leprous, physically incapacitated and so on.

Although this chapter is on poverty alleviation during the colonial period, however, reference is made to the pre-colonial period to provide the background for understanding subsequent developments and also to comprehend the magnitude of the issues involved in the British 'policy' on poverty alleviation in Northern Nigeria. The research for the chapter involved the combination of archival records, published and unpublished works and oral testimonies. A general quantitative study of the period is blended with sufficient qualitative data to support basic arguments.

Poverty Alleviation in Pre-Colonial Northern Nigeria

Pre-colonial Northern Nigeria implies what became the Northern Provinces beginning form 1906, since there was nothing like Northern Nigeria in this period. In the pre-colonial period, poverty alleviation was done collectively by the community and by the state in the form of a welfare function. Indeed, food security and poverty alleviation were the responsibilities of the community and the state. While the elders made the rules for economic activities for the communities, the people themselves were involved in determining and also preparing strategies for ensuring food security. Nyerere has argued that in African primal culture, "nobody starved, either for food or human dignity, because he lacked personal wealth; he could depend on the wealth possessed by the community of which he was a member" (Kalu, 2003:424). The roles of the family, nuclear and extended, age grades, associations and apprenticeship as poverty alleviation strategies were very central and paramount in the pre-colonial period.

Northern Nigeria during this era witnessed a lot of crises that called for state intervention in ameliorating and alleviating the suffering and poverty of the people. Many parts suffered from either flood or locust invasion or poor rainfall leading to famine and drought and causing food insecurity. For example, Kano suffered from severe and devastating famines in 1847 and 1855 as well as slight famines in 1863, 1973, 1884, and 1889, as a result poor rainfall and partial harvest failures within Kano Emirate (Watts, 1987:71). As a result, many of the rural famine victims moved into Kano city to get grains and alms from the state granaries. There were locust invasions of Abuja in 1851 and 1857, and a series of locust infestations of Bida in the 1880s. During these crises, the affected peasantries were assisted from the traditional central granaries as part of the welfare functions of the state. Indeed, community, culture, family and the state collectively served as structural agencies that staved poverty. It has been suggested that,

"neighbourhood associations, village community development agencies, and other types of civil societies – whether based on ethnicity or beyond boundaries – could serve as poverty alleviation agencies because they possessed organic roots and bonds that ensured viability" (Kalu, 2003:436).

As shall be seen in the next section, the realities of the situation in the colonial period demonstrated that the ability of the people to control the immediate disaster was less and the government did very little to ameliorate their sufferings. The colonial state had undermined the traditional welfare functions, and instead made new appropriations on the peasants.

Poverty Alleviation in Colonial Northern Nigeria

Colonial perception and response to poverty and its alleviation varied from 1900 to 1914, the war time period, the post-war era, the world wide great economic depression of the 1930s, the Second World War, and thereafter. Colonial state created a new face of poverty and transformed the geography by the creation of urban centers leading to rural-urban migration and population shifts. Colonial economy raised the problems of unemployment and a new class of labouring poor who emerged to earn meager wages. With the introduction of colonial tax from about 1903, dependence on wages for sustainability and the payment of the new taxes more and more replaced the reliance on land. In the 1930s, the vulnerability of peasant producers to price changes, natural disasters, the difficulty in controlling household production and weather fluctuations, increased taxes and reduction in salaries of government employees made for a highly volatile food security. Indeed, the urban poor and fixed-income groups suffered terribly from price fluctuations and the peasants from depressed prices. Official economic policy focused on agricultural cash crops and peasant-based export commodity production, principally groundnuts, cotton, palm oil, palm kernels, ginger, beniseed and so on. In fact, embattled traditional structures failed to buffer people from the new faces of poverty, and the colonial state was neither able to regularize the conditions of peasant production nor to resolve food security and poverty alleviation issues.

Up till 1939 relief was not in sight. The next six years or so were to see even more callous disregard of the rights and welfare of the colonial people. During the Second World War, an embattled Britain was galvanized in the battle against Germany and Japan and there was no 'sacrifice' too great for the colonial peoples of the British Empire to be forced to make to guarantee that the empire continued. New and harsh methods of central government controlled marketing monopolies were created which did not even pretend to benefit the producers. The control measures and other war time policies affected Nigerians. The fixing of produce prices and the role of the Marketing Boards enabled the firms to make substantial profits and the government to finance the war without raising taxes. Up to the 1940s, a combination of state control (interventionist) and the change of the existing economy in order to ensure the transfer of capital and wealth to Britain and indeed Europe comprised economic 'policy'. The 1950s was precisely the point when the colonial system began to reform itself and also began the final journey to dissolution. The period from the late 1950s through to 1960 was when ineffective, risky and contradictory reforms were initiated in order to alleviate poverty. The pressure from both the British and Nigerians led to important changes in the economy. The central and regional governments announced various incentives in order to promote business activities and provide social services– with intervention at those levels.

The fundamental problems of food crises, poverty and poverty alleviation in Northern Nigeria were highlighted early in the colonial period, 1904-1908. In 1904, there was a crop failure in many parts of Northern Nigeria. In fact, Zaria experienced food shortage as a result of the stationing of the colonial troops in the city (Abdulkadir, 2001:146). However, the British did nothing to alleviate the situation. When Lugard appealed to the Colonial Office for assistance, an officer of the Office pointed to the advantage of rural hunger. As noted by Shenton, "if there is a famine it ought to solve temporarily the difficulties which exist in obtaining labour for transport" (Shenton, 1986:130). Indeed, during this early period of colonial rule, the British were more concerned with cementing their authority than with social issues, coupled with little means of transport and personnel. In 1905, there was a severe and fatal outbreak of small pox in Dekina group of districts (*Annual Report, Northern Nigeria, 1900-1911*:499; Abdulkadir, 1990:315-316). In 1907, there were outbreaks of epidemics of black water fever, small pox and drought and crop failure in Dekina Division (Abdulkadir, 1990: 317). In Kano city and the surrounding districts, there was a severe pre-harvest famine which continued for almost six weeks prior to the millet harvest following the poor harvest of 1907 (Watts,1987:76). During the crop failure and ensuring famine of 1907-1908, the British were unprepared to assist the rural producer. The famine was so severe (in Kano) that it resulted in a considerable number of slaves been transferred because the possessors were unable to support them while the slaves were hungry and thus anxious to be transferred (Shenton, 1986:130). During these crises and specifically that of Kano in 1908, the Governor of Northern Nigeria did not appeal to the Colonial Office for famine relief because of the lame excuse that he only learned of it 1909. The acting Resident of Kano Province agreed that the mortality was considerable, but there was no remedy at the time. However, Mr. Festing, a former Resident of Kano admitted that' "the *talakawa* have suffered greatly....[due] to our having realized how great was their want, and for the last few months the old people, the women and children have literally been starving" (Watts, 1987:76). Kano consequently became dependent on the desert-edge granaries in Gobir and Damagaram for grain supplies.

In 1911, there were reports of drought and famine in many areas in Northern Nigeria (NAK/SNP 7, 466/1913). There was a severe drought in the 1913 wet season which caused substantial harvest shortfall in grains not only in Northern Nigeria, but also throughout the Central Sudan. 1914 also witnessed famine and rising grain prices. In Kano Province, a sample survey of prices in the twenty rural and local markets in 1914 indicated that 85% experienced grain prices at least ten times above 1911 level (Watts, 1987:78). In Kano Division alone between 30,000 and 40,000 people died as a result of the 1913-1914 famine. The famine was followed by an epidemic form of dysentery. In Sokoto Province some farmers were still badly indebted as a result of the 1914 famine that much of the 1915 good crop was used to pay their creditors (Shenton, 1986:132-133). Indeed, up till 1914, the British colonial officers showed little concern about poverty. Poverty alleviation was left almost entirely to the indigenous communities and missionaries, because for most Britons, indigenous structures and values had the capacity to respond to poverty. As the British push for colonial fiscal self-sufficiency continued, they abdicated their responsibilities of alleviating poverty. For example, in Kano Province, the British relief efforts in 1914 yielded no immediate assistance and failed to provide any support. First, the 1,000 tons of imported rice ordered only came to the capital – Kano -in October 1914 after the peak of the crisis. Second, the quantities of foodstuffs were very small compared to the huge demands for food relief. Third, several Residents proposed the establishment of local granaries at each district headquarters, so that self reliance could be obtained through the conversion of tax to grain. However, the British being obsessed with financial parsimony and afraid of the threat to welfarism aborted the scheme. According to the Governor, Goldsmith, the process was complicated and prone to petty oppression. Accordingly, he recommended moral pressure to urge farmers to produce food. Despite the seriousness of the crisis, the substantial cash balances in the Native Authority Treasuries were not utilized to avert the calamity (Watts, 1978:79). The market rigging and chaotic organization of the relief as well as the politics of disaster relief are what is termed famine crimes (de Waal, 1997).

In 1915 trade suffered in Hadejia Emirate as a result of the war, effects of famine and damage by locust on the farms (Abdulkadir, 2006:4-5). In Kano, the prices of local foodstuffs rose throughout the year. In many Provinces in Northern Nigeria, the general cost of living increased substantially, while "the breakdown of the regional and local self-sufficiency of the local producers….was at hand and its effects were felt throughout the entire economy" (Shenton, 1986:133). Although there was no serious threat of famine in most part of the war period, there were fears of famine as a result of the earlier disasters, increased agricultural exports, increased food prices and decreased food production. As a result of the fears of famine, the District Officer (DO) of Katsina proposed the collection of taxes in kind as an assurance against the danger of famine. Unfortunately, the plan was shelved by the Lieutenant Governor, Goldsmith in 1921, who argued that since there had been no serious alarm with regards to famine in the last 20 years (?), therefore a famine policy was not necessary and unwarranted (Shenton, 1986:135; Watts, 1987:79). However, events that followed proved Governor Goldsmith wrong.

1924 witnessed a bush fire resulting in a considerable destruction of crops (nearing a famine) and property in several places in Hadejia Emirate (Abdulkadir, 2006:8). In 1926 there was a drought in Dekina District in Kabba Province. The situation in the area was compounded by the continued drought in 1927 (Abdulkadir, 1990:384). Indeed, rural Northern Nigeria witnessed famine in 1927 mostly due to the failure of the rains the previous year. Food shortages were also experienced. The famine respite after 1927 was followed by the World-Wide Great Economic Depression of the 1930s.

The 1930s were characterized by the great economic depression. It was a disastrous period for rural Africa, witnessing a high degree of economic insensitivity and exploitation as well as establishing a crisis of colonial rule and poverty among colonial citizens. The era recorded declines in producer prices, increased prices for imported goods, locust invasions, flooding, unemployment and so on. In 1930, there were a series of locust invasions in Ilorin, Niger, Kabba, Benue, Azare, Plateau and Sokoto Provinces in Northern Nigeria. For example, in 1930, 1,336, 907 and 374 flying swarms were recorded in Niger, Benue and Kabba Provinces respectively (NAK/MINPROF: 1349; Crocker, 1936:115; Abdulkadir,

2000:52). Hadejia Emirate also witnessed locust invasion resulting in corn shortages. The Governor of Nigeria, Cameron, acknowledged this noting, "locust infestations and swarms of grasshoppers led to serious food shortage in the Northern Provinces" (*The Nigerian Gazette,* 1932:90). A colonial report of 1934 also stated, "Recently, Northern Nigeria has been subject to a plague of locusts. In 1930, the damage done by locusts was considerable..." (*Colonial Annual Report,* 1934:44). Crocker also wrote, "this locust problem is promising to become the outstanding economic menace of the country" (Crocker, 1936:138).

The British responded to the situation by the "destruction of the locust hoppers conducted chiefly by driving the swarms into trenches and pits...by poisoning the bands of hoppers with baits treated with arsenic". It is claimed that about 1,200 tons of bait were made, with over 150,000 acres of hoppers destroyed (*Colonial Annual Report,* 1934:44). However, these 'efforts' did very little to ameliorate the peasants' plight. For example, in July 1933 alone, about 162 and 193 farms were damaged in Kontagora and Abuja Divisions respectively, whilst 50 percent of sorghum was destroyed in three villages in Bida Division. In Arewa Gabas in Sokoto Province, the locust invasion of 1930-31 contributed to food shortages and a reduction of the area farmed (Shenton, 1986:135). In Sokoto and Zaria Provinces, locust plague and over-cultivation had resulted in famine. As a result of locust invasion, many places in Adamawa Province were hit by drought, with several farms and crops ruined (Fariku, 1974:42). In 1933, the Ham people in Kachia District suffered from locust invasion that severely damaged food crops, as well as drought (Abubakar, 1989:163). There was a local failure of crops and cotton around Ririwai village in Lame District in Azare Province (Crocker, 1936:115). An eye witness described poverty among the people in Lame District this way,

> "throughout the District I am convinced of the reality of their absolute poverty; they have nothing but a few fouls, a handful of old ragged clothes and just enough corn to keep them going until the next harvest. For the majority of the people, I should say 90 percent, there is no other way of obtaining the currency needed for their tax this year (1934) than selling some of their corn, and to do that will mean selling a large amount of it....it will mean short rations for most and in most cases hunger" (Crocker, 1936:115).

One of the major disasters of the 1930s was flooding. In most parts of Northern Nigeria, an abnormal rainfall in 1932 led to real food shortages and famine (NAK/LOKOPROF: 12; Abdulkadir, 2000:54). In Igala Division in Kabba Province, the exceptionally heavy rains in 1933 accompanied by severe flooding of farms caused a loss of 50 percent of the sorghum cultivated (NAK/SNP, 17: 19276). In Auyo, Mallam Moduri and Kirikasamma and other riverain Districts in Hadejia Emirate, there were abnormal floods in 1936 and 1938 leading to crop failure (Abdulkadir, 2006:13).

The general grain dearth occasioned by locust infestations, drought, famine and flooding was further complicated by the actions of the Central Government and Provincial Administrations, which had resulted in the prohibition of grain exports across Provincial, Divisional and District boundaries, in order to hold on to what ever grain they had. For example, when the District Officer (D.O), Kontagora Division sought assistance from Lapai and Agaie Divisions, the D.O stated, "I am afraid little help will be forthcoming from this Division". On his own part, the D.O of Abuja Division replied, "it is regretted that Abuja Administration is unable to help" (NAK/MINPROF, M68). The Secretary of the Northern Provinces further complicated the already terrible situation by his directives that food relief should only be sought from internal sources. The food crisis was again compounded by the action of 'lending' and 'investing' capital abroad by the Provincial Administrations in Northern Nigeria, which meant they could not liquidate their assets for grain purchase. For example, in the Financial Years 1930-34, 44.87 percent of Northern Nigeria Native Administrations' 'surplus' amounting to £2,508,354.1s.9d was invested in Crown Colonies, the Strait Settlements (Singapore), Trinidad, New Zealand and Australia (Abdulkadir, 2004:2). The reason for not liquidating the 'surplus' was, according to Resident Nash, that, '[the depression] would not appear to be a propitious moment for realizing investment' (Watts, 1987:82).

Since the government failed to support the people and the community and domestic resources were incapable of supporting them, the results were food shortages, famine, starvation and even death. In Kontagora Division, in order for some children to get food and survive the crisis, their parents sold them to those who had enough food. The Annual Report for Zungeru Division in Niger Province of 1932 contained evidence of an alarming number of deaths from disease and starvation. In Zungeru, Bida, Kuta and Agaie Districts, people ate all kind of grasses, tubers and leaves to survive the famine in the areas (Iyela, 1987:245-47).

The British in Northern Nigeria were found also to have slacked in the provision of water for the people, as part of the processes of poverty alleviation. A typical example will suffice. The Beeby Thompson Report of 1921-32 has shown that in rural areas of Kano there was an acute and serious shortage of adequate wells. Indeed, various Administrative Officers in Kano before the 1930s had noted this obvious neglect in favour of electricity and water works schemes. It has been pointed out that,

"Had even only 10 percent or 20 percent of the huge sum disbursed on the electric light and water works schemes been expended on digging and walling wells in the northern villages, and in construction of water troughs for the animals, a reform of quite unusual beneficence would have been wrought for several hundred thousand people" (Crocker, 1936:138).

Like almost all post-colonial governments in Nigeria, the British claimed that the sufferings of the people during these terrible times were not the result of governments' neglect, but due essentially to their laziness, backwardness, incompetence and lack of planning. This concept of a 'backward sloping supply of labour curve' is unacceptable. Perhaps, as shall be shown, the "Mixed Farming" of the British, the "Operation Feed the Nation", the "Green Revolution", the National Poverty Eradication Program" and even NEEDS were and are still attempts to blame the ordinary Nigerian for his/her problems (not enough food/work etc) rather than governments and their bad economic and even political policies and lack of adequate and sustained poverty eradication strategies.

During the 1930s depression (and even earlier) the Agricultural Department in Northern Nigeria had continued to pursue a misnomer 'policy' termed 'Mixed Farming'. This implies the use of animal husbandry especially cattle in cultivating the land. It was assumed that if the farmer was supplied with manure he could cultivate his land consistently without "the method of restoring soil fertility, by wasteful and tree destroying practice of shifting cultivation" (Crocker, 1936:131). It was equally wrongly assumed that with this method, the farmer would increase his productivity 8 fold. Even the Governor, as reported in the West African Review of June 1934 and quoted by Crocker, said, "an income of 10s can be increases to at least £10" (Crocker, 1936:131) – an increase of at least 2,000 percent. The problems with this 'policy' were that it downplayed the intercropping method utilized by the local farmer through which the legumes served as fertilizing agents; it was unmindful of the economic and social foundations of the local life; it assumed that the local farmers were not responsive to price incentives. As Crocker rightly pointed out, "it (Mixed Farming) illustrates the practice in Nigeria of failing to think out fundamental policies and the effects of that failure" (Crocker, 1936:132). Indeed, all what the Governor did, apart from his cynicism and knee-jerk actions, was to put a smoke screen to the Colonial Office in London and tried to blame someone else (anyone else) for the lack of poverty alleviation devises and policies to assist the ordinary Northern Nigeria citizens during this terrible time.

Until the 1940s the government was less than ready to promote development and to accelerate the pace of welfare provision and social change. The period witnessed state intervention in the economy as part of the efforts to win the war and to prevent Germany from extending its influence to Nigeria. The interventionist orientation which started during the war began at both the central and regional levels. Issues of development and welfare were often linked with production because if was when farmers produced that resources would be available to 'improve' their conditions, but not ameliorating poverty among the people. At the regional level, attempts were made to increase agricultural production through loan schemes, but such loans were misdirected to nonagricultural sectors including the building of personal residential homes (Falola, 2004:89). With the "First Development Plan" that spanned over ten years (1945-1955), resources were allocated to social services, education and projects that could create jobs.

However, despite acute regional food scarcity, the dire need of several Provinces for preserving their surplus grains as well as limiting inter-regional trade in basic foodstuffs had led to legislations by various Northern Provinces forbidding the private sale of millet and sorghum and inhibiting the movement of food commodities outside the frontiers of Native Authorities. During the 1940s, while the Council of Chiefs insisted on cash-crop regions maintaining reserves sufficient for government institutions, the Government started with the requisition of grains for military purposes and for workers on the Plateau tin mines. A quota was fixed for each of Province, Division, District, village and even on individual households. For example, the quota for Zaria Emirate was 3,330 tons of sorghum (Abdulkadir, 2001:149). Towards the end of the war, the Government, once again, started the storage and reserve policy occasioned by the aversion of local famine in 1943. Consequently, five permanent reserve stores were erected in four Northern Provinces with a capacity of 10,000 tons. This was done, one supposes, to relieve communities experiencing famine as well as to stabilize grain prices in urban markets such as Kano, Zaria, Kaduna and so on. Watts pointed out that the Emir of Kano was against the central store in order to avoid a dependency syndrome on the state. What is more, by November 1947 the grain requisition policy was abandoned along with the reserve system (Watts, 1987:83-85). All restrictions on the movement of grains were equally removed before the harvest. In fact, food requisition and forced labour for the tin mines created famine conditions and compounded the war-time food crisis and also discouraged farmers from increasing production. In the end, there was only limited poverty alleviation and relief but without any famine policy (Watts, 1987:83; Shenton, 1986:136).

One frequent occurrence during the war was flooding. For example, in 1946, extensive flooding in the Districts bordering the Hadejia River occurred, with damages done to sorghum, corn and millet farms. It was reported in 1947 that,

> "flooding from Hadejia river is becoming worse every year and is forming a serious menace to adjacent farmland. Owing to the unrestricted and variable flooding from this river and many branches and tributaries, more and more agricultural land is being carried away or ruined every year. A considerable amount of growing crops is also being destroyed from unexpected flooding from the river" (NAK/KANPROF, 348:159).

However, up to the 1950s nothing was practically done to minimize the flooding in the area. And so the local inhabitants of most of the Districts mostly affected like Auyo, Mallam Maduri, Kaugama and Guri had to erect considerable earthworks through communal and unpaid labour to minimize flooding (Abdulkadir, 2006:15-16).

By the 1950s and 1960s development dreams based on the surpluses from the marketing boards started, by which time food shortages had become an accepted life of most Northern citizens. Thus it should be possible to use part of the surplus as well as taxes to provide schools, hospitals and roads, and to create additional jobs. Despite these, in most rural and even urban areas in Northern Nigeria, the incomes of peasant farmers who depended heavily on food crops could hardly cope with post war inflation. The status and living standards of farmers declined compared to wage earners, with no relief in sight. Indeed, in the 1960s, food prices continued to rise due largely to increased population and declined production.

Conclusion

For most of the period discussed, the 'faces' of poverty have been demonstrated, but poverty alleviation and development strategies have failed to provide remedies. The British Government made little provision for the poor and for resolving the food security crisis. There were no provisions of social services or control against famine, drought and flooding. The Governor as well as Residents and District Officers provided little funds to relieve stress and poverty despite the substantial sums 'invested' abroad as well as the ones in Northern Nigeria Treasuries or in fixed deposits in Nigerian banks.

From the foregoing, the lessons in poverty alleviation strategies or lack of it from the colonial period are obvious. First, Nigeria must wake up to the scourge of poverty. Second, there must be an in-depth understanding of the ecological resources of communities and how people coped and what traumatized the coping mechanisms. Third, employment as one of the major routes out of poverty should be given priority in the development agenda. Fourth, there is the need to raise productivity and increase labour absorption in the agricultural sector in order to increase overall employment and address the problems of unemployment and underemployment. Fifth, a sustained human-centered development strategy capable of achieving a structural transformation and reduce poverty should be vigorously pursued. Sixth, parallel measures should be developed in order to improve living conditions and standards of the people. Seventh, government should tackle the structural causes of poverty through concrete, positive and sincere political and economic initiatives; and eighth, government should emphasize increased spending on social services and focus more on genuine and real job-creation and poverty alleviation strategy.

References

Abdulkadir, A. (2001), "Government and Food Distribution in Zaria : 1902-1966" in *FAISJournal of Humanities*. Vol. 1, No. 4,

Abdulkadir, M.S. (2006), *"Taxation in Hedejia Emirate, c. 1909-1950: The Archival Records"* paper presented at the Two-Day Conference of The British Conquest of Hadejia and Its Aftermath" to mark The Centenary of Hadejia Emirate's Resistance to British Colonial Invasion: April 1906-April, 2006 AD.

Abdulkadir, M.S. (2005), "Changing World Economy, Economic/Religious Problems and Immigration in Nigeria" in Rimmington, G (ed.) *Empire and Inter-Dependence: AMulti-Disciplinary Conference on the Post-Cold War World* , Wichita – Kansas: Friends University

Abdulkadir, M.S.(2004), *Structuring, Struggling and Surviving Economic Depression in Northern Nigeria: The 1930s as Preview of the Present* , Kano: Bayero University Inaugural Lecture Series. No. 9.

Abdulkadir, M.S., 2000, "Financial and Marketing Crises in Northern Nigeria during the Great Economic Depression: 1929-1935", in *Kano Studies*, New Series, Vol. 1, No.1,

Abdulkadir, M.S. (1990), *An Economic History of Igalaland: c1896-1939*. UnpublishedPh.D. History Department, Bayero University, Kano.

Abubakar, G.A.(2002), "Poverty Alleviation and Direct Job Creation in Nigeria", in Jega, A.M and Wakili, H (eds.), *The Poverty Eradication in Nigeria: Problems and Prospects* , Kano: Mambayya House

Abubakar, M.M. (1989), *A Neglected Nigerian Export Crop, The Growth of Ginger Production and Trade in Kachia District of Southern Zaria: c.1900-1953*. M.A.Thesis, History Department, Ahmadu Bello University, Zaria.

Ajakaiye, O.A., (2002), "Overview of the Current Poverty Eradication Programme in Nigeria" in Jega, A.M and Wakili, H (eds.) *The Poverty Eradication in Nigeria:Problems and Prospects* , Kano: Mambayya House

Annual Reports, Northern Nigeria: (1900-1911), London: Government Publishers.

Bauer, P.T., (1954/1969), *West African Trade* ,London: Routledge and Kegan Paul.*Colonial Annual Reports*, 1934 , Lagos: Government Printer

Crocker, W.R. (1936), *Nigeria: A Critique of British Colonial Administration,* London: George Allen and Unwin.

Crowder, M.(1968), *West Africa Under Colonial Rule,* London: Hutchinson.

De Waal, A., (1997), *Famine Crimes : Politics of Disaster Relief Industry in Africa* London: African Rights and the International African Institute.

Ekundare, R.O. (1973), *An Economic History of Nigeria: 1860-1960* New York: Africana Publishing Campany

Falola, T. (2004), *Economic Reforms and Modernization in Nigeria: 1945-1965*Kent and London: The Kent State University Press.

Fariku, K.S. (1974), *Uba District Under Adamawa Emirate: 1900-1939*. B.A. History History Department, Abdullahi Bayero College, Ahmadu Bello University, Kano.

Helleiner, G.K., 1976, *Peasant Agriculture, Government and Economic Growth in Nigeria* , Homewood Illinois: Richard D. Unwin Limited.

Iyela, A., (1987), *Colonialism and Famine in Niger Province, 1900-1945: A Survey of an Aspect of Colonial Under-Development*. M.A., History Department, Ahmadu BelloUniversity, Zaria.

Kalu, U.K., (2003), "Poverty and its Alleviation in Colonial Nigeria" in Oyebade, A (ed.)*The Foundations of Nigeria* , Trenton and Asmara: Africana World Press

NAK/KANPROF, 348.

NAK/MINPROF, M68.

NAK/MINPROF, 1349.

NAK/SNP 7, 466/1913.

NAK/SNP 17, 19276.

Shenton, R.W. (1986), *The Development of Capitalism in Northern Nigeria* (Toronto and Buffalo: University of Toronto Press

The Nigerian Gazette, (1932), Lagos: Government Printer

Watts, M., (1987), "Brittle Trade: A political Economy of Food Supply in Kano," in Guyer, J (ed.) *Feeding African Cities: Studies in Regional Social History*, Manchester: Manchester University Press

CHAPTER FOUR

POVERTY ALLEVIATION INITIATIVES IN NIGERIA: 'LEEMP' AS A REASSURING ALTERNATIVE STRATEGY

Kabiru Isa Dandago

Introduction

Poverty is a negative term, ordinarily denoting an absence, or lack, of material wealth. The term is used to describe situation of insufficiency, either in the possession of wealth or in the flow of income (Seligman & Johnson, 1933). In a more critical sense, poverty could be defined as an absence or insufficiency of human and material resources or absence of the leadership required to harness those resources for the betterment of the economy.

Poverty is one of the oldest enemies of mankind (Iqbal, 2002). Historically, the struggle between the "haves" and the "have-nots" has led to the decline of many empires and civilizations, while caring for the poor has invariably resulted in peace, progress and prosperity. These lessons have led to a universal recognition that alleviation of poverty should remain a high priority among the economic goals of mankind. The strategies and policies for poverty alleviation should, however, be dependant on the situation.

Poverty has a lot of detrimental effects, and is, therefore, a highly undesirable condition. A sudden reduction in the level of economic well being creates fear, depression, hopelessness and suicide. Chronic or absolute poverty has been responsible for most revolutions. Comparative or relative poverty causes envy, bitterness and self-depreciation of the ego. It is also mainly accountable for overvaluation of material goods as compared with intellectual and social values.

Poverty has political, economic, social and technological (PEST) implications. It slows down or frustrates PEST development and makes an environment or economy to be continuously stagnant or backward. A lot of efforts, therefore, must be made towards the alleviation of poverty, as its eradication may be too ambitious. Nigerian governments (at the federal, state and local levels) have initiated many programmes/strategies for the eradication, alleviation or control of poverty over the years, without success. Many non-governmental organizations (NGOs), community based organizations (CBOs), corporate bodies and individuals have made a lot of efforts to fight poverty in one way or the other, all to no avail. By all standards (international or local) the level of poverty is aggravating in Nigeria, despite the measures being adopted by government and private sector operators.

The continuous accentuation of poverty in Nigeria despite all the initiatives put in place to fight it out of the economy could be linked to the poor understanding of those initiated programmes by the people for whom the programmes were designed. A think-tank committee instituted by the Obasanjo administration to find out factors responsible for poverty in Nigeria and the way out found that a great majority of the poor did not understand the mechanism and mode of operations of the poverty programmes, mainly because they are not practically involved from the initiation to execution stages and, so, the success of the programmes could not be achieved due to lack of interest and disenchantment of the poor (Joshua, 2007). The committee, therefore, recommended for the design of a Programme that would involve the rural communities from projects inception to completion stages and enhance their capacity. The result was the conceptualization of the Local Empowerment and Environmental Management Project (LEEMP) in the year 2000. LEEMP is designed as a community driven development initiative aimed at empowering communities to identify, design, implement and manage priority poverty alleviation projects.

The objective of this chapter is to critically review the poverty alleviation efforts in Nigeria, with a view to making a case for LEEMP as an alternative strategy that is designed to be a community – based poverty alleviation/eradication Programme. The rest of the chapter is in four sections. Section two reviews conceptual issues and poverty indicators in Nigeria. Section three is an assessment of the poverty alleviation initiatives in Nigeria. Section four discusses the mechanisms and *modus operandi* of LEEMP, while section five summarizes and concludes the chapter.

Conceptual Issues and Poverty Indicators in Nigeria

In Nigeria and other developing countries where agencies like the United Nations (UN), World Bank, International Monetary Fund (IMF) and the like hold sway, the term poverty alleviation is more pronounced than actualized, for many years now. Other terms used interchangeably with poverty alleviation are 'poverty reduction', 'poverty eradication', 'poverty elimination', 'attack on poverty', 'action on poverty' and 'war against poverty'. The nomenclatures easily suggest various programmes, projects, activities and initiatives meant to bring about improvement in the standard of living of the poor. But first, what is Poverty?

Oyemomi (2003) describes Poverty as a state of lack or pronounced deprivation. This lack is primarily that of the basic needs of life such as food, shelter, clothing, education and health. The deprivation could be one that keeps the deprived away from leading the kind of life that everyone values. The poor people also face extreme vulnerability, natural disasters, violence and bad weather, which compound their sense of ill-being, exacerbate their material poverty and weaken their bargaining power.

Poverty may either be in absolute or relative terms. Absolute Poverty is where the person concerned is unable to satisfy his most basic elementary requirements of human survival, while relative poverty is a comparative state of deprivation among individuals, groups or nations of the world. It is, therefore, clear that while absolute poverty can be eradicated, relative poverty can only be controlled to bridge the gap in a set-up, as all people cannot be put at the same level of well being, even in the communist society.

Poverty could also be viewed as a condition in which the individual's income level is insufficient to meet his subsistence needs (Greenwald and Associate 1954). This implies that income level is the determinant of standard of living, which is the yardstick for measuring the well being of the people. All obstructions to the regular flow of income certainly bring about poverty. At the micro-level, for instance, issues such as death, illness, accident, old age and lack of employment of the head of the household are top on the list of causative factors of poverty anywhere in the world. These are complemented by lack of occupational training and excessive family size.

At the macro-level, Nigeria, for instance, is classified as a low income, severely indebted and, therefore, a poor economy (World Bank, 1994). Meanwhile, Nigeria has the largest population in sub- Saharan Africa and it is among the countries with the highest population growth rate in the world. From 64.7 million people in 1980, Nigeria's population increased to 95.2 million in 1994 (Arinze, 1995) and to 140 million (NPC, 2006).

As the aggregate income level of the country is low, its indebtedness is on the high-side, and its population rate is higher than its economic rate. Nigeria has all it takes to be rated as a poor country or, to be on the safe side, its citizens are qualified to be termed 'poor people'. This is to avoid the frowning of the World Bank which in 1999, described Nigeria as a Paradox: A rich country with poor people! According to the World Bank, Nigeria is "too rich to be poor". Be that as it may, it is absolutely clear that Poverty and its indicators are very glaring in Nigeria, and that despite the various poverty alleviation or eradication programmes introduced by the government, more people are being 'netted' than being redeemed from poverty.

Statistics on poverty in Nigeria are gloomier than in the so-called smaller economies in Africa. According to a World Bank report in 1999, Nigeria's Human Development Index (HDI) was only 0.416 with nearly 70% of its population of about 110 million living below the poverty line(spending not more than $365 a year), as against 15% at independence in 1960. National averages indicate that life expectancy at birth stands at 51 years; nearly 40% of the children below the age of 5 years suffer malnutrition; over 50% of the population lacks access to safe drinking water; and only 40% of the population is literate with only about 35% of the population living in urban areas.

Rural dwellers are among the hardest hit by all these statistics, with about 70% of their population having no access to potable water, health care facilities or electricity, amongst other vital facilities necessary for decent living. Onyemomi (2003) reports that the number of poor people in Nigeria has doubled over the last two decades, during which time the country received over $300 billion in oil and gas revenues.

The rate of poverty in Nigeria would be higher, of course, if a higher value than $365 a year is taken as the poverty line; a poverty line of $600 would have resulted in nearly 80% poverty in the country! This is very much contrary to the mass wealth of human and natural resources the country is endowed with, and the over $100 billion of private wealth kept by a few Nigerians abroad (Ighodaro, 2004). Why can't Nigeria attract its own private wealth back to the country for accelerated economic revival? Your answer might be as good as that of the questioner.

Nigeria is a very good show-case of a country where no one should be poor but not less than 70% of its population is consumed by poverty (World Bank, 1999). The irony is that the number of poor people (living on less than $1 per day) seems to be on the increase. All indicators of poverty: mortality, morbidity, fertility, access to water, sanitation, health, education and so on are increasingly deteriorating.

Poverty Alleviation Initiatives in Nigeria

As mentioned earlier, complete poverty eradication is rather too ambitious in any society, especially the widespread relative poverty. This poverty cannot even be alleviated through a short-term piecemeal approach (D'silva and By-South, 1992). According to Evbuomwan (1997), poverty alleviation does not simply mean short-term relief or the satisfaction of basic human needs, but also the development of strategies for increasing the long term productive potential and, therefore, the income of the poor. To achieve this long-term objective, it is necessary to effectively integrate macroeconomic policies, sectorial planning and sound project interventions. This would amount to government (at the federal, state and local levels) and the private sector players (companies, other firms, NGOs, CBOs, etc) coming together and joining forces to achieve the desired objective.

The World Development Report (1990) considers the mechanism which governments have at their disposal for overcoming poverty. Four measures are identified as having a major potential to increase the income of the poor. They are:

- Increase the demand and, therefore, the price for those factors of production that the poor own (e.g. their own labour).
- Transfer physical assets to the poor (e.g. land).
- Provide social services to the poor (e.g. education).
- Transfer current income to the poor (e.g. through cash or food subsidies).

Are these measures being taken in Nigeria? The honest and sincere answer to this question, even from the government quarters, should be "no"! These measures are in line with the South African initiative in human and infrastructure development aimed largely at providing access to education, health care, clean water, constant power supply, gainful employment and good judicial system for the poor, which would also contribute to overall economic growth. This would, in turn, allow further improvements in the lives of the poor (Hirsch, 2005).

The World Development Report (1990) further notes that the major obstacles to alleviating poverty are not so much the non-availability of financial, human and capital resources. The main constrain is lack of commitment among governments, individuals and organizations to achieving the goal of an end to poverty. This observation appears to be based on the Nigerian situation, where dogged commitment and dedication towards achieving set objectives are weak. The resources are there but, they are poorly managed to achieve the desired goals/objectives. In short, the report is blaming poor leadership as the major obstacle to alleviating poverty in countries suffering from it!

The International Community, through the platform of the United Nations Conferences in the 1960s, has set for itself several development goals to be achieved by the year 2015. These goals, if achieved, would have absolute poverty substantially eradicated and relative poverty greatly alleviated. These goals are:

- Reduce by half the proportion of people living in extreme income poverty (that is, living on less than $1 a day).
- Ensure universal primary education.
- Eliminate gender disparity in primary and secondary education (by 2005).
- Reduce infant and child mortality by two thirds.
- Reduce maternal mortality by three quarters.
- Ensure universal access to reproductive health services.
- Implement national strategies for sustainable development in every country by 2005, so as to reverse the loss of environmental resources by 2015 (Oyemomi, 2003).

To work towards achieving these seven goals, government and private sector operators must join hands together, with the government clearly defining the role each partner should play and ensure dogged commitment to the agreed plan of action. The period set for the third and seventh goals (2005) has passed and they have not been achieved at all in Nigeria. How could the other goals be achieved, by their target periods, given the same poor commitment of the government and the other stakeholders in the country?

In Nigeria, there are various actors who claim to be initiating, executing, co-ordinating, monitoring and reviewing activities meant to help the poor out of poverty. These actors include Community Based Organizations (CBOs), Non-Governmental Organizations (NGOs), government at the local, state and federal levels, the private sector group (corporate bodies and individuals) and international organizations. For poverty alleviation activities to have any meaning and direction, all these actors must work together as a force led by the federal government. They must be honest, sincere, prudent, transparent, accountable and committed as they play relevant roles towards the realization of the set goals/objectives in helping the poor out of poverty.

Ayeni (2004) recounts that successive Nigerian governments from 1970 started to adopt various mission-oriented strategies to achieve specific national economic development objectives which, in general, were targeting poverty alleviation. These strategies are: Operation Feed the Nation (OFN); the Green Revolution (GR); Agricultural Development Projects (ADPs); technology transfer; backward integration; small scale industries programme; Directorate of Food, Roads and Rural Infrastructure (DFRRI); National Directorate of Employment(NDE); Better Life for Rural Women; Family Support Programme; and National Poverty Eradication Programme (NAPEP). These strategies could not achieve the desired results, due to lack of dogged commitment and insincerity of purpose. Another vital reason is the fact that the poor, for whom the programmes were designed, did not understand their mechanism and *modus operandi* (Joshua, 2007:19).

Close working relationships were also established several times between the government and external agencies to develop poverty alleviation strategies. For instance, the federal government launched a poverty assessment Programme in 1994 in partnership with the World Bank, UNICEF and the Oversea Development Administration (ODA) (World Bank, 1998). The result of the assessment (completed in 1995) was discussed at federal, state, local and community levels. Vision 2010 was another all-involving programme in which it was broadly acknowledged that Nigeria needed to re-orient its development strategy and set real objectives to address the poverty and welfare concerns of its people.

The government of Chief Olusegun Aremu Obasanjo, had NEEDS (National Economic Empowerment and Development Strategy) as its 'bible' for achieving the sustainable economic development objective of the country and, in particular, for achieving the poverty reduction/alleviation objective. The NEEDS document has clearly spelt out the role government, private sector, Community Based Organization (CBOs), Non-Governmental Organizations (NGOs), foreign agencies and other interest groups are to play towards achieving set objectives.

The federal government, in addition to pursing the process of Poverty Alleviation Strategy, has established the National Poverty Eradication Programme (NAPEP) to perform the following functions:

- co-ordinate and monitor the activities of all federal ministries and agencies and other relevant organizations on poverty eradication nationwide; and
- Intervene in areas requiring action to be initiated, further action and/or intensified action.

NAPEP's activities are hinged on four schemes; each having programmes to be executed at all levels of government, namely:

- Youth Empowerment Scheme (YES).
- Rural Infrastructures Development Scheme (RIDS).
- Social Welfare Service Scheme (SOWESS).
- National Resources Development and Conservation Scheme (NRDCS) (Oyemomi, 2003).

The overall target of NAPEP is to eradicate absolute poverty in Nigeria by the year 2015. NAPEP is set to achieve this target through relevant well-articulated and focused policy formulation, policy continuity, transparently sustainable practical programmes, full coordination, full monitoring, timely impact assessment and adequate funding. More significantly, the programme is designed to be sustained at all levels of the three tiers of governance.

Direct funding for NAPEP activities is drawn from the Poverty Eradication Fund (PEF), which has both internal and external sources. The internal sources include budgetary allocation; contributions from states and local governments, contributions from the private sector; and special deductions from constituted funds of the federal government. The external sources include funds sourced from the World Bank, United Nations Development Programme (UNDP), the European Union (EU), Department For International Development (DFID), Japanese International Corporation Agency (JICA); German Technical Assistance (GTA) and other international donor agencies.

Looking at the way NEEDS and NAPEP are well designed and articulated, the present administration of Alhaji Umar Musa Yar'Adua needs only to develop the required 'political will' and exhibit a sincere and honest commitment to the implementation of the two programmes for the country to achieve the set objectives before the target period. But since the programmes are not clearly community-based, involving practically the poor in the community set-up, LEEMP should be amplified as a complementary or alternative strategy for poverty alleviation in the country, ensuring that its presence is felt in all the rural and urban communities in Nigeria.

Local Empowerment and Environmental Management Project (LEEMP)

LEEMP was conceptualized in the year 2000 in line with the recommendation of the presidential think-tank committee set up to find out factors responsible for poverty in Nigeria. The committee recommended for the design of a Programme that would involve the rural communities from inception and enhance their capacity.

LEEMP is, therefore, designed as a community driven development initiative aimed at empowering communities with ideas and resources for them to manage priority poverty alleviation projects. It was approved by the federal executive council in May, 2003 as a poverty interventionist Programme. The International Development Association (IDA) and the Global Environmental Facility (GEF) also bought the idea and objectives behind it. This led to the subsequent approval by the World Bank board on 31st July, 2003.

The development credit agreement for LEEMP was signed between the federal government and the World Bank on 3rd December 2003 and was declared effective, by the World Bank on 29th April, 2004. The agreement encourages the IDA and the GEF to jointly support LEEMP with a sum of$78.5million, with the IDA contributing the higher chunk of $ 70 million.

LEEMP implementation took effect on April 29, 2005, hoping that it would make tremendous impact in improving economic governance, creating conditions for private sector-led poverty reduction and economic growth programmes. It is also expected to improve environmental management, capacity building and accelerate the development of rural areas.

To ensure successful implementation, LEEMP was designed with an in-built monitoring and evaluation mechanism. This mechanism consists of seven monitoring groups at various levels. These are:

(i) Community project management, drawn from the benefiting communities; (ii) the multi – facilitation implementation teams, made up of experts from various fields; (iii) the local government authorities; (iv) the local government review committees; (v) the state project support unit (SPSU); (vi) the federal project support unit(FPSU); and (vii) the donor agencies. A federal government programme advisory committee (FPAC) is to provide overall policy guidance and implementation advices, while the federal project support unit (FPSU) will be responsible for overall planning, coordination and monitoring. LEEMP currently has five components:

- Multi – sectoral community- driven investments.
- Local government assessment and capacity building.
- Protected areas and biodiversity management.
- Strengthening environmental institution framework.
- Programme management.

The present participating states are: Adamawa, Bauchi, Bayelsa, Benue, Enugu, Katsina, Imo, Niger and Oyo. At initial stage three local government areas were selected from each of the nine states, while ten communities were chosen from each local government area. LEEMP is currently operating in more than 80 local government areas and about 1350 communities, with aggregate micro projects of 4000. These projects have transformed the lives of the rural dwellers within a short while. It is hoped that LEEMP would soon be launched in the remaining states of the Federation and FCT.

LEEMP is the only World Bank assisted project that involves the active participation of beneficiary communities in the project initiation and execution. It empowers communities and local governments; it creates opportunities for realigning responsibilities between tiers of government; it entrenches transparency and accountability and government business; it inculcates the principles of participatory development, improved management capacities of the communities as well as increased awareness on sustainable environmental management.

With just about $50,000 (₦6.5million), the LEEMP initiative could sunk boreholes to ensure safe water supply; construct blocks of classrooms to provide shelter for pupils/students; construct clinics/ dispensaries, etc for a community. LEEMP contribution is like a matching grant to be complemented by the contributions of the able and willing members of the community.

If state governments and local governments are to be investing just ₦6million from their monthly Federation Account allocation to develop their rural communities, in line with the LEEMP philosophy, it should not take the state or local governments' chief executives up to the four year in their tenure to eliminate substantially the absolute poverty in their communities and alleviate the relative poverty in them. Even if LEEMP is not yet launched in a state, the State Governors and the Local Government Council Chairmen in the state should adopt LEEMP strategies in their own ways, as the amount to be invested in stimulating rural empowerment and development is nothing big to Write home about, especially when compared with the benefits that would accrue to the masses.

LEEMP is the long awaited solution to Nigeria's poverty problem and a gateway to the country's ambition for achieving rural industrialization and sustainable national development. It should be wholeheartedly welcomed by all the three tiers of government in Nigeria, the organized private sector operators, NGOs, CBOs, CSOs and the entire Nigerians.

Conclusion

Based on the foregoing discussion, it is clear that Nigeria and/or Nigerians are deep in the 'mud' of poverty and that several efforts were claimed to have been made through different 'window-dressing' programmes of government to help the country or its citizens out of the 'mud'. Instead of redeeming the poor from the hard-bite of poverty, the biting is just becoming harder, with more people falling below the poverty line. It has been established that the cause of this unfortunate situation is lack of a dogged commitment to the implementation of agreed plans and policies and, of course, non-involvement of the poor in the initiation, planning, execution and reporting of poverty alleviation projects.

The chapter argues for the speedy introduction of Local Empowerment and Environmental Management Project (LEEMP) in all the 774 local governments in Nigeria for all Nigerians to take their fate strongly in their hands and accelerate their communities' process of economic, social and political development on a sustainable basis. This is the real and practical strategy for poverty alleviation or eradication that is very much suitable in the Nigeria context.

A successful attack on poverty requires the full participation of, not only government and the private sector but, all other stakeholders as well. For the government, it has to create an enabling investment environment, in real sense; create and promote opportunities (roads, education, credit, business etc); facilitate PEST empowerment, and enhance security at all levels. To achieve economic growth and alleviate poverty, there must be prudent fiscal and monetary policies with incentives to: (i) create more and wider sources of growth; (ii) support the development of the private sector as the catalyst for growth; and (iii) carry the poor along in the design and implementation of projects that would alleviate or eliminate the poverty in them.

In conclusion, the chapter argues that Nigeria is not basically suffering from the poverty of resources, poverty of income or poverty of ideas. No-matter how much money, time and energy the country invests in fighting these variants of poverty (especially poverty of income, which this paper has focused on), the end result would still be zero or negative improvement since the real target is essentially ignored. The hard fact is that the country is suffering principally from poverty of leadership! Fighting this poverty which is the cause of the marginalization of the poor in project initiation and execution, should be the starting point for any realistic and sincere battle against all the other variants of poverty in Nigeria.

References

Arinze, A.I. (1995), "Review of the 1994 Human Development Report: UNDP" in CBN EFR, Vol. 33, No. 1, March.

Ayeni, F. (2002), "Stimulating Economic Growth Through Entrepreneurship", paper presented at the 34th Annual Accountants Conference of ICAN, Sheraton Hotel & Towers, Abuja, October.

D'Silva, E. and Bysouth, K. (1992), "Poverty Alleviation Through Agricultural Projects", in *Economic Development Institute of the World Bank*, Policy Seminar Report, No. 30.

Evbuomwan, G.O. (1997), "Poverty Alleviation Through AgriculturalProject: A Review of the Concept of the World BankAssisted Agricultural Development Projects in Nigeria",in *Bullion*, a publication of CBN Vol. 21, No. 3, July/Sept.

Greenwald, D. (1965), *The Mc Grow-Hill Dictionary of Modern Economics*, A Handbook of Terms and Organizations, New York: McGrow Hill.

Hirsch, A. (2005), *Season of Hope: Economic Reform Under Mandele and Mbaki*, Scottsville: University of Kwazulu –Natal press.

Igbal, M. (ed) (2002), *Islamic Economic Institutions and the Elimination of Poverty*, Leicester – UK: The Islamic Foundation.

Ighodaro, C. (2004), "Corporate Governance: Everybody's Business", Paper presented at the 34th Annual Accountants Conference of ICAN, Sheraton Hotel & Tower, Abuja, October.

Jashua, S. (2007), "Nigeria's Many Fight Against Poverty", in *Empowerment News*, a publication of LEEMP, Vol. 1, No. 1, May,

National Population Commission (2006), *Result of Population Census in Nigeria*, Abuja: Government printers.

Oyemomi, E.O. (2003),"Poverty Reduction: NAPEP and the NGOs", in *the Nigerian Accountant*, the official journal of ICAN, Vol. 36, No.2 April/June,

Seligman, E.R.A. and Johnson, A. (1933), *Encyclopedia of the Social Sciences*, New Jersey: Macmillan Company

World Bank (1994), *World Development Report: Infrastructure for Development*, World Development Indicators, Oxford: Oxford University Press.

World Bank (1999), "Nigeria: Poverty in the midst of plenty, the Challenge of Growth Inclusion", *World Bank Poverty Assessment*, May.

World Bank (1998), "Poverty and Welfare in Nigeria", Washington, DC: American Writing Corporation.

World Bank (1999), "Human Development Index", New York: World Bank HDIReports

World Development Report (1990), "Mechanism for Poverty Reduction", the United Nations Impact Assessment.

CHAPTER FIVE

THE NIGERIAN GOVERNMENT AND WAR AGAINST POVERTY: VICTORY VERDICT, 1999 – 2007

Murtala S. Sagagi

Introduction

Persistent rise in Poverty level is a malaise to African countries. Today, 60% of the world 6.4 billion population lives in abject poverty and most of them live in the African continent (Sampson, 2006). Nigeria is one of the few countries in the world blessed with large population and massive mineral resource deposits. With more than 130 million people, vast fertile land and irrigation opportunities; massive oil reserve, zinc, platinum, traces of gold and others, Nigeria stand a great chance of achieving economic growth and poverty reduction. Unfortunately, the country has failed over the years to have policy direction that would help harness the country's diverse resources to produce enduring wealth. This makes Nigeria one of the oil rich countries and at the same time one of the poorest.

In 1999, Retired General Olusugun Obasanjo emerged as the democratic President of Nigeria. His Administration came with the promise to fight poverty and restore prosperity to the nation which was devastated by the failures of the past military dictators. So, it is reasonable to point out that Obasanjo inherited economic deterioration from the past unsuccessful governments. Ogwumike (2003) maintains that the implementation of Structural Adjustment Programme (SAP) from 1986 to early 1990s has worsened living condition in Nigeria. The Programme not only failed to deliver its economic growth objectives, but succeeded in weakening economic growth, engendering unemployment leading to unprecedented poverty in the country. For this, the task before Obasanjo's Administration was to stimulate economic growth and improve general economic management leading to poverty reduction. This was believed to be the key for winning the war against poverty.

However, evidence from national Core Welfare Indicators Questionnaire (CWIQ), National Living Standard Survey (NLSS) and data obtained from international agencies reveal that the number of people living in poverty in Nigeria has increased from 1996 to 2006. Also, the structure of the economy has not changed significantly in the same period. This is regrettable considering the oil wind fall that Nigeria enjoyed over the last seven years and the huge amounts invested in poverty reduction strategies. So, it is not clear whether the funds directed at poverty reduction and economic growth were misdirected or squandered. This paper is aimed at addressing poverty incidence before and during Obasanjo's regime, and shows 'what went wrong' in poverty reduction efforts. The analysis of various data collected would help proffer possible measures of formulating genuine and sustainable poverty reduction strategies in Nigeria. It is hoped that the paper may help the next regime avoid certain pitfalls that prevented Obasnajos's administration from winning its battle with poverty incidence in real terms.

A Review of Poverty Incidence in Nigeria

Breaking the vicious cycle of poverty should be the real goal of any purposeful government in Africa. Today, poverty is the greatest obstacle to achieving economic growth in Nigeria. At the same time, inadequate economic growth is the main cause of poverty. Thus, poverty cannot be reduced unless growth and economic diversification is achieved. Frequently, Poverty Incidence is used to show the gravity of poverty in a particular country. Poverty Incidence is the proportion of the population for whom consumption falls below poverty line. The poverty line is an international accepted measure that divides the poor and non-poor. The most commonly used measure of people living below Poverty Line is that portion of the population who live below $1 per day. The World Bank (cited by Friedman, T. L (2005) reported that the number of people living below Poverty Line in Sub Saharan Africa (SSA) increased from 227 in 1990 to 313 million in 2001. This figure is projected to increase to 340 million by 2015.

Fwatshak (2003), reported that Nigeria belonged to the group of middle income countries in 1980, but by 1989, it degenerated to the group of poorest nations. Recently, CWIQ Survey (2006) revealed that Nigerian people consider themselves as poor because of the following main reasons:

- Hard economic condition
- Prices of commodities are too high
- Inability to meet basic living requirements
- Lack of capital to start or expand business/agriculture
- Lack of employment opportunities
- High prices of agricultural inputs
- Low prices of agricultural outputs

In Nigeria, general economic mismanagement, lack of domestic capacity and weak social and economic infrastructure are identified as the main cause of increased poverty (Khor, 2001). The issues discussed below are indication of how far away Nigeria is from combating poverty.

Economic Mismanagement

Mauro (1995) argues that corruption is negatively and significantly associated with the accumulation of physical capital/GDP growth. Evidently, Nigeria neither lacks material nor the human resources to create enduring wealth. The country earns hundreds of billions of petrodollars which could have been utilized to improve living standards and infrastructure. Unfortunately, the national poverty level remains as high as 54% (NLSS, 2006). The issue is how the government deployed such massive resources.

Nigeria is still the 6th most corrupt nation among the 155 counties ranked by the Transparency International. It is to be noted that Nigeria was ranked second most corrupt nation on earth just few years ago. DFID, (2006) similarly reported that Nigeria had the worst score -1.13 in the Rule of Law Index and also ranked poorly on other institutional and governance indexes. Again, a survey by the DFID indicated that the quality, integrity and efficiency of most public institutions are very poor. The survey also reported that companies pay bribes to secure government contracts. It could therefore be inferred that Obasanjo's Administration has slightly improve the negative image of the country by improving the nation's corruption ranking. However, considering the level of resources pumped into the economy in the last seven years and the increasing poverty in most part of the country, it is difficult to qualify the CPI upgrading as improvement on national economic management. This is clearly a misfortune for a nation aspiring to catch-up with other developing countries. Table 1 shows how Nigeria lags behind other developing nations in improving living standards and human capital development.

Table 1: Indicators of Size and Quality of Human Capital

	Literacy rate		Life Expectancy at birth		Public expenditure on Education % GDP
	1970	2003	1970	2003	2004
Nigeria	20.1	66.8	43.5	44.9	1.02
Indonesia	56.1	87.8	49.2	66.9	1.3
Korea			61.4	74.2	4.3
Mexico	73.5	90.0	62.6	73.6	5.2
South Africa	69.5	86.0	53.9	45.7	5.4

Source: World Development Indicators and CBN Statistical Bulletin (in DFID, 2006)

Table 1 above indicates that from 1970 to 2003 Nigeria performed worst than its peers in raising literacy level of its people and the country was also a low performer as far as health delivery system is concerned. This is given by the low life expectancy rate when compared to other similar developing countries. Again, while South Africa spent 5.5% of its GDP on educating its citizens, Nigeria spent only 1.02%.

Clearly the federal government of Nigeria has the ultimate responsibility to devise policies and command actions that would build human capital which would, in turn, reduce poverty. But at the same time, the state governments also play significant role in the creation of social and economic capital in their respective states. Where a state depends almost exclusively on federal revenue allocation, and failed to allocate resources wisely, the effect would be devastating for its own people. In the 21st century, natural resources (such as oil, gold, fertile land etc) are not the key to achieving growth and poverty reduction. Otherwise, Nigeria would be one of the richest in the world considering its vast fertile land, oil and other mineral resources. So, it does not matter what type or how much resources a state possess as long as available resources are deployed productively and judiciously.

Table 2: Net Federal Revenue Allocation to oil Producing States and Ten other most Populated States in Nigeria*

		Revenue in Billions (Naira)			Population (millions)	Revenue per head	Level of poverty
		2005	2006	Total 2001 – 2006			
1	Abia	20.6	26.2	100.7	2.8	9,357	22.27
2	Akwa Ibom	76.7	93.6	303.9	3.9	24,000	34.82
3	Bayelsa	102.4	116.9	357.2	1.7	68,764	19.98
4	Cross rivers	22.4	27.5	95.9	2.8	9,821	41.61
5	Delta	83.6	-	385.3	4.0	3,500	45.35
6	Edo	22.6	28.9	95.7	3.2	9,031	33.09
7	Imo	23.7	30.2	105.4	3.9	7,743	27.39
8	Ondo	32.6	46.5	145.4	3.4	13,676	42.14
9	Rivers	124.9	153.3	428.4	5.1	30,058	29.09
10	Anambr	19.2	25.5	85.6	4.1	6,219	20.11
11	Bauchi	23.4	28.1	103.9	4.6	6,108	86.29
12	Benue	20.7	26.7	94.9	4.2	6,357	55.33
13	Borno	22.5	28.5	101.5	4.1	6,951	53.63
14	Jigawa	19.9	27.1	92.6	4.3	6,302	95.07
15	Kaduna	23.1	28.5	109.3	6.0	4,750	50.24
16	Kano	31.8	38.8	144.6	9.3	4,127	61.29
17	Katsina	24.6	30.5	110.9	5.7	5,350	71.06
18	Lagos	29.0	38.8	152.2	9.0	4,311	63.58
19	Oyo	24.5	29.0	108.9	5.5	4,454	24.08

Source: Author's computation of data from the Federal Ministry of Finance, 2007; Federal Republic of Nigeria Official Gazette 4 (94) January, 2007; and NLSS, 2006.

Table 2 shows that in the last five years there is no state government in Nigeria that receive less than 80 billion naira regardless of weather it belonged to Niger delta region or not. However, the incidence of poverty remains high especially in the most populated northern states. This is an irony in view of the economic opportunities and past glories of the North. These states have not been able to tap the creative talents and productiveness of their larger population to create their own wealth. They have also not judiciously utilized the enormous financial resources accruing to them over the years.

Clearly, the choices of leaders at both states and federal levels greatly affect poverty level. Lower poverty incidence in the southern states could not be totally explained by the federal allocation alone. On the contrary, productivity and human capital development play a significant role in lower poverty incidence. Unfortunately, the North has the highest number of unproductive adults and has the lowest human capital development in the country. This point is even clearer in table 3 and 4.

Table 3: States with the highest poverty incidence (po) in Nigeria

	2004	1996
Jigawa	95.7	71
Kebbi	89.65	83.6
Kogi	88.55	75.5
Bauchi	86.29	83.5
Yobe	83.25	66.09
Kwara	75.5	85.22

Source: NLSS, 2006

Table 4: State with the lowest poverty incidence (po) in Nigeria

	2004	1996
Oyo	24.08	8.7
Osun	32.35	58.7
Imo	27.3	56.2
Bayelsa	19.98	44.3
Abia	22.27	56.2
Ogun	31.73	69.9

Source: NLSS, 2006

From these tables it is apparent that northern states recorded high incidence of poverty when compared to the southern states. As emphasized earlier, this is not a coincidence. About 40% of Nigeria's 'head of households' have no formal education. CWIQ survey (2006) reveals that the South West has the highest literacy rate of 78% and the North East has the lowest 42.2%. So, it could be said that the South has higher human capital required to achieve growth than the North.

Many people believe that the South benefited from colonial legacy. However, it is an open admission of failure to use past disadvantages to justify present inaction. It is true that the federal government has over the years neglected educationally disadvantaged states in human development programmes. But, the governments of northern states also contribute significantly to the educational backwardness of their people.

Poor Infrastructure

Electricity supply in Nigeria is both inadequate and costly. DFID, (2006) reported that an average Nigerian (small) enterprise spent US$576 per annum on electricity while a comparable enterprise in Egypt spent $201. Again, in Nigeria, electric generators and related accessories accounted for 22 percent of the total cost of machinery and equipments used in running the business. The president has publicly accepted major problem with his approach to power supply in Nigeria. For eight years Obasanjo's regime was unable to diagnose and take appropriate actions to considerably improve power supply.

The situation of Nigerian roads is equally pathetic. Table 5 compares the condition of Nigerian roads with that of other similar developing countries. Compared to Indonesia and Mexico, Nigeria has the least road networks. Also, about 46% of its limited roads are in bad shape. It is to be noted that Indonesia and Mexico are also oil producing developing countries. So, lack of power supply and good road contribute greatly to increasing cost of production which, in turn, makes prices of manufactured goods and services very high. And, this is a bad new for business growth and poverty reduction.

Table 5: Assessments of Condition of Classified Roads in Three Oil-Producing Countries

	National Roads		Regional Roads		Local Roads		Overall Network	
	% of Total	% poor	% of Total	% poor	% of Total	% poor	Total kilometers1	% poor
Indonesia	8.5	<10	12.5	>35	79.0	<50	311,000	42
Mexico	16.2	31	27.5	40	56.3	55 ?	302,000	47
Nigeria	16.4	30	15.9	40	67.7	>50	195,000	46

Sources: DFID, (2006).

Anti Poverty Programmes Before and DuringObasanjo's Regime

The wrong implementation of Structural Adjustment Programme (SAP) in the mid 1980s through 1990s was attributed to worsening condition of living standards in Nigeria. In recognition of the harshness of the policy on people, a number of programmes and agencies were introduced to reduce its pains on the ordinary citizens. The main programmes/agencies introduced include:

Agency/Programme	Year establ.	Activity
Directorate of Food Road & Rural Infrastructure (DFRI)	1986	Water, feeder roads & electrification
National Directorate for Employment (NDE)	1986	Youth training, finance & guidance
Better Life Programme (BLP)	1987	Rural women skills, health care
Peoples' Bank of Nigeria (PBN)	1989	Savings and credit facilities
Family Support Programme (PSP)	1994	Health, child care & youth devt.
Family Economic Advancement Programme (FEAP)	1997	Credit & supporting cottage industry

Unfortunately, all these measures fell short of any meaningful poverty reduction in Nigeria. In fact, lack of sincerity of purpose of the government crippled most of the programmes and agencies. In recognition of the failure of the past poverty reduction measures, Obasanjo's Administration created Poverty Alleviation Programme (PAP) by attempting to provide job opportunities to hundreds of thousands of Nigerians. A total of N470 billion budgeted in 2000 was directed towards poverty reduction in the country. The budgetary provision on poverty reduction was increased by 150% in 2001 and salaries were reviewed upward from 2001 to 2002. These efforts could not achieve significant results because of fuel shortages, increase in tax and increasing unemployment due to slow economic growth (Ogwumike, 2003).

PAP was later changed to Poverty Eradication Programme PEP to increase states participation in poverty reduction. This policy was later supported by the World Bank. The Bank assisted in formulating Interim Poverty Reduction Strategy (IPRSP). This Strategy was completed in 2004 when National Economic Empowerment and Development Strategy (NEEDS) was introduced. NEEDS is a medium term agenda (2003-2007) to reduce unemployment, stimulate growth, improve governance and increase access to basic education. States and local governments are required to formulate their own (SEEDS and LEEDS) strategies in line with national strategy. The SEEDS has recorded certain improvement in poverty level (CWIQ, 2006). However, the strategy has not significantly reduced

unemployment and cost of doing business. Today, 49.8% of Nigerians were unemployed and in 2004 there were more poor people in Nigeria than in 1996 (see
table 6).

Table 6: People living in poverty in Nigeria

1980	18.26
1985	34.73
1992	39.07
1996	67.11
2004	68.70

Source: NBS, 2006.

It is important to emphasize that the high incidence of poverty is not unconnected to the fact that Nigerian economy is still backward; it relied on primary
sectors. This makes it difficult to classify Nigeria as a developing country. Countries are often classified as 'developing' when they are shifting away from natural resources and agriculture to industry and knowledge (service). Table 7 shows
that from 1980 to 2004, the structure of Nigerian economy has not been any different. If Nigeria had improved on its economic successes of the 1970s, the country would have at par or even ahead of Indonesia, Malaysia and South Africa.
Unfortunately, the country still relies heavily on oil sector and small holder agriculture as the main contributors to GDP. The high value added manufacturing
sectors is yet to be fully developed and utilized.

Table 7: Sector Contribution to GDP

	1970	1980	1990	2000	2004
OIL	6.0	29.1	39.3	48.2	48.2
Agriculture	41.3	20.6	29.7	26.3	16.6
Industry	7.8	16.4	7.4	4.5	8.5
Service	45.0	33.8	23.6	21.0	26.5

Source: NBS/IMF, 2006.

One measure of knowing the depth of poverty in Nigeria is to look at what
people use on daily basis. It is unthinkable to imagine that Nigeria export oil and
gas, but its citizens rely on bushes as the main sources of fuel for cooking. Table 8
shows different fuel of cooking used by Nigerians. Fire wood is the main source
of fuel for an average household in Nigeria. This awful condition is mainly due
to the decreasing disposable income arising from high unemployment and slow
economic growth.

Table 8: Fuel for Cooking Used by Nigerians

Fire wood	69.98
Charcoal	0.84
Kerosene	26.53
Gas	1.11
Others	1.54

Source: CWIQ Survey, 2006.

Table 9 is an evidence of Obasanjo Administration's failure to achieve economic diversification and halt inflation essential for poverty reduction. One could be right to argue, judging by the regime's priority actions over its two term period, that the government has succeeded in raising cost of living (given by high inflation) through fuel price and tax increases without reasonable increase in nation's productiveness (GDP) due to weak infrastructure and social capital.

Table 9: GDP Growth and Inflation Rate 2002-2006

	GDP	Inflation
2002	4.63	12.2
2003	9.57	14.0
2004	6.58	15.0
2005	6.51	-
2006	6.9	-

Source: NBS, NLSS, 2006.

Akinkuotu (2006) concluded that Obasanjo's administration was able to reduce the burden of debt on the country and has attempted to improve the image of the country in the eyes of the outside world. However, the author added, the Administration has woefully failed in its mission to reduce unemployment and improve infrastructure essential for poverty reduction. Perhaps, this conclusion is a fair assessment of the Obasanjo's two term rule. With this record, it is very hard to imagine how government could justify the trillions of naira spent over the last eight years when most Nigerians could not afford basic living. Therefore, one could be right to infer that Obasanjo's regime is either naïve or confused about the key requirements for achieving poverty reduction in Nigeria.

The Way Forward

It is apparent that President Obasanjo would like to be involved in the political affairs of the country even after leaving office in May, 2007. While it is important to learn from the past successes and failures, the next Administration would be better off with a radical rethink of development and poverty reduction strategy. To achieve the radical transformation essential for creating prosperity for Nigerian citizens, the following should be seriously considered.

Economic Transformation

The government must embark on sustained efforts with effective collaboration with the private sector to diversify the economy away from oil. Consider the shift in Vietnam's economy in Table 10. Vietnam has been transformed away from 'excess baggage' or primary sectors into medium technology sectors that are easily traded and have the most potential in creating wealth and employment. No society is condemned to subsistence and peasant life style. Societies can always reinvent themselves with the right mindset, education, enlightenment, dialogue and broad policy guidance. Thus, Economic development should not simply be 'one of the policies'; it should be 'the only policy' upon which all others are based. Nigeria needs a development strategy that would encompass reduced cost of doing business, improve investment climate and infrastructure; and encourage savings and investments. This would hopefully bring the desired shift in the structure of the Nigeria economy from resources based sectors to high value added sectors as presently being experience by many Asian countries.

Table 10 Country Structure of Production (% of GDP)

	Agriculture	Industry	Service
Brunei	3	46	51
Indonesia	16	44	40
Malaysia	11	45	44
Philippines	19	32	49
Singapore	0	35	65
Vietnam	26	32	42
Thailand	11	39	50
Chile	8	35	56
Mexico	6	29	66

Source: IMF, Direction Of Trade Statistics (2002).

Redirecting Local Government Administration

As the country attempt to boost the economy from the top, it should not be forgotten that development has to be taken closer to people. From Table 11, it could be seen that there is no local government (LG) in Nigeria that gets less than 600 million naira in 2006. This means that any local government with a 5 years vision has the capability to produce at least 30 professionals and expertise in various professions. Again, with active public-private partnership, a number of small of medium scale businesses can be promoted annually. Education and entrepreneurship development are the *yin yang* essential for poverty reduction and

powering people is much more than a political statement or a media giggle. It requires concerted efforts to change the way people think about their self-worth and how they could create their own future.

Rethinking Agriculture

More than 60% of Nigerians live in rural areas. The primary occupation for rural dwellers is agriculture and related activities. In Nigeria, the size of land required by an average farmer for massive production is so small to achieve any radical improvement in food production. Smallness of land makes antiquated method of farming considered more economically than mechanized farming. It should also be emphasize that over the years, agricultural policies in Nigeria produced very limited results because they mainly serve the interest of importers of fertilizer, machinery and other inputs. Governments at federal and state levels spend billions of naira annually on the procurement and distribution of fertilizers. Unfortunately, according to a NLSS (2006) more than 70% of farmers in Nigeria obtain their fertilizers and other inputs from the open market.

Revitalizing agriculture requires land reform, year round food production, promoting large scale farming, institutional funding, and mechanized farming and embedded processing. Developing processing and light manufacturing in rural areas would absorb farmers who would likely be displaced by large scale farming methods. When resources are freed from fertilizer imports, massive irrigation structures, extension services and support can be funded. Again, a number of states have agricultural supply companies. Some of them have the capacity to use local expertise and resources to produce agricultural inputs such as pesticide, seedlings, implements and fertilizers. With active public-private partnerships these establishments could be resuscitated and be made competitive.

Refocusing of Industrial Growth

A society cannot develop simply because of its accomplishments in agricultural transformation. This is because returns to agriculture tend to be much lower than most other sectors. A speedy growth of the industrial sector requires power to energize it and the will to sustain growth. The first priority of the next administration is to vigorously expand generation of power and create efficient market mechanisms for distribution. Private sectors should also be allowed to compete in power generation and distribution. On their parts, state governments should vigorously pursue Independent Power Project with active collaboration with private investors. The project could better be executed jointly among neighboring states. Today, Nnewi in Anambra State has succeeded in becoming the old Taiwan because of massive industrial activities. Ogun State has benefited from massive Foreign Greenfield Investments leading to massive industrial growth. Cross Rivers is presently leading the nation in tourism. Other states need to make their investment climate right in order to attract more investors. When governments at all levels focus on industrialization, massive unemployment would be significantly reduced.

Growth of Formal Sectors

There are areas where policies, not big budgets, are required to boost growth and reduce poverty. Among them is building a viable formal sector. Today, many businesses in Nigeria are not registered. The government is denied of substantial revenue from taxes and business registrations fees by the failure to create a strong formal sector. In the 21st century, people and businesses need to be re-oriented on the need to unlearn past ineffective practices that are mostly based on history and traditions. A comprehensive programme should commence to ensure that genuine businesses are registered, supported and streamlined not just for the revenue purposes but also to sanitize towns and cities from chaos emanating from misuse by petty traders. Above all, formal businesses have better access to government support and facilities from the financial sector.

Conclusion

Many people believe Nigeria is backward because of excessive corruption. This could be true to certain extend. In reality, lack of genuine economic agenda that would boost growth and reduce poverty is as tragic as corruption. So, Nigeria must fight bad governance and poor policy direction at the same time. Globally, governments are not the creators of prosperity, but it is the sole responsibility of government to provide policy guidance, capacity, and infrastructural framework to support social transformation. With government intervention around these areas, people would rationally search for opportunities and exploit them on their own. Where government fails to provide these necessities, it compensate by embarking on aggressive social policies that encourage consumption, laziness and under utilization of human resources.

The last thing Nigeria needs is a repeat of the last eight years which were both painful and quite disappointing. Obasanjo's Administration might have good intentions on the on-set but evidence presented suggests a complete diversion from the path of development and lessening the pains of poverty in Nigeria. The goal of every leaders should be to make a difference in peoples lives by given them opportunity to explore life potentials to the fullest. With massive oil revenue and overwhelming public support, Obasanjo's Administration was equipped with the right ammunition to combat poverty. Unfortunately, the Regime could not even find an interim solution to erratic power supply, slow growth, and increasing poverty. The next Administration would face a greater challenge of unlearning the past ineffective policies and strategies leading to the reinvention of the nation's economic future. With the right mindset, strategy and willingness to listen, the challenges of poverty reduction in Nigeria are surmountable.

References

Akinkuoku, A. (2006), "A pencil Called Obasanjo", *TELL*, No.25 June 12.

DFID, (2006), Nigeria Competitiveness and Growth, Poverty Reduction and Economic Management 3, Country Department 12, Africa Region, Report No. 36483 – NG

Dunklin, A.L. (2005). Globalization: A portrait of Exploitation, inequality and limit, http://globalization.icaap.org/content/v5.2/dunklin.html

Federal Office of Statistics, (2005), The *Nigerian Statistical Fact Sheets on Economic and Social Development*, Abuja and Lagos.

Federal Office of Statistics, (2005), Draft *Poverty Profile for Nigeria*, Abuja and Lagos.

Friedman, T.L. (2005), The *World is Flat*, New York: Farrar, Straus &Giroux.

Fwatshak, S.U.(2003), "Globalisation and Economic Development in Nigeria: the Challenges of poverty reduction through E-commerce", in Maduagu, M.O & Onu, V. C. (eds.), *Globalisation and National Development in Nigeria*, a publication of Fulbright Association of Nigeria

Federal Office of Statistics (2006), *"Core Welfare Indicators Questionnaire, A survey:"* www.nigerianstat.gov.ng/index.php

IMF, (2005), *Nigeria: 2005 Article IV Consultation* – Staff report; Staff Supplement; and Public Information Notice on the Executive Board Discussion, IMF Country Report No. 05/302.

Khor, M. (2001), Globalization and the South: Some Critical Issues, Ibadan: Spectrum Books Ltd

Mauro (1995), . "Nigeria Competitiveness and Growth, Poverty Reduction and Economic Management", in *DFID*, 3, Country Department 12, Africa Region, *Report* No. 36483 – NG

National Living Standard Survey (2006), *A Report*, Federal Office of Statistics, www.nigerianstat.gov.ng/index.php.

Ogwumike, F. O. (2002), "An appraisal of poverty reduction strategies in Nigeria", in *Central Bank of Nigeria, Economic and Financial Review*, Vol. 39 (4)

Sampson, E. (2006, "Capital Market and Wealth Creation: The Global Picture", Zenith Economic Quarterly, July 1/1

CHAPTER SIX

STATE GOVERNMENTS AND THE WAR AGAINST POVERTY IN NIGERIA

Kabiru Isa Dandago & Ahmad Audu Maiyaki

Introduction

The attainment of high socio-economic well-being has been the desire of all individuals as well as all nations in history. While every individual and nation that have weak socio-economic well being struggle hard to advance their status, the nations/individuals that attain high living standard strive vigorously to maintain and improve on that status. In other words, everybody whether an individual, society or nation tries as much as possible to get rid of poverty. As such, poverty is a phenomenon that is being avoided by everyone as much as possible. Conversely, high socio-economic well-being is always targeted and cherished by all.

Poverty is the state of extreme deprivation, in which the basic necessities of life are grossly lacking (Oyemomi, 2002). Poverty always goes hand in hand with undesirable phenomena such as poor healthcare condition, violence, malnutrition, illiteracy, unemployment, high infant mortality rate, and general economic deprivation, in some cases, dislocation among others.

Several reasons account for poverty in modern societies. For example, Africa is one of the few continents in the world that are ridden by poverty (Sachs, 2005). Nigeria is situated in Africa. The country is hit hard by poverty; perhaps more than several other countries despite its huge natural and human resources endowment. The inability of Nigerians to exploit the resource potentials of the country for their betterment, coupled with the lack of political will in the country, further pushes the country deeper into poverty. These factors, among others, resulted in the current international position of Nigeria as one of the poorest countries in the world, despite all her abundant resources. For example, Nigeria has more than four hundred and fifty different types of solid mineral resources-the highest in the world (Dandago, 2005: 109).

It is against this backdrop that both the Nigerian government and the government of the rich countries set out to fight poverty vigorously. This can be seen in the different ways the government and donor agencies make efforts to fight poverty in Nigeria and beyond: Millennium Development Goals; through its Poverty Reduction Strategy, United States Agency for International Development

(USAID), British Government's Department for International Development (DFID), United Nations Development Projects (UNDP), Non Governmental Organizations for Literacy Support (NOGALS), National Poverty Eradication Programmes (NAPEP), National Directorate of Employment (NDE), National Economic Reconstruction Funds (NERFUND), National Agricultural Land Development Agency (NALDA) and the National Economic Empowerment and Development Strategy (NEEDS).

These are some of the institutions and programmes set to reduce or eliminate poverty in Nigeria and other parts of the world. National Poverty Eradication Programme (NAPEP) is among the most recent programmes established by the Nigerian government to eliminate poverty. The efforts of both international and local organizations are yet to show significant impact in the war against poverty in Nigeria.

It is worth mentioning that various state governments in the federation have an important and inescapable role to play in the fight against poverty in the country. This is because the states have a lot of human and natural resources and, therefore, they have all it takes to attain sustainable economic development, thereby attacking poverty to the end (Dandago, 2005). It is against this backdrop that this study focuses on the role of States governments in the war against poverty in Nigeria.

Literature Review

Perspectives of Poverty

Several scholars have defined poverty from different perspectives. It is defined as a dreaded condition of absence of capacity to maintain at least basic level of decent living. Poverty is a hydra headed condition which tends to restrict people from socio-economic opportunities (Garuba, undated; Oyemomi, 2003). According to Garuba, poverty as a complex and multi dimensional phenomenon goes beyond condition of lack of resources and extends to social inequality, insecurity, restricted or total lack of opportunity for personal growth and self realization. Individuals who are victims of poverty are usually referred to as poor while nations suffering from it are called poor nations.

Onibokun and Kumuyi (1996) corroborate this view when they defined poverty as a way of life characterized by low calorie intake, inaccessibility to adequate health facilities, low quality education, inaccessibility to various housing and societal facilities. This view is also shared by Canagarajah (undated) who argues that a large number of Nigerian population live below poverty line and consume not more than 2,100 kilocalories. In Oyemomi's view poverty could either be in an absolute term or in relative terms. While absolute poverty is a situation whereby the victims are unable to meet their most basic and elementary requirements of human survival, relative poverty is situation whereby the victims experience deprivation when compared with other individuals, groups or societies (Oyemomi, 2003). While it is possible to eradicate absolute poverty, relative poverty can only be controlled by appropriate policy measures. Nevertheless disparities of income distributions between mankind could be reduced drastically. Unequal distribution of income is viewed as a serious cause of poverty which could be recognized by some specific indices.

Poverty Indicators in Nigeria

According to UNDP (1998; cited in Garuba) the poor are those who are unskilled and unemployable who, as a result of little or no income, are totally dependent on others for the satisfaction of their daily needs. Poor countries are marked mostly by low productivity, alarming high population growth rate and pronounced gap between the haves and the have-not especially in terms of access to health facility; quality and quantity of food intake and wide urban-rural divide.

One indicator of poverty is the lack of social services, such as clean water, education, and health care. Another is lack of assets, such as land, tools, credit, and supportive network of family and friends. Also lack of income, including food, shelter, and clothing constitute another category (Sattaur, 2004). According to Garuba (undated), the 1998 UNDP Human Development Report (HDR) for Nigeria described the country as 'a rich country with a poor population and the poorest and most deprived OPEC country' (UNDP 1998:145). The HDR for the country in 2003 is as follows:

Table 1: Socio-Economic Indices in Nigeria

1	Life expectancy at birth (years), 2001	51.8
2	Adult literacy rate (% age 15 and above), 2001	65.4
3	Combined primary, secondary and tertiary gross enrolment ratio (%), 2000/01	45.1
4	GDP per capita (PPP US$), 2001	850
5	Life expectancy index, 2001	0.45
6	Education index, 2001	0.59
7	GDP index, 2001	0.36
8	Human development index (HDI) value, 2001	0.46
9	GDP per capita (PPP US$) rank minus HDI rank	13.0

Source: http://www.undp.org/hdr2003/indicator/cty_f_NGA.html

The above statistics show how poor and backward Nigeria is with regard to socio-economic standard of living. This situation presents a nation wallowing in abject poverty in the midst of abundant human and material resources. The effect of poverty is more pronounced on women since they have to combine the direct impact of poverty with several cultural restrictions and perceptions that tend to prevent them from exploring socio-economic opportunities (Garuba, undated). The situation of poverty becomes more apparent when her socio-economic indices are compared with those of other countries. For instance, consider the following figures from the World Bank Report (2005) with respect to Nigeria:

- 52% of the population, i.e. over 70 million people, live on less than one dollar a day (Nigerian National Bureau of Statistics, Poverty Profile, 2006).
- Gross National Income (GNI) per capita is $560. UK = $37,600.
- National net primary education attendance ratio is 60%, although there are wide regional and gender disparities between the North and the South of the country. But in UK the ratio is 100%.
- Average life expectancy in Nigeria is 44 years. UK = 79 years.
- 1 in 5 children (20%) dies before the age of 5. UK = 0.6%.
- Approximately 800 per 100,000 women die in childbirth, although this may exceed 1000 per 100,000 in some regions. UK = 11 per 100,000.
- 4.4% of 15-49 year olds (2.6 million people) are living with HIV and AIDS. UK = 0.11% (Nigerian National Planning Commission, Sentinel Survey, 2005).
- The average annual growth rate over past 5 years was 5.7%.
- 48% of the population has access to safe and clean water (UNICEF/WHO Joint Monitoring Programme, 2004). UK = 100%.
  Source: hppt//www.dfid.gov.uk.

The forgoing data show how critical Nigeria's social indicators are. Surprisingly, even among some African countries such as Cote d'voire, Ghana, Kenya and Zambia; Nigeria's profile is still not encouraging (Canagarajah, undated). Based on this situation, Oyemomi (2003) posits that statistics on poverty in Nigeria are even gloomier than in the so-called smaller economies in Africa.

Characteristics of Poverty in Nigeria

The spread of poverty in Nigeria is alarming; about two-thirds of the population is poor, despite the fact that Nigerians live in a country with vast potentials (Sattaur, 2004). Revenues from the sales of crude oil have been on the increase (especially in the last eight years) and yet the citizens are stricken harder by poverty. For example, while the total federally generated revenue in 1997 was N582, 811.0m, it increased to N1, 731.8b in 2002 (Kiyawa, 2007). The revenue continued to increase tremendously and today, the revenue accrues to Nigeria is in trillions. See the table bellow:

Table 2: Revenue Generation in Nigeria by Different Tiers of Government

Generated Revenue	2002	2003	2004	2005	2006
Federation Account (billion)	N1,731.8	N2,575.1	N3,920.5	N5,547.5	N5,965.1

Federal Govt. Re-tained Revenue (billion)	N7,18.8	N1,023.2	N1,253.6	N1,660.7	N1,836.7
State Govt. (mil-lion)	N688,317.2	N854,997.1	N1,112,944	N1,419,537	N1,543,770
Local Govt. (mil-lion)	N172,151.1	N370,170.9	N468,295.2	N597,219.1	N674,255.7

Source: adapted from Kiyawa, A. I. 2007

From the above it can be seen that the revenue accruing to the federation account increased from N1, 731.8b in 2002 to N5, 965.1b in 2006, an increase of N4, 233.3b over a period of 4 years. Similarly, during the same period, the revenue generated by states and local governments increased by N855,453.0m and N502,104.6m respectively. Nigeria as a country is generating adequate revenue to meet the basic needs of its citizens and to be on the path of development (Kiyawa, 2007).

Despite all these rising revenues, Nigerian citizens are still wallowing in abject poverty. Poverty levels vary across the country with the highest proportion of the victims living in the rural areas; the number of rural poor is roughly twice that of urban poor (Canagarah, undated). The depth of poverty i.e. the average short fall from the poverty line, was more than double in rural areas. Canagarajah (undated) itemizes some features of poor household in Nigeria which include lack of access to education; most poor people are illiterate. Most of the poor live in rural areas and are involved in farming. Agricultural sector employs about 72 percent of the labour force in Nigeria, most of whom use local and less efficient implements.

Poor households have many members with few jobs. Per capita health spending is low and does not focus on quality. Per capita health expenditure of US$9 in Nigeria is much lower than in other African countries, for instance, in Ghana, it is US$14 and in Kenya it represents US$16. While children health is a good indicator of the health of Nigerians, because it covers a significant percentage of the overall population, Nigerian children have poor health, worse than what is obtainable in most other African countries (Canagarah, undated). The nutritional welfare of most Nigeria's children is poor and childhood malnutrition is common. Considering the negative and devastating effects of poverty on humanity, wars have been waged against it globally and in various countries.

Global War Against Poverty

The need to reduce poverty to the barest minimum has been the major concern of experts, policy makers and academics the world over. Ending global poverty requires concerted actions by the rich as well as the poor countries (Daudu, 2005; Sachs, 2005). The growth of poverty among the developing societies has assumed an epidemic proportion, so much so that poverty reduction took a centre stage in the United Nations Millennium Development Goals. The 191 member nations of the organization have collectively resolved that by 2015, extreme condition of poverty and hunger will be eradicated.

In addition, the proportion of those living on less than a dollar a day and those suffering from hunger would be halved (UNDP 2003, in Garuba). It is against this background that a lot of agencies and programmes at the international level have been introduced. Some of these agencies/programmes have already been mentioned. They include: USAID, DFID UNDP, NOGALS, MDGs, National Special Programmes for Food Security (NSPFS), United Nation's Children Funds (UNICEF), Japanese International Corporation Agency (JICA), and German Technical Assistance (GTA).

Interestingly most of these agencies/programmes have made some impact in one way or the other in fighting poverty, but their efforts are not enough. For instance, in its West African Water Initiative, USAID's contribution of $4.4 million over three years for the whole West African countries is grossly inadequate. Ethiopia needs $70 per person annually based on a reasonable estimate under UN Millennium project, it receives only $14 person per year (Sachs, 2005). According to DFID statistics (2007), a lot of headways have been made. For instance, in 2005, Nigeria received £489 million of aid; of this DFID provided £75 million. DFID has adopted a three-pronged strategy for contributing to the achievement of the Millennium Development Goals (MDGs) in Nigeria.

This is done through supporting the Nigerian government's strategy for growth and poverty reduction as outlined in the National Economic Empowerment Development Strategy (NEEDS) and State Economic Empowerment Development Strategy (SEEDS); Improving governance and the accountability of government to the Nigerian people; contributing directly to improve human development, particularly in the areas of health, education and HIV and AIDS. Although, some of these efforts by international agencies have been criticized and considered as being grossly inadequate, Sachs (2005: 267) maintains that a pitiful contribution of $4.4 million over three years by USAID to the whole West Africa with 250 million people, means less than a penny per person per year; enough perhaps to buy a cup, but probably not enough to fill it with potable water.

War Against Poverty in Nigeria

Like the international community/agencies, a lot of efforts have been made by both the Federal and state governments and of course local governments. Right from Gowon's regime (1967-1975) almost every regime made some attempts in one way or the other to fight poverty. Unfortunately, most of the efforts have been either a colossal waste of public funds or supported the enrichment of the elites at the detriment of the poor whom the programmes were supposed to assist (Maduagwu, 2000).

The earliest poverty alleviation programmes were the 1972 General Yakubu Gowon's National Accelerated Food Production Programme (NAFP P) and the Nigerian Agricultural and Co-operative Bank, an institution that is entirely devoted to funding agriculture. In the end, the programme achieved very little if anything at all. Similarly, with the coming to power in 1976, Obasanjo focused on food production and he launched Operation Feed the Nation (OFN). This was premised on the fact that improved nutrition would enhance healthy living standard for people (Garuba, undated). The scheme only succeeded in creating awareness of food shortage and the need to tackle the problem without feeding the nation (Maduagwu, 2000). The Second Republic under the leadership of President Shehu Shagari witnessed the introduction of the Green Revolution programme with focus similar to his predecessors.

When General Muhammadu Buhari came to power in 1984, he introduced the 'Go Back to Land' programme to fight against poverty. His major emphasis was on fighting corruption and inculcating discipline in the citizenry which was expected to have some positive impact on poverty in the country as corruption and indiscipline were seen as the two major causes of poverty in Nigeria. According to Garuba (undated), the most pronounced effort was during the regime of General Ibrahim Babangida (1985-1993). It was during this period that the first institutional structures and policy framework for poverty alleviation in the country were put in place.

Most of these structures are still in place today, though with modifications in some cases. Among these structures are the National Directorate of Employment (NDE) with responsibility for fighting unemployment through provision of opportunity for self employment for school leavers, Peoples Bank, National Economic Reconstruction Funds (NERFUND) and Community Banks all for provision of capital for funding small businesses without stringent collateral requirements; the Directorate of Food, Roads and Rural Infrastructure (DFRRI) which focused on integrated rural development with emphasis on opening of fresh rural roads for easy access to the urban centers, while the National Agricultural Land Development Agency (NALDA) had its focus on clearing of arable lands for cultivation. The wives of the military president and Heads of State, Babangida and Abacha also 'contributed' in the war against poverty in Nigeria through their various programmes i.e. Better life for Rural Women and Family Support Programme respectively.

State Governments and the War Against Poverty in Nigeria

The fact that Nigeria is the seventh largest producer of oil in the world, by OPEC rating, a country with the largest number of solid minerals in the world, and with a population of one hundred and forty million people, such a country should not be poor. Nigeria produces over 2 million barrels of oil per day with the proven reserves of oil amounting to 34 billion barrels, enough to last for 37 years at the current rate of production. Similarly, the natural gas reserves amount to 174 trillion cubic feet, the equivalent of 30 billion barrels of crude oil. About 20 percent of this is used to generate electricity. At the present rate of production the nation's gas will last for 110 years (NEEDS, 2004). However, the states governments have a great and a vital role to play in the effort of reducing poverty in the country, thereby leading to a sustainable economic development.

State governments in Nigeria have a lot of human, natural and agricultural resources to explore and exploit for their development and eventually for the development of the country as a whole (Dandago, 2005). It is, therefore, surprising that state governments are always waiting for the monthly federal government allocation to run their affairs. In the following paragraphs various resources that state governments are endowed with are explained.

Natural Resources

Mineral resources agricultural resources and human resources endowments of the 36 states and FCT are too numerous to be put to use in fighting out poverty from the shore of Nigeria, if the required political will to do just that would be developed by those in the helm of affairs. A highlight of the resources are presented and discussed below:

Mineral Resources

Mineral in general is any naturally occurring, chemical element or compound, but in mineralogy and geology, chemical elements and compounds that have been formed through inorganic processes. Petroleum and coal, which are formed by the decomposition of organic matter, are not mineral in the strict sense (Redmond, 2006). Each of the 36 states constituting Nigeria has some solid minerals endowments, with Nassarawa taking the lead (Dandago, 2004). Let us take a look at the sample of solid minerals in various states:

1. Gold Osun, Niger, Edo, Akwa Ibom, Borno, Kebbi, Lagos, Ogun, Ondo and Plateau
2. Bentonite Abia, Ebonyi, Borno, Akwa Ibom and Gombe
3. Barytes Borno, Yobe, Plateau, Benue, Gombe and Nassarawa
4. bauxite: Adamawa, Taraba and Cross River
5. Lead, Zinc: Enugu, Ebonyi, Abia, Niger, Plateau, Kano, Bauchi, Gombe, Taraba and Benue
6. Feldspar: Borno, Kogi, Ogun, Kwara, Oyo, Niger, Kaduna, Gombe, Katsina, Nassarawa
7. Brick: Lagos, Enugu, Kano, Plateau, Oyo, Borno, Borno, Kogi

8. Tin: Plateau, Nassarawa, Kano, Bauchi, Gombe, Benue and Taraba
9. Calcium & Marble: Cross River, Anambra, Ebonyi, Sokoto, Kebbi, Edo, Kwara, Delta, Adamawa, Benue, Oyo, Plateau, Nassarawa and Kaduna
10. Ceramic: Plateau, Nassarawa, Katsina, Bauchi and Gombe
11. Uranium: Borno, Yobe, Cross River, Akwa Ibom and Gombe
12. Iron ore: Kwara, Kogi, Borno, Bauchi, Kano, Kaduna, Enugu, Gombe, Anambra, Katsina and Nassarawa
13. Phosphate: Sokoto, Abia, Ogun, Bauchi and Gombe
14. gypsum: Sokoto, Kebbi, Bauchi, Gombe, Abia, Enugu, Edo, Yobe, Anambra and Borno
15. Gemstone: Katsina, Nassarawa, Bauchi, Gombe, Kaduna, Kogi, Kano and Jigawa
16. Bitumen: Ondo, Ekiti, Ogun and Lagos
17. Diatomite: Borno and Yobe
18. Clay Ball: Imo, Edo, Delta, Katsina Akwa Ibom, Rivers, Cross River, Ondo, Ekiti, Ebonyi, Nassarawa, Enugu and Anambra
19. Kaolin Clay: Delta, Imo, Edo, Kwara, Kogi, Gombe, Nassarawa, Plateau, Kaduna, Katsina, Kano, Ogun, Sokoto, Jigawa, Kebbi and Borno
20. Fire-clay: Anambra, Enugu, Kwara, Katsina, Kebbi, Ebonyi, Ogun, Sokoto, Zamfara and Nassarawa
21. Dolomite: Kwara, Kogi, Oyo, Osun, Niger, FCT and Nasarawa
22. Limestone: Anambra, Ebonyi, Cross River, Akwa Ibom, Benue, Ogun, Nassarawa, Sokoto, Kebbi, Gombe, Edo, Delta, Plateau, Enugu, Adamawa, Kano, Niger and Ondo
23. Sand (Glass sand): Edo, Delta, Ondo, Ekiti, Rivers, Bayelsa, Anambra, Enugu, Ebonyi, Imo, Abia, Kogi, Lagos and Nassarawa.
24. Salt: Ebonyi, Benue, Imo, Abia, Enugu, Anambra, Cross River, Plateau, Nassarawa, Akwa Ibom and Kebbi
25. Soda Ash: Borno, Yobe, Kano and Jigawa
26. Talc: Oyo, Osun, Ondo, Ekiti, Niger, Kogi, FCT, Kwara and Nassarawa.

The different types of solid minerals are just few out of the numerous minerals state governments are blessed with. However, the problem is that of inability to exploit them effectively (Dandago, 2004). Due to laxity on the part of the authorities, unlicensed miners have dominated the mining sites to the extent that an estimated 95% of the mining and exploration activities are being done by them, and this cost the country about N400 billion annually (Ademowo cited in Dandago, 2004:110). If these solid minerals could be exploited and processed meaningfully by the various state governments, then poverty would have been attacked seriously. This is because, all the mineral resources we have could serve as raw materials in one industry or the other in the economy, and consequently, provide job opportunities to the nation's teeming population thereby fighting poverty from another angle.

Table 3: Different Solid Minerals and Their Possible Industrial Uses

S/N	Minerals	Main Industries	Related Economic Activities
1.	- Limestone - Gypsum - Brick clay - Bitumen	Cement Construction	Construction of: Bridges Houses Roads, etc
2.	- Feldspar - Ceramic clay - Clay Ball - Kaolin clay - Fire-clay	Ceramic Plastic	Plastics Production Paint Production Pottery Tiles Bowls
3.	- Iron Ore - Bauxite	Steel Rolling Mills Aluminum Production	Alumina Refractries Building Construction Manufacturing
4.	- Phosphate	Fertilizer	Agricultural Agro-allied

Source: Adapted from Dandago, K. I. 2004

The above table highlights a few industries that could be aided if governments (states and federal) are to be committed to industrialization, using the country's solid mineral endowment as bases. However, it is rather unfortunate that despite all these solid minerals the state governments continue to import some manufactured goods which could have been produced by local manufacturers of goods, using local resources as raw materials. Exploiting and harnessing resources by states governments in Nigeria would lead to mass employment generation; higher purchasing power in the economy, proliferation of service businesses, among others benefits (Dandago, 2004).

Agricultural Resources

Agriculture has suffered from years of mismanagement, inconsistent and poorly conceived government policies, and the lack of basic infrastructure. Still, the sector accounts for over 41% of GDP and two-thirds of employment. Agriculture provides a big chunk of non-oil growth, which in 2006 reached 9%. Once the biggest poultry producer in Africa, corporate poultry output has been slashed down from 40 million birds annually to about 18 million (Bureau of Public Affairs, 2007). The oil boom of the 1970s led Nigeria to neglect its strong agricultural and light manufacturing bases in favor of an unhealthy dependence on crude oil. In 2002 oil and gas exports accounted for more than 98% of export earnings and about 83% of federal government revenue.

Despite these setbacks, Nigeria has no reason for not being able to become self-sufficient in terms agricultural products. Had that sufficiency been obtained in the country, the cry on poverty would not be heard in the country at all. The country has all it takes to be a major exporter of agricultural products for its foreign reserve to be as strong as possible, thereby becoming one of the biggest economies in the world. The table below shows agricultural resources endowment distributed in various parts of the country:

Table 4: Agricultural Resource Endowments of States in Nigeria

Food Crops	Cash Crops	Animal Products	Processing Industries
• Yam • Cassava • Maize • Millet • Guinea corn • Rice • Beans • Plantain • Fruits • Vegetables • Edible aquatics • Tomato • Wheat • Cocoyam • Potato • Sorghum • Banana • Sugarcane • Ginger • Cowpea • Coconut	• Palm produce • Cocoa • Rubber • Timber • Groundnut • Cotton • Gum Arabic • Kola nut • Cowpea • Sugarcane • Soy beans • Tobacco • Kenaf • Melon	• Poultry • Fishery • Livestock	• Foodstuff processing • Cocoa processing • Oil milling • Rubber production • Timber production • Cotton ginnery • Meat processing • Groundnut oil milling • Dairy processing • Palm produce canning • Cassava, rice and yam processing and bagging • Fruits canning • Flour milling • Furniture making • Fish canning • Timber and Rubber processing • Tomato canning • Guinea corn processing • Textile milling

Source: Adapted from Dandago, K. I. 2004

The table above shows that Nigeria is not only rich in mineral resources but it is also blessed with large number of agricultural resources. Each state in Nigeria has a combination of food crops, cash crops and animal products which could be exploited and thereby becoming a self sufficient nation as far as food is concern. In addition to feeding the nation, the excess agricultural products could be exported to generate more revenue for the country. Again maximum exploitation of agricultural resources in Nigeria will ensure drastic reduction of unemployment in the country.

Human Resources

According to the last population census, Nigeria has population of 140 million people (2006 estimates). Being the most populous country in Africa, Nigeria accounts for over half of West Africa's population. It is estimated that one in every six black person in the world is a Nigerian (NEEDS, 2005). Although less than 25% of Nigerians are urban dwellers, at least 24 cities have populations of more than 1,000,000 people each. The variety of customs, languages, and traditions among Nigeria's 250 ethnic groups gives the country a rich diversity (Bureau of A.A., 2007). Nigeria's 80-plus universities have produced an educated labour force which is being high exported to other countries of the world, her adult literacy level remains at 49% of the population, and 76% percent of children of primary school age attend school while less than 76% of children of secondary school age attend school (NEEDS, 2005). With its large population, coupled with diverse natural resources, Nigeria has the human resource capacity to achieve sustainable economic development objective, thereby successfully fighting out poverty in the process.

Conclusion

In line with the analysis and discussion conducted above, the paper is summarized and concluded as follows:

- Nigeria has a lot of human, natural and agricultural resources which are yet to be tapped for poverty eradication from the sore of the country. Exploiting these resources will hopefully results into a meaningful development which consequently would deal decisively with poverty.
- Despite abundance resources available in the country and specifically the plenty revenue from crude oil, the income of average Nigerian is less than US$1 per day; this is a big paradox- suggesting poverty in the midst of plenty!
- Rural dwellers suffer incidence of poverty more than their urban counterparts and the menace is more apparent in people without education. State governments appear to be paying less attention to rural industrialization strategies and their mass educational efforts are not effective.
- Agricultural sector employs larger percentage of the population, most of whom use primitive tools which are virtually less efficient. Mechanized farming is he order of the day in the globalize environment.
- International community is committed more than ever before to eradicate extreme poverty by 2015 through the United Nations' Millennium Development Goals (MDGs).
- A lot of efforts have been made by different regimes in Nigeria through various programmes to curb poverty but the results of such programmes were not very signifi-

cant. This suggests that the ace for poverty eradication or alleviation in Nigeria is not in the hand of the Federal Government but, in the hands of the 36 States.

- It is clear that state governments in Nigeria have a vital role to play in the fight against poverty; this is because all the huge resources the nation has are spread in the 36 states and FCT and, so, the utilization of these resources should be spearheaded by the states with a view to achieving the desired objectives.

Based on the examination of the resource endowments of the states in Nigeria, the following summary and conclusion are drawn:

- All the state governments in collaboration with the federal government should ensure maximum exploration and exploitation of our natural resources and utilize them for the betterment of the citizens. This could be achieved through giving adequate attention to their development to an appropriate standard (local or international).
- Considering the number of agricultural products the country is endowed with, state governments should come up with favorable agricultural development policies that will stimulate farmers to work towards feeding the country and eventually achieving self-sufficiency. Again developing agricultural sector means improving the source of employment for over 70% of Nigerians, particularly the rural dwellers.
- State governments should endeavor to invest in the relevant industries that will assist in processing both the food crops and the cash crops; this again creates employment for a sizeable Nigerians. Doing this is enough to deal with poverty to a great extent.
- All the 36 states in the federation should work towards achieving the objective of industrialization. This could be achieved through supporting and encouraging Small and Medium Scale Industries, especially those in the agricultural, manufacturing and extractive sectors of the economy. State governments should not depend heavily on national source of power (PHCN)), rather they should create their own sources of power with one name or another, and this is very possible given the number of dams that have been created in almost all the states in the country.
- Each state should ensure capacity building of its teaming population by means of appropriate training and other educational development measures. This means that the government should show a high sense of commitment towards the educational sector.

The recent government programmes NEEDS/SEEDS should focus on laying a solid foundation for sustainable employment generation, wealth creation and value reorientation as necessary measures for poverty reduction or even poverty elimination.

References

Achor, U. (2001), Managing the Environment in Popular Neighbourhoods: A Manual for Action, Lagos: Shelter Right Initiative (SRI).

Agbebiyi, H.A. (2000), 'Poverty Alleviation: Channel NYSC into Food production', *The Nigerian Accountant*, Official Journal of the Institute of Chartered Accountants of Nigeria (ICAN), Vol.33, No.3

Bureau of African Affairs [BAA] (2007), Background Note: Nigeria, U.S. State Department, Bureau of Public Affairs, Electronic Information and Publications Office,http://www.state.gov/

Canagarajah, S. (undated), *Poverty and Welfare in Nigeria*, Washington, D.C: American Writing Corporation,

Dandago, K.I. (2005), *Beyond Slogans: How States Hold the Ace for Nigeria's Industrialisation*, Kano: Benchmark Publishers Ltd

Daudu, R. (2005), Impact assessment of two poverty reduction projects in Nigeria confirms participation as key components of strategies for poverty alleviation, University of Agriculture, Makurdi

Department for International Development (2007), About Nigeria, www.dfid.gov.uk, retrieved on 10/05/07

Garuba, A. (undated), "Adult Education and Poverty alleviation Programmes in Nigeria: A Case for Harmonisation", Unpublished Thesis, Federal College of Education Yola, Nigeria

Harrison, G.W., Rutherford, T.F., Tarr, D.G. and Gurgel, A. (2004), 'Trade Policy and Poverty Reduction in Brazil', *The World Bank Economic Review*, Vol. 18, No.3

Kiyawa, I.A. (2007), Improved Revenue Generation for Sustainable Development, A paper presented at a Seminar Organised for newly elected/appointed public officials in Jigawa State.

Maduagwu, A. (2000), "Alleviating Poverty in Nigeria", in *Africa Economic Analysis*

Redmond, W.A. (2006), Mineral (chemistry), "Microsoft Student Encarta Premium 2007" (DVD): Microsoft Corporation

Oyemomi, E.O. (2002), "Poverty Reduction, NAPEP and the NGOs", in *the Nigerian Accountant*, the Official Journal of the Institute of Chartered Accountants of Nigeria (ICAN) April/June 2003, Vol.36, No.2

Sachs, J.D. (2005), *The End of Poverty: How can we make it Happen in our Life time*, London: Penguin Books

Sattaur, O. (2004), National Economic Empowerment and Development Strategy (NEEDS), Abuja: National Planning Commission

CHAPTER SEVEN

REPOSITIONING THE LOCAL GOVERNMENTS FOR THE POVERTY ERADICATION AGENDA IN NIGERIA

Shehu Dalhatu

Introduction

For a responsive and functional living in the modern world every person needs a means of survival and proper sustenance which requires material wealth, development opportunities, saleable production skills, security, safety, peace, decent housing, food security, mobility, access to information technology, and participation in basic democratic processes. It is on the basis of this that poverty is essentially described as a state of perpetual want, absence of or the inadequacy of basic and essential means of survival and or proper human sustenance (federal Government of Nigeria, FGN, 2001).

For every society, jettisoning poverty and ensuring that the effects of the phenomenon are kept at bay of the people is a since qua-non for development. Hence, all tiers of governance have key roles to play in any poverty eradication agenda in society.

The Concept of Poverty

According to Nwachukwu (2000) poverty is the scarcity of human basic needs or inability of an individual, group or society to acquire these basic needs for existence. The perspectives above explain that any societies or communities that would not provide basic needs for its members are perpetrating poverty amongst the people.

Olaitan et al (2000) asserted that poverty is a more permanent feature where there exists relatively wide spread insufficiency of materials for existence. Thus, it is an undesirable social phenomena that subject people, groups and communities to effects of incidences of malnutrition, starvation, sickness, lack or poor education, mental torture, vulnerability to hazards, underdevelopment of personal talents etc. All of these are indicators that help to highlight what is meant by poverty both in urban and rural communities. Peter Townsend (1974) argued that

"individuals, families and groups in the population can be said to be in poverty when they lack the resources to obtain the types of diet, participate in the activities and have the living conditions and amenities which are customary or at least widely encouraged and approved in the societies to which they belong".

Furthermore, Haralambos and Heald (1983) opined that fluidity perspectives of the societies and variations in standard of living among societies must be judiciously assessed to determine the extent of poverty among people. In other words, because societies keep changing along with people depending on the indices of wealth distribution and opportunities available, poverty indicators keep changing. Such phenomenal changes occur at individual levels, places, societies and nations. Consequently, an objective view point of the definition of poverty must see it from absolute, relative and subjective perspectives. That way, the style of analyzing poverty would provide insights into the functional and operational ways of addressing the issues arising in poverty eradication efforts.

The following characteristics help to explain what poverty is and its effect on individuals, groups and societies as enumerated by Olaitan et al (2000) inter-alia (a) Low income (b) Large family size (c) Low level of productivity (d) High dependence (e) Sickness (f) Political instability. The diagram below shows the symbiotic system of poverty in its interrelated network.

Figure 1: Symbiotic System of Poverty

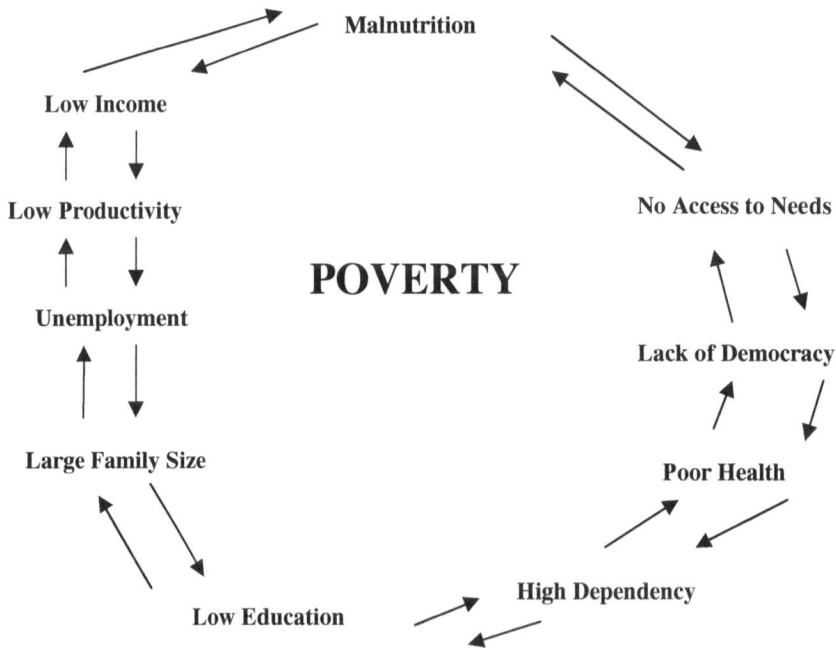

Feedback System of Poverty Chain (Haralambos, 1983)

Poverty Eradication

Olaitan et al. (2001) define poverty eradication as the removal or minimizing of the factors which contributes to poverty among people, groups, societies and nations. It would be observed that poverty alleviation is a conceptual framework based on the provision of citizens, groups and societies with those congenial opportunities that would enable them provide the basic and essential means of achieving socio-economic independence. For instance, Haralambos (1993) describes alleviation of poverty to mean the synchrony of efforts aimed at combating the after effects of poverty such as crime, illiteracy, unemployment, high cost of services, instability, security, poor and inadequate or complete absence of municipal services which must be addressed head on or controlled to a manageable rate. To achieve the tasks of poverty eradication, the psychology of individuals, communities and the entire nation has to be repositioned through a conscious effort of involving the third tier of government that is closest to the grassroots where 90% of the poor live.

Antecedents of Poverty Eradication Initiatives in Nigeria

Federal and state governments during military and civilian administrations since independence in Nigeria often floated Poverty eradication programmes. However, such programmes have generally suffered from poor articulation, planning and even truncated execution (Olaitan, 2000).

According to Nwachukwu (2000), "each new programme in shape and ideology appeared better than the last but lacked the needed commitment on the part of the initiators and implementers to make it a success." Experiences show that such programme did not go beyond the policy pronouncements. In many cases, as soon as funds were set aside by Federal Government of Nigeria for successful implementation of the programme, it almost become a scramble for all to get a share of the 'national cake'.

In the last three decades several programmes all aimed at poverty alleviation have been initiated at national and state government levels. Such programmes are elucidated herewith:

- *Operation Feed the Nation*
  The programme was initiated by General Obasanjo Government in 1976 to improve food sufficiency and increase the earning of peasant farmers and civil servants. The programme was expected to enhance farming by all Nigerians to compliment their meager earnings and create a culture of food sufficiency and security.

- *Green Revolution*
  This was initiated by Alhaji Shehu Shagari's Government in 1980 as a more responsive alternative to Operation Feed the Nation (OFN). The scope was cen-

tered on producing more food to eradicate hunger and increase income. The programme was short lived due to many operational bottle-necks that posed problems to effective implementation.

- *Directorate of Foods, Roads and Rural Infrastructure (DFRRI)*
  This was established to coordinate the opening up of the rural areas to supply
  them with infrastructural facilities and empower them with rapid rural transformation. The initiative induced construction of feeder roads, sinking of bore-holes
  and wells, construction of bridges, food-silos in the rural areas. The programme
  failed due to operational and bureaucratic bottle necks.

- *National Directorate of Employment (NDE)*
  The increase in the number of young school leavers prompted the government in 1986 under General Babangida to create the NDE to cater for yearly increasing graduates and non-graduates. Programmes of NDE till date includes
  farming schemes, mass transit scheme, vocational training of school leavers, release of loans to school leavers for business ventures, etc. although the glamour of
  the laudable programme has simmered a great deal, the institution still lives up to
  it responsibilities.

- *The People's Bank Initiatives*
  Ogbogodo (1993) wrote that this programme was introduced to empower rural dwellers and the urban poor through the release of public funds for managing
  businesses and alleviating their sufferings as regards getting credit facilities. Such
  loans were given on long and short term basis to better the business chances of the
  rural and urban poor. Like the previous programmes, it soon lost its focus and fell
  short of meeting up with the expected targets.

- *Community Banks Initiatives*
  This was also Babangida's initiatives configured to alleviate poverty. It was to
  serve the broad purpose of rural investment and capitalization of rural business, it
  failed colossally due to poor implementation.

- *Better Life Programme (BLP)*
  This was meant to improve the living condition of rural women through
  contributory efforts of communities in partnership with social development stake
  holding institutions in public and private sectors. It was an initiative of Babangida's wife, Maryam Babangida, and soon lost its euphoria as soon as they
  were out of power.

- *(NAPEP) National Poverty Eradication Programme*
  This is a recent initiative housing a lot of sub schemes like Youth
  Empowerment Scheme, Capacity Acquisition Programme (CAP), Mandatory
  Apprenticeship Programme (MAP), etc. the Programme generally aims at ena-
  bling the Nigerian citizenry to be self-sustaining.

Despite all of these initiatives by Federal and State Government the following problems reduced the potency of their operational success. These inter-alia includes, misuse and abuse of opportunities created, corruption in all its ramifications, and in many cases, lack of commitment to the ideals and success of the programmes by those charged with implementation responsibilities.

The Imperative for Local Government Councils Involvement in Meaningful Poverty Eradication Initiative

The efforts of the federal and state governments in poverty alleviation schemes in the past have been interwoven and because local governments were not given their rightful places and recognition as direct owners of the programme for poor people, impact of the programme was not strongly felt. Hence, poverty continues to unleash on the people and societies. Unless a re-assessment is done to strategically reposition local government councils in the rightful places of poverty eradication, its alleviation could continue to be a wasteful venture.

Looking at the frequency in failures of even well conceived poverty alleviation programmes of the Federal and State governments, coupled with the colossal lost of resources and time, it is imperative that community based approaches at the local government levels are necessary. Many reports have indicated that there has been progressive increase of poor people year in year out to the extent of more than half the population of the world (United Nations Development Programme – UNDP 2006). Indeed the population is far higher in some countries such as Sir Lanka and Burma where 90% of the people are living below poverty line. Nigeria has about 67.1 million of her people living below poverty line.

Of the 67.1 million people, more than 50% live in rural areas directly under the control of local government councils (Olaitan, 20000; Nwachukwu, 2000). For these reasons local governments have the following roles to play in alleviating poverty in Nigeria:

- A more effective advocacy and sensitivity approach to ensure participatory approach for sustainability. This is possible only with the local governments who are custodians of the rural local inhabitants and their ways of life that need to be changed. Thus, local government councils can better carry out a more meaningful and educative sub-programme for the rural people.
- Nwachukwu (2000) suggested virile community capacity building to ensure efficient and long lasting rural developmental group activities. Local government councils are better positioned to do this because of proximity to target beneficiaries. The local government councils therefore owe these groups a responsibility of strategizing for their leadership, training, technical training, women empowerment, skills training, etc for such groups with a more effective supervision. With this, transparency and accountability would be guaranteed to some extent.

- Provision of the platform for a more functional implementation framework. Local governments are better positioned to provide this framework accordingly to endorse effective coordination for impact creation and sustainability.

- A re-strategizing stakeholder's consultative forum with intermittent progress evaluation report roles. Haralambos (1984) wrote that Miller and Zoby argued that the poor will remain stubbornly poor despite investments in poverty eradication if the efforts are not geared to re-engineering changes through consultation and interactive forums with the poor for purposes of feedback and re-strategisation. In doing so local government councils in Nigeria being the tier of governance that has direct access to the larger populations of the poor in Nigeria should be charged with the consultative responsibilities and reporting periodically on progress made in the gesture.

Strategies Towards Sustainable Role of Local Governments in Poverty Alleviation

- Collaborative grassroots and participatory approach towards planning poverty alleviation initiatives
- A more strategic re-focusing of poverty eradication programme on the basis of enhancing efficacy for target groups.
- Collaborative funding and ownership at grassroots level.
- A reinvention and incorporation of the traditional education curriculum in the pedagogy of implementation in poverty alleviation initiatives to forestall cases of conflicts with traditional taboos.

Conclusion

The realization of the alternating positions of success and failure in a developmental initiative towards poverty eradication provides the input for analysis of future efforts. Poverty alleviation initiatives would be better handled by the local governments, considering their proximity to the larger population of citizens in the poverty bracket. Haralambos (1983) pointed out that the war on poverty would be far harder to wage than the previous ones since it would require considerable sacrifice by the rich and powerful and reconsideration of direct and indirect involvement of the target group in the policy planning, development and implementation.

References

Federal Government of Nigeria – FGN, (2001), *National Poverty Eradication Programme (NAPEP)*. A Blue Print for the Schemes. Abuja: Author.

Federal Government of Nigeria (2004), *National Economic Empowerment and Development Strategy – NEEDS*. Abuja: National Planning Commission.

Haralambos, M. and Heald, R.M. (1983), *Sociology: Themes and Perspectives*. Slough: University Tutorial Press Limited.

Olaitan, S.O. eta'l (2000), *Poverty and Poverty Alleviation Initiatives in Nigeria*, Nsukka: Ndudin Printing Press.

Ogbogodo, G. (1993), *Seven years of CBB: Vol. III LAbour and Social Development*: Lagos; Daily Times of Nig. Plc.

Nwachukwu, C. (2000), "Women's Role in Poverty Alleviation". *Punch* News Paper Time.

Townsend, P. (1974), "Measures and Explanation of Poverty in High and Low Income Countries", in Wedder Burn (ed.) *Poverty as Relative Deprivation,* London: Heinemann.

United Nations Development Programme – UNDP (2006), *Human Development Report,* New York: United Nations.

CHAPTER EIGHT

THE ROLE OF THE BUSINESS COMMUNITY IN THE WAR AGAINST POVERTY IN NIGERIA

Garba Bala Bello

Introduction

There is no generally acceptable definition or a measurement technique to compare poverty across countries or even within a country. Rein (1970: 46) identified three broad concepts of poverty that seem to encompass most of the difficulties associated with poverty analysis: Subsistence, inequality and externality. Subsistence is concerned with the "Minimum of provisions, needed to maintain health and working capacity (capabilities)". Inequality is concerned with the relative position of income groups to each other". Externality is concerned with the "Social Consequences of poverty for the rest of society rather than in terms of the needs of the poor – it is not much the misery part of the community which is crucial to this view of poverty". Therefore, the concept of poverty must be seen in the context of society as a whole and cannot be fully understood by isolating the poor and focusing on their behavior as a special group. It is equally important to understand the behavior of the rest of the society especially the richer segment.

According to Oyemomi (2003) poverty may either be in absolute or relative terms. Absolute poverty in the sense that the person or group of persons concerned is/are unable to satisfy his/her/their most basic and elementary requirements of human survival. Poverty in the relative term would be a comparative state of deprivation among the individuals, groups or segments of the society. It is generally accepted that while absolute poverty can be eradicated, relative poverty can only be controlled to bridge the gaps in the society.

The social responsibility clause in most private sector companies make them go for community based projects in the communities where they operate. These organizations and individuals, out of the profits made from their operations, plough back to develop the communities around them. Nigeria is blessed with socially responsible corporate bodies and individuals in the private sector that develop the human, natural, physical, financial and social assets of the poor around them. Such development has been noticeable in the health, education, infrastructural, social and agricultural sectors of our economy. The poor people in such communities have had the turn-around in their status attributable to the private sector operator's interventions (Oyemomi, 2003).

This chapter attempts to examine the meaning and practice of business community to alleviate poverty and hence better the life of the populace. Emphasis will be given to the practice of corporate social responsibility as obtained amongst indigenous firms and individual business people. Before delving into the roles of the business community in the fight against poverty, it will be imperative to understand the Nigerian corporate governance frame work, its socio-economic conditions and the implication both have for corporate social responsibility (CSR).

It is important to note that the present Nigerian firms as institutions of socio-economic production and exchange originated within the context of colonial imperialism and have therefore evolved in the context of modernization and contact with the western world. Nigeria gained her independence from Britain in 1960. Before the contact with the west the mode of production was largely agrarian and peasantry in nature. Nigerians were mainly engaged in agriculture, hunting, cattle rearing and trading. The trading was in the main internal until the contact with North African in the Trans – Saharan trade (Orojo, 1992). With the growth of trade during colonial era, the imperial masters felt that it was necessary to promulgate laws to business activities locally. The first company law in Nigeria was the companies Ordinance of 1912, which was a local enactment of the companies (Consolation) Act (1908) of England; and even the current company law of Nigeria (now known as the companies and Allied Matters Act 1990-(CAMA) is largely modeled on the UK company Act, 1948 (Guobadia, 2000).

Socio-Economic Condition

Nigeria is composed of different tribes, cultures, languages and religions necessitated by the imperialist interest of the then British government to ease the governance of this amalgamated entity. The country has abundant natural and human resources, with a population of about 140 million (2006 census) the Nigerian economy is largely dependent on its oil sector which supplies 95 percent of its foreign exchange earning. Thus, Nigeria is very rich in natural resources and earns significant revenue from her oil reserves. However, the presence of oil in the country has remained more of a curse than a blessing. This is because, first, it has destabilized the past emerging strong agrarian economic based of the county. Before the discovery in the 1960's, agriculture was the dominant sector accounting for well over 50 percent of Gross Domestic Product (GDP). Secondly, it has continued to unleash untold devastation on the people where the oil resources are extracted i.e. the Niger Delta region of the country.Their main sources of livelihood (rivers and farmlands) are polluted and destroyed. These damages often lead to conflict between the oil firms and the host communities (Amaeshi, et al, 2006).

Despite her rich natural resources, Nigeria as a country has a per capital income of around $390 and life expectancy period of 45 years (World Bank Report, 2006). Also, Nigeria's infrastructural development is poor. The road network is under developed and there are some communities and cities that are cut-off from each other due to unassailable transportation network. The education system is under funded and illiteracy rate is up to 40 percent. More than two-thirds of Nigerians are poor. In 1980, an estimated 27 percent of Nigerians lived in poverty. By 1999, 70 percent of the population had income of less than $1 a day – and the figure has risen since then (NEEDS, 2005). Nigeria has one of the worst health care delivery system, in the world with doctor – patient ratio getting to 1:1000. The public sector is very weak and corrupt (Ameashi et. al, 2006). In short businesses wishing to operate in Nigeria face many constraints, including poor infrastructure, particularly road network and electricity supply, inadequate physical security, corruption, weak enforcement of contracts and the high cost of finance. These factors have deterred foreign entrepreneurs from investing in Nigeria and induced many Nigerians to take their money and skills abroad (NEEDS, 2005).

The Nigerian oil sector is mainly dominated by the multinational corporations (MNCS). For instance, Shell spelt its strategies as sustainable development, community investment etc. Thus, its corporate social responsibility (CSR) activities are focused on remedying the effects of its extraction activities on the local communities. Therefore, the oil firms operating in this sector have often provided pipe-borne water, hospitals, schools etc. However, these provisions have often been on a temporary rather than a permanent basis. In its report on the activities of Shell in this region, for instance, the Christian Aid (2004) asserted that some of the schools, hospitals and other social amenities, claimed to be provided by some of the firms in this sector have been abandoned or did not meet the needs of the communities they were meant to serve.

On the little influence of traditional values in the Nigerian business practices, Moon (2002) identified religion, ethnicity and language as the three major factors that shaped Nigerian business practices and social responsibility. A common phenomenon among the different peoples of Nigeria is the communal philosophy of life and concern for the less privilege. This belief is rooted in the concept of "intended kinship", and "being one brother's keeper". The family bond is very important in Nigeria and almost all ethnic groups believe that individual responsibility extend beyond the boundaries of immediate family. This practice has been described as Nigeria's form of social security. In establishing a farm, the founder represents not only the company but also the family. Therefore, in his business judgment the business man balances the demand of business with his responsibility to the extended family which could be the whole community (Amaeshi, et al., 2006).

Specific Cases of Nigerian Business Community Response to the Society

In terms of philanthropy, writing on its social responsibility philosophy and practice, Zenith Bank, one of the first four banks in Nigeria states:

> At Zenith, Corporate Social Responsibility is not just a buzzword; it is a way of life. To emphasize this belief, Zenith bank set up Zenith philanthropy, a fully functional department responsible for identifying areas, sectors and causes deserving of philanthropic aid – Zenith philanthropy is a channel through which Zenith Bank gives back to society. One would invariably ask why we have set up a department just to give money out? At Zenith Bank, we see giving back to society as a serious and passionate cause
> (http//w.w.w.zenithbank.com/philanthropymn.cfm.objectives).

Philanthropy, goodness to society charity are conceived within the moral economy of kin-based solidarity and reciprocity (Adi, 2006) A traditional and informal sector example of this would be the case of auto spare parts business cluster found in Nnewi, Eastern Nigeria that play crucial roles in their local community development including, provision of city-work security (see Brautigam, 1997).Another case is the Kwara Business community in Kano, Northern Nigeria contribution in the building of boreholes, Mosques and Islamiyya Schools.

In November, 2002, the British American Tobacco (BAT) Nigeria established a British American Tobacco Foundation with the task of identifying and implementing community enhancement programmes across Nigeria. The foundation has commenced a series of Poverty Reduction Projects (PRP) for unemployed youths in different states of Nigeria. Also, the foundation is working with the International Institute of Tropic Agriculture (IITA) to provide maize seedlings and cassava to farmers from communities of production. BAT Nigeria in the same year also introduced an under graduate Internship Programme to contribute towards the development of promising undergraduates and prepare them for life in corporate world. Even though, this programme is a strategy by BAT to enhance the quality of its employable labour pool but it could also benefit the wider society in form of knowledge spill over as BAT may not be in a position to employ all the interns (Amaeshi et al., 2006).

Similarly, Shell Nigeria also has a programme for enhancing the science and engineering skills required in the Nigerian oil and gas sector. Generally, therefore, while indigenous firms are more involved in philanthropic CSR, the multinational firms are more Strategic – their CRS activities (e.g. poverty alleviation and capacity building) cut across both the market and non-market environments corporate Strategy (Baron, 1995, Lantos, 2001)

Other contributions of business community to the society include offsetting pollution, transformation of rural environment through provision of infrastructural facilities and provision of employment. Such organization, such as UAC, Unilever, and John Holt contribute to educational development through award of scholarship to deserving children, provision of classrooms, equipment and facilities, funding research and development efforts, sponsoring professorial chairs in different fields of study such as Business Administration, finance etc .

As a corporate citizen, Mobil has been contributing to its host communities especially in the Cross Rivers state. The company has made direct cash donations to the state's School of Nursing, Emmanuel Hospital Eket, and the Community Secondary School Ibeno and to Health Projects of the Eket Local Government. The company has supplied pipe-borne water to the local villagers at Mkpanak. Also, it sponsors candidates to University level. For instance, in 1984, it sponsored 30 students in various disciplines to Nigerian Universities. Since 1977, some Children of Junior employees of the company have been benefiting from the company's post Primary school Scholarship (Public Affairs Department, NNPC, 1988).

Texaco has engaged in pioneering venture to assist in the development of Nigerian agriculture and particularly in the production of a basic staple food – Gari. In doing so, it has set up and operated a Cassava plantation and Gari Factory, using advanced technology to produce Gari from the cassava grown on its farm. The Gari produced by Texaco goes by the trade name "Texagari"(Public affairs Department, NNPC, 1988).

Elf also, believes in identifying with the aspirations of the environment in which it operates; for instance, company awards about 300 post primary and 20 post secondary scholarships annually to employees children and to children living in the areas of its operations and other parts of the country. Moreover, it sponsors sporting competitions, contributes to community development and lends support to the enhancement of formal and informal education in the country (Public Affairs Department, NNPC 1988).

Conclusion

It is clear that socio-cultural characteristic of Nigeria are unique and as such the role of the business community in the war against poverty is mainly shaped by the socio-economic conditions in which these business operate. Therefore, the social responsibilities of the business community in Nigeria are aimed at addressing the peculiarity of the socio-economic development challenges of the country i.e. poverty alleviation through health care provision, infrastructural development, educational support etc. and are informed by the socio-cultural factors of communalism and charity. This might not reflect the popular western standard of corporate social responsibility which includes consumer protection, fair trade, green marketing, climate change concerns etc.

References

Adi, A.B.C (2006), "The Moral Economy and the Possibility of Accumulation in Africa: How the IFIS can help to West Africa" *Review* Vol.5.

Amaeshi, K. et. al (2006), "Corporate Social Responsibility in Nigeria: Western Mimicry or indigenous practice", @ http:/www.nottingham.ac.uk/business/ICCSR

Baron D.P (1995), "Integrated Strategy: Market and non Market Components", in *California Management Review*, 37(2)

Brautigam, D. (1997), "Substituting for the State; Institutions and Industrial Development in Eastern Nigeria", in World *Development*, 25(7)

Christian Aid (2004), "Behind the Mask: The Real Face of Corporate Social Responsibility"@http://www.christian-id.org.uk/indepth/040.csr/index.ltm.

Guobadia, A. (2000), "Protecting Minority and Public Interests in Nigeria Company Law: The Corporate Affairs Commission as a Corporations Ombudsman". In a McMillan, F. (ed.), *International Company Law Annual* Vol. I , Oxford – Portland Oregon: Hart Publishing

Lantos, G.P (2001), "The boundaries of Strategic Corporate Social Responsibility" *Journal of Consumer Marketing* 18(7)

Moon, J. (2002), Corporate Social Responsibility: An overview. In International Directory of Corporate Philanthropy. London: Europa.

NEEDS (2005), *National Economic Empowerment and Development Strategy*, Abuja: Central Bank of Nigeria (CBN)

Orojo J.O (1992), Company *law and practice in Nigeria*, Lagos, Mibeya & Associates Nig. Ltd, (3rd Ed.)

Oyemomi E. U. (2003), "Poverty Reduction: NAPEP and the NGOs,"in *The Nigerian Accountant* April/June, Vol. 36. N02.

Public affairs Department (1981), Nigerian National Petroleum Corporation (NNPC)

Rein, M. (1970), "Problems in the Definition and Measurement of Poverty", in Peter Townsend (ed.), *The Concept of Poverty*, London: Heinemann Educational Books

World Bank (2000), *World Development Report*, Washington DC, U.S.A

World Bank (2006), *World development Report*, Washington DC, U.S.A Zenith-Bank(2006), http//www.zenithbank.com/philanthropy.mn.Cfmt//objectives.

CHAPTER NINE

THE ROLE OF THE MASS MEDIA IN THE FIGHT AGAINST POVERTY IN
NIGERIA

Balarabe Maikaba

Introduction

The greatest problem facing the African continent and Nigeria in particular
is the rising level of poverty amongst the vast majority of the populace. The rising levels of poverty in Nigeria, the so-called "giant of Africa", manifested in
widespread hunger, diseases including HIV/AIDS, illiteracy and high crime
rates, among others, has proven difficult to contain by successive governments
that governed the country. Although Nigeria is the seventh largest exporter of oil
in the world, it is one of the poorest countries in terms of human development
(HDR, 2006).

Even though poverty is a global phenomenon afflicting people all over the
world, the case of Nigeria is pathetic and irritating in view of the vast human
and natural resources that the country possesses. As Osinubi (2003) contended,
the most pathetic feature of Nigerian society is that majority of its members are
living in a state of destitution while the remaining relatively insignificant minority are living in affluence. Due to mismanagement and corruption, the Nigerian
economy has been seriously battered paving the way to pervasive poverty. In the
sub-Saharan Africa, Nigeria's economic, social and political statistics is ranked
low in view of widespread poverty and the poor living conditions of its people
(Ali-Akpajiak and Pyke, 2005). The World Bank has observed that the poor of
Nigeria have 'a cash income [that] is insufficient to cover minimum standards of
food, water, fuel, shelter, medical care and schooling (World Bank Report 2001).
In a 1998 UNDP publication Nigeria's ranking as one of the poorest countries in
the world was further underscored: "Nigeria is worse off today than in the
1980's. The poverty profile of the country does indeed present a somber picture
of a rich nation in decline."

Currently, Nigeria belongs to the group of lower-income countries and poverty is continually rising. In addition, at the level of global poverty measurement
using the Human Poverty Index (HPI), Human Development Index (HDI), Gender Development Index (GDI) and Gender Empowerment Index (GEM) indices,
Nigeria has remained at the bottom ladder of the rankings due to the prevalence
of poverty across the country. The HPI is measured by considering the survival

rates of the population in terms of life span, illiteracy rates and standards of living in terms of access to basic human needs. The HDI measures the incidence of human poverty in a country. Nigeria's HPI is 41.6, which ranked it 54th out of the 78 poorest countries in the world in terms of the provision of education, and services such as portable water, public health measures and sanitation (UNDP, 2001). Nigeria's HDI index is 0.456, ranking it 156th in the world. As a result, the UNDP concluded that at the turn of the new millennium and twenty-first century Nigeria belongs to the "lowest of the low".

The Gender Development Index (GDI) assesses disparities between males and females in relation to the HDI result. The closer the GDI to the HDI the lower the gender disparity prevailing in a country. Nigeria's GDI is 0.425 ranking the country 124th in the world. The income disparity between men and women in Nigeria shows that the real GDP per capita of women is only 12.8% of that of men is lower than the average of Sub-Saharan Africa (SSA), which is 54.9% (UNDP, 2001, p. xvi). The Gender Empowerment Index (GEM) measures the gender inequalities in economic and political opportunities in a country; it focuses on the mechanisms available which would empower men and women to take advantage of these opportunities. The GEM in Nigeria for men is 0.456 and for women is 0.442, which shows that men are marginally better off than women in Nigeria.

Therefore, by all measures and statistics it is clear that Nigeria's poverty incidence is high and as Alayande and Alayande (2004) noted the implication of this is that about 67 million Nigerians are languishing in poverty out of an estimated population of about 100 million. By 2007, more than 70 percent of the 140 million inhabitants in Nigeria was poor. Several measures have been taken by successive governments to address the rising poverty in the country. A number of poverty alleviation programmes and policies were put in place and yet, Nigerians still wallow and lurch in abject poverty.

Poverty in Nigeria as the World Bank reported in 1997 has no geographical boundary. It is all over the place as seen in the North, West, South and East. It is found in rural as well as the urban areas even though, it is more pronounced in the rural areas (Alayande and Alayande, 2004). Therefore, the greatest challenge facing Nigerians is how to minimize or completely eradicate the rising incidence of poverty in the country. Even though there are many prescriptions made in that regard, this paper would argue that an effective use of the mass media comprising radio, television, newspapers, magazines, the film media and the emerging media of the internet and the GSM in creating awareness and educating the populace could effectively curtail or reduce the incidence of poverty in the country.

The main objective of this chapter is to explore the ways and means by which the mass media in Nigeria could assist in curbing and curtailing the rising levels of poverty among the vast majority of the population. The chapter also discusses other measures of poverty control and advocate the need for other agencies like the family, schools, civil society organizations, religious bodies, peer groups and government to rise up to the challenge of minimizing or completely eliminating poverty in our midst.

Methodology

The methodology used in this chapter is qualitative content analysis of relevant literature found in texts (herein refers to books and journals) on the effective utilization of the mass media in addressing societal problems to which poverty is a major part. Qualitative content analysis as opposed to quantitative content analysis according to Gunter (2000), is concerned with interpretive and hermeneutic styles, and does not utilize the use of statistics in data reduction and analysis. The procedures of qualitative content analysis in media studies according to Gunter (2000: 82) were influenced by the writings of Weber (1907), Blumer (1933) and Levi-Strauss (1963).

Literature Review

How and to what extent does the media report poverty issues in Nigeria? In a study titled "How the news media covers poverty" among the poor of New York City which can be narrowed to Nigeria's context, Jones (2004) contended that there is an ideological shift (owing to ownership) to the right in the manner in which the news media report the poor. "News stories in general, have become more focused on trivial issues, celebrities and sensationalist trash than on hard news that affects peoples' lives. Many stories about the poor tend toward stereotypes. "They don't have jobs; they use drugs; they lack moral fiber." This can lead to the conclusion that there is no need for public investment in poor neighborhoods - the problem is the poor, not society.

Similarly, Butler (2007) while discussing media's portrayal of poverty issues in the news observed that the mainstream media presents those who live in poverty as being inherently different from the rest of society by creating artificial divisions and similarities. Butler (2007) further identified two main reasons why poverty issues do not receive much attention or positive attention in the media. The first reason is for the lack of such stories because they may not be news worthy. For the media poor people out of work is not news. The second reason why the media does not give adequate coverage to poverty issues is because poverty itself is linked to certain class of people such as women, ethnic minorities and blacks. And these, particularly in the US are not news worthy for the majority of news consumers in view of racial inequalities and hatred there.

In Nigeria even though not much literature exist on media's coverage of poverty issues one may discern from the day to day reporting of events that the Nigerian media are really not much concerned about poverty issues. They are more concerned with sensational and trivial issues touching on politics and scandals in the lives of celebrities, politicians and ordinary people.

Theoretical Framework: Development Media Theory

Issues of poverty are issues of development. How the media portrays and projects poverty issues is related and linked to development. The development media theory is the theory that is linking the media with development issues particularly in developing countries. The theory emerged as a result of the short-comings of other theories of the mass media to cater for the needs of developing countries (McQuail, 1983). This is owing to some certain characteristics of devel-oping countries such as inadequate supply of requisite communication infra-structure or equipments, lack of professional skills as well as cultural and pro-duction resources; a large number of audiences are illiterate, and lastly over de-pendence on the developed world for aid, skills, technology and other cultural products.

The primary objective of the development media theory, McQuail (1983) contended, is to positively use the mass media in national development. This po-sition was further expatiated by Oso (2003: 85) who stated that:

> "the normative elements of the theory are shaped by the peculiarities of the developing nations, which have led to the belief that the mass media have a positive role to play in stimulating development and economic change."

The major tenets of the development media theory as McQuail (1983: 121) enunciated are:

- Media must accept and carry out positive development tasks in line with nation-ally established policy.
- Freedom of the media should be open to economic priorities and development needs of the society.
- Media should give priority in their content to national culture and languages.
- Media should give priority in news and information to links with other develop-ing countries, which are close geographically, culturally or politically.
- Journalists and other media workers have responsibilities as well as freedom in their information gathering and dissemination tasks
- In the interest of development and media operation and devices of censorship subsidy and direct control can be justified.

Whether the media can be able to attain adequately these tenets is still sub-ject of debate. In most cases, the media does not assist in carrying out positive developments. They are supportive of the status quo and are being controlled and influenced by their sponsors.

Causes of Poverty in Nigeria

What are the major reasons behind the prevalence of poverty in the country? Several scholars and writers, (Dudley 1975, Anyanwu 1997 and Echemeri 1997) have proffered reasons for the rising levels of poverty in the country which may be broadly classified into economic, political, social, cultural and environmental factors. For the purpose of this paper however, the major causes of poverty in Nigeria are enumerated thus:

- **Corruption:** This is a leading cause of poverty in Nigeria. Several of Nigeria's resources are stolen by officials of government, resulting in the pauperization of the masses and increasing affluence of the few, minority rich. Indeed, the Transparency International has continuously ranked Nigeria as one of the leading corrupt nations in the world. This is in spite of attempts by the current democratic leadership in entrenching agencies like the ICPC and EFCC to minimize and curb the incidence of corruption in the country. Early this year, precisely on the 3rd February, 2007 , the chairman of the EFCC, Malam Nuhu Ribadu on a Nigerian Television Authority (NTA) programme "One-on-One" stated that his commission had confiscated over N90 Billion (USD 700 Million) of stolen money from government functionaries which is indicative of the deep rooted nature of corruption in Nigeria.
- **Bad Leadership:** Successive governments (both military and civilians) that came to rule the country are often blamed for Nigeria's poverty. The bad policies and programmes they initiated and implemented such as SAP are behind the destruction of the country's economic base leading to widespread poverty.
- **Overpopulation:** This is another cause of poverty in Nigeria. The factor of overpopulation, which may be linked to political, cultural and religious beliefs, is manifested in youth unemployment and high crime. Nigeria's borders are also open and porous resulting in neighboring citizens migrating to settle in Nigeria. This has overburden the economy, overstretching facilities and resources of the country.
- **Illiteracy:** The greatest poverty, which may afflict a set of people, is lack of education. In a world, that is science and technology oriented a society that is illiterate or semi-literate may find it difficult to survive. Nigeria's rising poverty level is attributed to the illiteracy level of its people especially in the rural areas.
- **Greed and Selfishness:** The "get rich quick" syndrome and greed are the bane of our society today. The consequence of this is the majority chasing few scarce resources resulting in friction and wars. The result is poverty and deprivation amongst the vast majority of the people.

Consequences of Poverty

What are the consequences of poverty in countries affected? These are quite numerous as enumerated thus:

- **High Crime Rate**: High level poverty among the populace breeds crime. Cases of fraud in government ministries, armed robbery, drug addiction and several other crimes are rampant in Nigeria and a clear manifestation of poverty.
- **Poor Infrastructural Development**: With poverty one finds decaying infrastructure all over the place; lack of drinking water, roads, electricity, hospitals and other infrastructure. Even where these facilities are found, they are either obsolete or not functional.
- **Diseases**: Rampant cases of diseases among the population are a manifestation of poverty. Such diseases like HIV/AIDS, Tuberculosis, malaria and several others that are difficult to control and contain. Cases of drugs defying treatments and fake ones all have to do with poverty.
- **Conflict and wars**: Because of competition for scarce resources, tension is likely to be generated leading to conflict and sometimes war. Most of the conflicts in Nigeria be it ethno-religious, political, boundary disputes and several others could be linked to the rising levels of poverty.
- **Overdependence**: This is another manifestation of poverty. With rising levels of poverty in Nigeria majority of the citizens who could not be gainfully employed may resort to begging and destitution.

Media's Intervention in the Fight Against Poverty

Contemporarily, the mass media of communication comprising the print, electronic, film, the internet and telecommunications media touches every sphere of our lives. Indeed, the mass media are central to the organizations of our lives. Without the media, one can imagine how life could be. It is a life of silence where we shall be left in the dark about the happenings around us and in other settings. This may explain why several communication scholars and writers have ascribed certain roles, which the media must perform in a given society. Traditionally the role and function of the mass media in any society is to inform, educate and entertain. This means that on any given issue the media must inform, educate and entertain the people. In the process of performing these roles the media either wittingly or unwittingly sets the agenda for public discourse on that issue.

Ojo (2000) identified five specific functions which the mass media performs in a given society or any democratic polity, which are relevant to our understanding of the media's role in the fight against poverty in the country. They are:

- **Reporting the News:** The media should strive to report issues on poverty for the people to really know that it really exists. By frequently reporting on poverty, the media is reminding the leaders and the led on the problem so that concrete measures are taken to address it.
- **Interpreting the News:** The media should not only report on the poverty problem but, also provide a detailed interpretation of the scourge by providing data and statistics of its prevalence. This will assist government in handling the problem from areas most affected.

- **Influencing the Opinions of Citizens:** The media can in several ways influence the views and opinions of citizens in favour or against an issue. As an example, previous government programmes on poverty alleviation such as Better Life for Rural Women, FEAP e.t.c. relied on the media for publicity and influencing the citizens for their acceptability.
- **Setting the Agenda for Government Action:** By giving prominence to poverty issues the media may influence government policy on it. Agenda setting whether it is the media's or public agenda is one key responsibility of media in modern societies.
- **Socializing Citizens:** The media creates awareness on issues including poverty. By "shining the light" on issues of poverty the media would create a room for further understanding of the problem.

Lasswell (cited in Wright, 1960) provided a different version of the supposed roles and functions of the media in society to include; surveillance of the environment (informing people of what is going on), correlation of parts of the society, bringing about different viewpoints and opinions for people to debate and deliberate on. Transmission of social heritage from one generation to another considered the educational and socialization function of the media is the last in Lasswell's (1948) classification.

Gurevitch and Blumler (1990) renowned media and politics scholars identified six functions and roles, which the media must perform in a given society. These functions are:

- Media's surveillance of the sociopolitical developments,
- Media's identification of the most relevant issues (agenda setting),
- Media serving as a platform for debate across a diverse range of views,
- Media holding officials to account for the way they exercise power (watchdog role),
- Media providing avenue and incentives for citizens to learn, choose and become involved in the political process and lastly,
- The media resisting efforts by forces outside the media to subvert their independence.

Several media critics, Fog (2004), Herman and Chomsky (1988), Keane (1991), Herman and McChesney (1997) had argued that in reality the modern mass media are not performing these functions effectively. In view of the nature of their ownership and control, and the nature of capitalist economy to which the media is 'fourth estate' the modern mass media are elitist and are not supportive and concerned about issues of the downtrodden poor. Poverty is not part of the agenda they set because the media does not identify with the poor. For the purpose of this paper however, the mass media in Nigeria may assist in the fight against poverty by:

- **Putting Poverty Issues as Leading Agenda**: The mass media whether print or broadcast should give prominence in their leading and cover stories to poverty and related issues./ In this way it remains with the leaders and the led for debates and discussions for a solution to be found..

- **Issue Reminders**: From time to time, the media must remind its audience about the existence and prevalence of poverty in our midst. This is done through news reporting, commentaries, feature articles, letters, documentaries and drama shows.

- **Organize Workshops on Poverty Reporting**: Media organizations should organize workshops and conferences to educate and enlighten their reporters and staff on how best to report and handle issues of poverty for societal development. It is in this regard that Dobmeyer (1995) developed ten (10) tips, which the media can utilize to improve its coverage of poverty issues. They are:

    Be Honest: in their coverage of poverty issues the media should be honest, have the facts straight, avoid stereotypes, and seek to break away from conventional wisdom on poverty issues.

    Be Aggressive: dig for the details. Go directly to community sources for interviews if you need confirmation of a fact or a quote for the story.

    Be Persistent: Go to the communities and its organizations for interviews. Include the views of the poor, not just the politicians on an issue. Actively seek background material and position from community organizations.

    Be Creative: Employ fresh approaches to present complex issues to the public Use interviews, case studies and illustrative graphics.

    Be attentive: Do follow up stories that will detail the impact of an issue on people and the community.

    Be factual: Tell the facts, get all sides, but leave the editorializing on the editorial pages.

    Be Analytical: Ask hard questions about crucial and often complex proposals. Measure the impact of all policy ideas on people who are affected. Think bottom line: *How will this policy impact family, single people and communities?*

    Be Informed: Take time to inform yourself of an issue and its effect on the community.

    Be Open: Keep your eyes open to new ideas. Avoid reporting on something that won't work, just because a politician say it won't fly; and

    Be Watchful: Watch out for creeping cynism if you have covered a particular issue extensively. Avoid rehashing the same old story if you have grown tired of covering the issue.

Conclusion

In an attempt to find out how the mass media could be used effectively to address the burning issue of poverty in Nigeria, this paper examined several texts and materials that offer varied prescriptions. Jones (2004) in his *"How the news media covers poverty: The Urban Agenda"* identified reasons behind news media's neglect of poverty issues. They include issues of profit making motive. Media's job especially in a capitalist economy is to cover news stories and make money out of advertisement placement. Jones (2004) contended that these two roles of the media do not go together or "reconcile" with issues of poverty because in their news coverage role poverty news in most cases is not news worthy. Any media organization that emphasizes on poverty issues may be doing so at their own peril because they may not be patronized after all. The same argument is applicable to media advertisements most of which are not concerned with the interests of the poor. The media are largely ignoring issues of poverty because they may be irrelevant to peoples' lives, "poor people out of work isn't news."

Another reason for media's neglect of poverty related issues in their coverage is to do with ownership. As the saying goes "who pays the piper dictates the tune." Because media investment is capital intensive, the poor do not have the means and capacity to own and control a media organization. Media ownership and control is mostly in the hands of the elite and those in power and their priorities are never inclined towards poverty or the poor.

In these lights therefore, the mass media and other agencies could help if the following recommendations are taken into account:

- Community based media should be established in the nooks and crannies of the country to cater for the needs of the rural poor. Community based media in the form of a local FM station; a small newspaper in the local language would go a long way in educating and enlightening the people on poverty issues and how to overcome them.
- Media owners and practitioners must be made to understand the implication of widespread poverty amongst the population, which may not be in the interest of their businesses. They should therefore, consider poverty issues as a leading agenda in their cover and leading stories. They should shine more light on it.
- Other agencies of socialization and orientation such as the family, religious bodies, schools, peer groups and the like should perform their roles sufficiently to make the work of the media easier.

Indeed, one may claim that the media in Nigeria are not doing enough in the fight against poverty. As Uyo (1996: 59) pointed out "The media in Nigeria is not doing enough, or can do much more than it is doing now towards fighting what is critically wrong with the civil society." The civil society in Nigeria is critically pauperized and the mass media should rise up to the challenge of leading the fight against poverty in all its ramifications. This can be done by letting the public know the latest about poverty, projecting statistics and areas mostly affected. The media should also launched a campaign through news coverage, news analysis, features, editorials, cartooning, documentaries and commentaries to achieve the objective of poverty reduction and possible alleviation.

References

Alayande, B. and Alayande, O. (2004), "A Quantitative and Qualitative Vulnerability of Poverty in Nigeria." *Paper* Presented on CSAE Poverty Reduction Conference, Growth and Human Development in Africa, March, 2004.

Ali-Akpajiak and Pyke (2005), *Measuring Poverty in Nigeria:* Oxfam Report

Anyanwu, E. (1997), "Poverty in Nigeria: Concepts and Measurement and Determinants", in *Poverty Alleviation in Nigeria.* Proceedings of the 1997 Annual Conference of the Nigerian Economic Society.

Butler, K. (2007), "Portraying Poverty in the News" a paper on http://mainstream Journalism.suite 101.com/article.cfm/

Dudley, B. J. (1975), "Power and Poverty" in *Poverty in Nigeria.* Proceedings of the 1975 Annual Conference of the Nigerian Economic Society.

Dobmeyer, D. (1995), "20 Steps to Improving Media Coverage of Poverty Issues" A Paper developed for Chicago Community, USA

Echemeri, R. N. (1997), "The Structure of income, inequality and poverty in Rural Southeastern Nigeria." Proceedings of the 1997 Annual Conference of the Nigerian Economic Society.

Fog, A. (2004), "The Supposed and Real Role of the Mass Media in Modern Democracy." A working paper 2004/5/20

Gunter, B. (2000), *Media research methods.* California: Sage Publications.

Gurevitch, M. and Blumler, J. G. (1990), "Political Communication Systems and Democratic Values" in Lichtenberg, J (ed.) *Democracyand the Mass Media.* Cambridge: University Press

Herman, E.S. and Chomsky, N. (1988), *Manufacturing Consent: The Political Economy of The Mass Media.* New York: Pantheon

Herman, E.S. and McChesney, R.W.(1997), *The Global Media.* London: Cassell Human Development Report (2006)

Jones, D. R. (2004), "How the News Media Covers Poverty", *Urban Agenda Index*

Keane, J. (1991,) *The Media and Democracy.* Cambridge: Polity Press

McQuail, D. (1983), *Mass Communication Theory: An Introduction.* London: Sage

Ojo, E. O. (2000), "The Military and Democratic Transition in Nigeria: An Indepartment Analysis of Gen. Babangida'sTransition Programme (1985-1993)" *Journal of Military and Political Sociology* 28(1)

Osinubi, T. S. (2003), "Urban Poverty in Nigeria: a case study of Agege area of Lagos State, Nigeria," Unpublished paper, University of Ibadan, August, 2003

Oso, L. (2003), *Communication and Development: A Reader.* Abeokuta: Jedidiah Pub.

United Nations Development Programme (UNDP) Report (1998)

United Nations Development Programme (UNDP) Report (2001)

Uyo, A. (1996), "The Press and Civil Society in Nigeria", in *The Mass Media and Democracy.* Lagos: CLO

World Bank Report, (2001)

Wright, C. R. (1960), "Functional Analysis and Mass Communication," in *Public Opinion Quarterly*, 24.

CHAPTER TEN

ETHNO-RELIGIOUS CONFLICTS IN KANO STATE: POVERTY AS A MAJOR EXPLANATORY FACTOR

Fatima Oyine Ibrahim

Introduction

One major issue which poses a challenge to the citizens and government of the Federal Republic of Nigeria today is the incessant occurrence of ethno-religious as well as communal conflicts among the various groups that form the country. This situation contrasts with the past when ethnicity and religion were the instruments of unity and peaceful co-existence and not the sources of discord and strife among different groups in the country.

A body of literature abounds (see Elaigwu 2005; Jega 2004; Ibrahim 2004) which shows that throughout the world, contemporary events provide enough evidence to indicate that societies which were hitherto co-existing peacefully now resort to the use of deadly violent confrontations along ethnic, religious, re-gional, economic, cultural and other divisions. It is true that Nigeria in general and Kano state in particular, for the purpose of this chapter, do not have the mo-nopoly of being the theatre of ethno-religious conflicts in the world. The cause for concern is the devastating impact of such crises on the people even many years after each occurrence. Adamu (2005) expresses his concern when he states that:

> Nigeria has become a killing field as a result of the growing social, ethnic and religious intolerance. In the past few years, Kano, Kaduna, Jos, and Yelwa, the Southern Senatorial district of Nassarawa...Were convulsed in inter-ethnic and religious crises in which thousands of people died, private and public prop-erties worth millions of naira were destroyed (Adamu; 2005:53).

Recently, the spate of ethno-religious crises in Nigeria has made the country "polarized along political, ethnic, religious and economic lines" (Adamu, 2005:53}. As a result, the gap between Muslims and Christians is widening by the day. The same applies to the growing social inequality in the country which is a perfect recipe for social discontent. History has taught us that the pauperization of the people ultimately leads to social upheavals in which the rich as well as the poor and the innocent become the victims.

In Kano state, not less than 12 ethno-religious conflicts have occurred between 1953 and 2007. Out of these conflicts, 10 occurred since the 1980s. Thus, it
can rightly be said that though Kano state does not have the monopoly of being
the flash point of ethno-religious conflicts in Nigeria, the frequency of its occurrence, calls for a concern. This is because evidence abounds to show that in the
state, like other parts of Nigeria, the poverty level is a major cause of conflicts in
the society. The level of poverty in Nigeria in general and Kano state in particular (the focus of this chapter) has been a major challenge which successive governments have contended with over the past few decades. Despite various public
policies which have been designed to tackle the problem over the years, poverty
level is on the increase.

The period since the 1980s has been spectacular for many African societies as
the harsh economic conditions of the people have resulted into an upsurge of
internal crises. The period proved that there is a symbiotic relationship between
poverty and internal conflicts in these societies. The Nigerian experience to a
large extent, and that of Kano in particular, fits into these characterizations as the
country has witnessed "Civil War, ethnic, regional, religious, class and communal conflicts that have taken a major toll on national development" (Kwanashie,
2005:110).

It is therefore proposed that poverty is a major cause of frequent occurrence
of ethno-religious crises in Kano State. This is, in line with Makarfi's (2005) position that "as economic crises dwindle people's fortunes, they tend to perceive
their enemies as those who belong to the other – ethno-religious groups" (2005:
28).The situation is further worsened by the conspicuous consumption of political office holders whose economic backgrounds, according to Elaigwu (2005),
were well known before they assumed public offices. Therefore, people's abject
poverty in the midst of plenty not only alienates but could generate hatred
(Elaigwu, 2005: 73).

Elaigwu (2005) and Kwanashie (2005) positions have been substantiated by
Jalingo (2001)who argues that in Kano state, like other parts of Nigeria ,the prevailing situation is abject poverty. This chapter therefore, attempts to analyze the
extent to which the prevailing poverty situation in Kano state has contributed to
the frequent occurrence of ethno-religious conflicts in the state using the results
of a study conducted in Kano state in 2003.

Methodology

This study used two sources of data namely, the empirical and library research. The empirical source involved the use of data obtained from 200 questionnaires administered on respondents whose categories included the local
populace who are resident in Kano and adherents of Islam and Christian religions. The administered questionnaires covered the three major ethnic groups in
Kano: Hausa, Yoruba and Ibo, and other minority ethnic groups. Also, an un-

structured interview schedule was administered on the following categories of specialized groups: *Ulamas*, priests/pastors, community leaders, security agents (The State Security Service and the Nigerian Police), local and state government officials. Twenty four persons were interviewed among in these categories. The library research was through such sources as Federal and State Government official gazettes, books, journals, research theses (M.Sc. and Ph.D.), magazines and newspapers that are related to the subject matter.

Conceptualizing Poverty and Ethno-Religious conflicts

Poverty is a multidimensional social phenomenon. The definitions of poverty and its causes, according to Narayan et. al (2000:32):

Vary by gender, age, culture, and other social and economic contexts. For example, in both rural and urban Ghana, men associate poverty with a lack of material assets, whereas for women, poverty is defined as food insecurity.

In the past classical works, various academic literature defined the concept of 'poverty' in terms of lack of income necessary to ensure access to a set of basic needs. With passage of time, the concept of poverty has been redefined to mean not only the lack of income but also the lack of access to health, education, and other services. Of recent, the definition has been extended to include powerlessness, isolation, vulnerability and social exclusion (FRN, 2006:67) To Sen (1984), however, poverty is the lack of certain capabilities such as being able to participate in society with dignity, or when peoples' standard of living is below a minimum accepted level (cited in Ibrahim, 2003: 401). Makarfi (2003) defines poverty thus:

> Poverty is being conceptualized in absolute and relative terms... absolute poverty is a state of having little income too little to purchase the necessities of life such as food, shelter, clothing, health care and education. This essentially means absolute poverty is perceived in terms of earnings of individuals in relation to the general market condition (2003: 370).

The usage of poverty in this study is in line with the FRN 2006's explanation of poverty. This is because in Kano State, many of the residents lack basic necessities of life like potable water, electricity, health facilities and so on .Also, many of the residents are powerless as they are not gainfully employed when compared with other States of Nigeria (see FRN,2006:290-292).

Ethno-religious conflicts on the other hand have been seen by Elaigwu (2005) as "all conflicts which regiment primordial identities of a group in competitive relations with other groups" (2005:59). Ibrahim (2005) on her part defines ethno-religious conflicts as the "disputes arising from ethnic and religious differences. Such conflicts are often associated with ethnic or religious sentiments" (2005: 321). The usage of the concept in this chapter denotes the fact that all crises that

have religious and ethnic undertones are ethno-religious conflicts i.e. either of
the two can give way to the other.

Literature Review and Theoretical Framework

Available Literature attribute frequent occurrence of ethno-religious crises in
a society to prevailing poverty situation. Scholars like Adamu (2005), Lawan
(2000), Jega (2004) and Omorogbe and Omohan (2005) argue that the increasing
pauperization of Nigerians under the regimes of poor economic management has
worsened the situation of the poor. To these scholars, the situation has led to frequent eruption of ethno-religious crises across different parts of the country. In
Jega's words:

Mass poverty served to condition the minds and attitudes of Nigerians and
made them susceptible to elite manipulation and mobilization of negative identities. As the state becomes unable to satisfy basic needs of the people, they in
turn withdrew from the sphere of the state into ethno-religious and communal
cocoons, with heightened sensitivity to the roles of the "others" in their marginalization and immiseration (cited in Lawan, 2000: 54).

Lawan (2000) argues that poverty and illiteracy are antithetical to the survival of democracy. Therefore, democracy is unsafe with the persistence of these
factors in Nigeria. This is because a poverty stricken and illiterate person can
easily be mobilized in the event of ethnic and religious conflicts. Thus, poverty
and illiteracy contribute to perpetuating and fuelling ethnic and religious violence in Nigeria.

Omorogbe and Omohan (2005), acknowledge the fact that societies the world
over experience various forms of civil unrests irrespective of their level of development. However, the frequent occurrence of ethno-religious crises in Nigeria is
of great concern to all stakeholders, because of the devastating effects of such crises. They therefore deemed it fit to investigate why ethno-religious conflicts take
place frequently in Nigeria. In their investigation, Omorogbe and Omohan explain that:

> Given the position of Nigeria as the sixth oil producing nation in the World,
> one would naturally expect that the resources accruing to the country will be
> more than sufficient to cope with the needs of her citizens... Sad to say, that has
> not been the case. No year passes without the eruption of severe conflicts within
> and between ethnic and religious groups in Nigeria (2005: 550).

They therefore conclude that among other factors, mass poverty experienced
by Nigerians over the years is one of the factors responsible for the generally
high level of instability in the country. Invariably, this has found expression in
ethic and religious outbursts .To further give credence to the claim that poverty
is the major cause of frequent ethno-religious crises in recent times in Nigeria,

Jega (2004) argues that the failure of the Obasanjo regime to resolve the socio-economic crises in the country on assumption of duty worsened the situation. He puts it thus:

> ...the more the Obasanjo regime seemed unable or unwilling to address these problems, the more heightened the crisis of rising expectations. As all the major economic indices have not changed appreciably for the better, expectations have been shattered and disappointment and disenchantment have increased, and all these have created conducive atmosphere for rising protests and ethno-religious confrontation and conflicts (Jega; 2004:8).

Worried about the spate of ethno-religious crises especially in the Northern parts of the country, the Executive Goverrnor of Nasarawa State, Alh. (Dr.) Abdullahi Adamu (2005) expressed his dismay when he stated that:

> ...Never in the history of Nigeria has it been as polarised as it is now. It is polarised along political, ethnic, religious and economic lines. The gap between Muslims and Christians is widening by the day. The same applies to the growing social inequality in the region...This growing inequality is a perfect recipe for social discontent. This is because pauperisation of the people ultimately leads to social upheavals (Adamu, 2005:10).

There are existing theories that explain why poverty is the genesis of ethno-religious crises in a society. Among such theories are Feierabend and Feierabend's (1972) Frustration-Aggression theory, Schock (1996) Conjectural Model, the Marxist (1887) theory of rebellion as well as Ethnic Mobilization and Conflict theory.

This study however has adopted Feirabend and Feirabend's Frustration-Aggression theory as an explanatory framework on why the high rate of poverty level in a society, Kano state for the purpose of this chapter, is one of the major causes of ethno-religious conflicts. To Feierabend and Feierabend (1972), political instability is aggressive politically relevant behaviours which can be defined:

[A]s the degree or the amount of aggression directed by individuals or groups within the political system against other groups or against the complex of officeholders and individuals and groups associated with them. Or conversely, it is the amount of aggression directed by these officeholders against other individuals, groups or officeholders within the polity (1972: 136).

Feierabend and Feierabend's Frustration-Aggression theory postulates that "aggression is always the result of frustration" (1972: 136). Frustration may lead to other modes of behaviour. Thus, political instability is identified as aggressive behaviour which results from situations of unrelieved, socially experienced frustration. Such situations could result from conditions in which levels of social expectations, aspirations and needs are raised for many people for significant periods of time and still remain unmatched by equivalent levels of satisfaction. Fierabend and Fierabend's frustration-aggression theory can aptly give theoretical explanation of the poverty situation in Kano state as a major cause of ethno-religious conflicts in the state. This is in line with the saying that a hungry man is an angry man.

Some Cases of Ethno-Religious Conflicts in Kano State

Nigeria has experienced uncountable ethno-religious and communal conflicts. Like other parts of the world, it had its share of violent ethno-religious and communal conflicts. The source of worry however is the frequency of ethno-religious conflicts in the Northern States of the Federation since the 1980s. For instance, between 1980 and 2004, there were at least 50 ethno-religious conflicts in the Northern States out of which Kano State witnessed 10(Elaigwu,2005). The average of crises per Northern state shows that Kano State has witnessed the highest cases of ethno-religious crises in the Northern States.

According to Elaigwu (2005:6), tracing causality of conflicts is a very difficult business but all the same, reasons must be adduced for all conflicts which had occurred in Kano State as illustrated in the following paragraph by the chronology of selected ethno-religious conflicts in the state.

Between 1953 and 2007, not less than twelve ethno-religious crises have occurred in Kano state. Out of these conflicts, only two i.e. those of the 1953 and 1966 occurred before the 1980s. Thus, the period since 1980 can be said to have been characterized by series of conflicts in the state. The psychological impact of these crises remain with the citizens to date. The 1953 ethnic conflict in Kano was fuelled by the then existing local grievances against the Sabon-Gari settlers in Kano. The conflict originated following the rejection of a motion by Chief Anthony Enahoro (Action Group) for Nigeria's independence on the floor of the Federal House of Representatives by the Hausa-Fulani members of the House who were mostly members of the Northern People's Congress (NPC). Both their Igbo and Yoruba colleagues in the parliament openly insulted the Hausa-Fulani of being stooges of the British.

The campaign for self-governance come 1956 was taken by members of AG to the Northern parts starting with Kano on 15th May 1953. A mass demonstration broke out in Sabon-Gari where the kinsmen of the Yoruba and Igbo collaborators could be found. Many lives (mostly Igbos) and property were lost. The 1953 riot was the genesis of the victimization of the Igbo and Christians in Kano.

The 1966 crisis was as a result of the first military coup d'etat in Nigeria staged by young Igbo officers led by Major Chukwuemeka Kaduna Nzeogwu in which many prominent Hausa-Fulani leaders were killed. The result of this was the replacement of Sir Tafawa Balewa by General Aguiyi Ironsi, an Igbo man as the Nigerian Head of State. The Unification Decree promulgated by the new Head of State on March 29, 1966 led to demonstrations in Kano in which between

100 and 200 Igbos lost their lives in Sabon-Gari. In July the same year, some Northern Military Officers staged another coup to avenge the death of their leaders in the January coup.

After a span of fourteen years, the Maitatsine riot occurred in Kano in December, 1980. Kano played host to different Islamic Scholars from neighboring African countries. This led to the existence of different sects like the Kadiriyya, Kabalu, Tijjaniyya etc. The confrontational attitude of the Maitatsine sect towards other Islamic sects made it to be seen as a social misfit whose activities must be checked. Hence, on November 26, 1980, the then Kano State Governor, Alhaji. Muhammad Abubakar Rimi in a letter gave the Maitatsine sect fourteen days ultimatum within which to demolish and evacuate the illegal structures erected by Marwa (their leader) and his men. The crisis that followed led to the loss of over 500 lives including Marwa himself and goods worth several millions of Naira were destroyed by the fundamentalists (Albert, 1999: 274).

Two years after the Maitatsine riot came the Fagge crisis of 1982 which was an inter-religious conflict caused by a violent reaction of the Muslims against the reconstruction of a dilapidated Church which they felt was too close to the Abdullahi Bayero Mosque in Waje quarters.The disorder resulted in the burning of three churches and the vandalization of several others (Ekoko and Amadi, 1989). The Federal Government resolved the issues by paying ₦75, 000.00 as compensation to the Christian Association of Nigeria in Kano.

For almost a decade, conflicts of ethnic and religious nature did not occur in Kano until October, 1991 when a German Preacher, Reinhard Bonke was invited by the Christian Association of Nigeria (CAN), Kano Branch, to come and preach the Gospel in a Crusade which was supposed to hold in Kano at the Race Course. The publicity given to the event attracted the attention of the Muslims who felt aggrieved because the same government who granted a license to Reirchard Bonke to preach in Kano had earlier refused to grant same permission to Sheikh Ahmed Deedat, a South African Muslim Preacher to come and preach in a religious revival programme for the Muslims in Kano. The above reason, coupled with the provocative posters and handbills written in Arabic text inviting people to the crusade which read "JESUS FOR ALL... BY THE YEAR 2000" was protested by the Muslims. Their protests however fell on deaf ears. This led to a peaceful march by the Muslims on October 16, 1991 to the Emir's Palace to lodge their complaints. However, some hoodlums and the unemployed hijacked the peaceful demonstration which led to violent attack on the Christians living around Sabon-Gari, Rimin Kebe and Tudun Murtala. It was reported that several hundreds of people were killed on the two sides and properties worth several millions of Naira were destroyed (Ibrahim, 2004: 66).

Barely three years after the Reinhard Bonke conflict, another round of ethno-religious violence took place in Kano on December 6, 1994 when an Igbo man, Gideon Akaluka detained in Bompai Prison awaiting trial for defecating on a leaflet of the Quran, was beheaded. The Shiite (an Islamic sect) who spearheaded the unfortunate event stuck Gideon's head to a spear and took it round Kano City. This annoyed the southerners and hence, the atmosphere was charged and ready to explode at any slightest provocation. The Kano State Government diplomatically calmed down the charged atmosphere. It is the opinion of this paper that the 1995 ethno-religious conflict resulted partly from this "bottled-up" emotion.

The Kano State Government was not as lucky on May 30, 1995 when a battle of words which developed into a scuffle between Mr. Aurthur Nwankwo an Igbo man and Mallam Abubakar Abdu alias Dan Fulani, a Fulani man in Sabon-Gari market developed into an ethnic conflict which left twenty five people dead. Other consequences of the crisis, according to Albert (1999) include a total of twenty two vehicles, eighty-one motorcycles and forty-nine shops which were vandalized by the rioters.

Poverty as a Major Cause of Ethno-religious Conflicts in Kano State

With the resurgence of several forms of identities like ethnic, religious and gender, Nigeria can be described as undergoing the age of resurgence of identity politics. This poses a challenge to the state. The 1980s witnessed series of ethnic and religious conflicts in different parts of the country with their devastating impact on social lives and destruction of properties worth millions of Naira. Suddenly, communities and religious groups which had co-existed peacefully since Independence are at logger heads. The ethnic and religious violence is the extreme manifestation of conflict rooted in the crises of identity.

At this juncture, it is pertinent to ask, why the persistence of crises in Kano State since the 1980s? Like any other social phenomenon, the causes of the conflicts in Kano State can be traced to many factors. These are: poverty; ignorance of the doctrines of the two religions by their adherents; religious fundamentalism; unemployment etc. It is the argument of this paper however that the prevalence of poverty in Kano state is the dominant factor responsible for the frequent occurrences of ethno-religious crises in the state. For instance, Kano State in 2004 was ranked amongst the states with very high prevalence of poverty (See FRN 2006:79) in Nigeria with 73.11% of the population of the State classified as poor. In short, the North-West Geo-political Zone where Kano State is situated, has witnessed an increase in the level of poverty as illustrated by the data below:

Table 1: Trends in Poverty Level by Zones (1980 - 2004)

Zone	1980	1985	1992	1996	2004
South South	13.2	45.7	40.8	58.2	35.1
South East	12.9	30.4	41.0	53.5	26.7
South West	13.4	38.6	43.1	60.9	43.0
North Cen-	32.2	50.8	46.0	64.7	67.0

tral					
North East	35.6	54.9	54.0	70.1	72.2
North west	37.7	52.1	36.5	77.2	71.2

Source. Adopted from Federal Republic of Nigeria (2005), *Poverty Profile for Nigeria,* Abuja: National Bureau of Statistics, p. 22.

To consolidate the point that poverty is a major cause of ethno-religious crises in Kano State, a survey research was carried out in 2003 (see Ibrahim, 2003) in which questionnaires were administered on 200 carefully selected sample in Kano state. Non-structured interviews involving twenty four individuals were also conducted. In the course of the research, attempt was made to know the reasons for frequent occurrences of ethno-religious crises in the state. Poor economic base of the populace (among other factors) was adduced to be a major cause of ethno-religious crises in the State as affirmed by the result of the 2003 survey as presented in Tables 2 and 3 below.

Table 2: Reasons for Frequent Occurrences of Ethno-Religious Crises in Kano

Sample Size	192
Poor Econ. Base of the Populace	67 (34.9%)
Religious Fundamentalism	61 (31.8%)
Occurrences at the Int'l level	8 (4.2%)
Diverse Social Culture	22 (11.5%)
Incapacity of Security Apparatus	16 (8.3%)
Other factors	18 (9.4%)
Total	192 (100%)

Source: Survey Research 2003

From the table, poor economic base of the populace has 67 (34.9%), religious fundamentalism 61 (31.8%), diverse social cultures 22 (11.5%) other factors 18 (9.4%), incapacity of security apparatus 16 (8.3%) and occurrences in international area 8 (4.2%). It is therefore, easy to infer that the poor economic base of the populace is mainly responsible for ethno-religious crises in Kano State. This reason is further strengthened by what the interviewees asserted. For instance, Alhaji Abdulmalik Yakubu (Interviewed August 14, 2003, Alhaji Ahmed Isa (Interviewed July 30, 2003), Alhaji Aminu Sabo (Interviewed May 15, 2003), and the CAN President, Kano State Chapter Rt. Rev. Foster Ekeleme (Interviewed October 15, 2003) all share similar views that poverty and youth unemployment are the major causes of frequent ethno-religious crises in Kano State. Also, on the reasons for the direction of attacks on Igbos and Christians in the 2001 crisis in Kano State, the data in Table 3 below provide the reasons:

Table 3: Reasons for the Direction of Attacks on Igbos and Christians in the 2001 Crisis

Sample Size	192
Ignorance on the part of the attackers	67 (34.9%)
Hatred of Non-Muslims and Non-Indigenes by the Attackers	61 (31.8%)
Economic Motive of the Attackers	8 (4.2%)
Inability of the State Govt. to Protect Non-Indigenes Resident in the State	22 (11.5%)
Other Reasons	16 (8.3%)
Total	192 (100%)

Source: Survey Research, 2003

The respondents were asked to proffer reasons why the attack in the 2001 crisis was directed against Igbos and Christian particularly. From the data in the table, one can see that majority of the respondents numbering 80 (41.7%) were of the view that ignorance on the part of the attackers was the major reason. A substantial number of the respondents 45 (23.4%) held the view that sheer hatred of non-Muslims and non-indigenes by the attackers contributed immensely to the above phenomenon. Following this set of respondents are those who felt that economic motive of the attackers was responsible for the direction of attacks against Igbos and Christians. This set of respondents numbered 37 which represent 19.3% of the sampled respondents. Other respondents, 19 (9.9%) in all, opined that the above incident was caused by the inability of the state to adequately protect non-indigenes resident in the state. Those respondents who had reasons other than the ones specified in the questionnaire collectively numbered 11 (5.7%).

From the interviews conducted, Alhaji Ahmed Ibrahim and Mallam Saidu N.T. held a common opinion that the attackers had the economic motive as their reason for attacking Igbos and Christians. Alhaji Ahmed Ibrahim however, categorized the attackers into what he termed as 'real attackers' and the *area boys*. According to him, the 'real attackers' were motivated by the American attack on the Afghans who are Muslims, while the *Yan daba* were motivated by the economic factor, that is, to loot the Christians' shops. Still giving credence to the economic motive of the attackers, Alhaji Danladi Yahaya Mai (Interviewed, June 17, 2003) and Alhaji Aminu Sabo (Interviewed, May 15, 2003) were of the opinion that it was the possession of wealth by those who were attacked that attracted the attackers with the aim of looting their possessions for economic reason(s) irrespective of whether the attacked persons were Christians or Muslims.Most strategic areas in Kano like Kofar Ruwa, Sabon-Gari, Ibo Road, Galadima Road etc. are dominated by the Igbos. Thus, these areas are often targets of attacks by hoodlums with the aim of looting their wares for economic motive.

From the analysis arising from the data in Table 3 above, it can be deduced that the poverty situation in the state is responsible for the frequent occurrences of crises in the State. Other reasons however abound.. For instance, the highest number of respondents constituting 80 (41.7%) is of the opinion that ignorance on the part of the attackers is responsible for the frequent occurrence of crises in the state. This view is held by scholars like Bashir (2005) who stated that:

The mutual ignorance of the doctrines of the two religions by their adherents. Nigerians are very prayerful but not religious. They are largely ignorant of the substance and spirit of the religions that they profess. That is why they can be easily manipulated by mischief-makers who put on the toga of Imam, Priest/pastor (2005:104).

Religious fundamentalism as a cause of frequent ethno-religious crises in the state attracts 61 (31.8%) of the respondents (See Table 2 above).while this number is significant, it should be noted that Islam as a religion does not approve this kind of crises. Islam is a religion of peace which invites its followers to be just and kind in dealing with the non-Muslims as long as they do not wage war against them on account of their faith nor support one another to drive them out of their homes or support an enemy against them. Allah, the exalted says "Allah does not forbid you to deal justly and kindly with those who fought not against you on account of religion nor drove you out of your homes. Verily, Allah loves those who deal with equity" (See The Noble Quran; Surah Al -Mumtahanah, 60:8).

On equity and justice to the non-Muslims, the Prophet (PBUH) said "Whoever wrongs a non-Muslim ally or demeans him or over burdens him, I will be his opponent on the day of Resurrection" (cited in Al-sawy, 2002:78). It is the view of this author that religious fundamentalism as a cause of frequent occurrence of crises in Kano State does not hold water. This is because in the research carried out by the author in 2003, it was found that not all those who carried out the dastardly acts were Muslims or Kano indigenes. Some of the hoodlums who asked their victims to recite specific verses from the Qur'an often sought confirmation from others to ascertain the correctness of such texts (See Ibrahim, 2004).

Conclusion

In this chapter, efforts have been made to highlight the factors that are responsible for the frequent occurrence of ethno-religious conflicts in Kano State. This paper however, holds that poverty is predominant among them. Therefore to nip the menace in the bud, there is need for multi-faceted approaches. Among such approaches are: societal re-orientation, bottom-up poverty programmes, efficient use of public resources, provision of infrastructural facilities, human development, good governance and pro-poor government policies. The societal re-orientation which the Shekarau government adopted from 2003 to 2007 as an approach to abate frequent occurrence of ethno-religious crises in the state is the right step in the right direction. In this approach, the business community, public servants, the urban and rural communities, educational institutions, women and youths were targeted. However, this is like a tip of the iceberg because after many years , the poverty level is still high as many children are still roaming the streets aimlessly, hawkers still litter the streets with their wares in the State.

Therefore, the issue of *almajiranci* as a practice needs to be critically addressed if ethno-religious conflicts in Kano State are to be curtailed. This is because the pathetic condition to which less privileged children are exposed due to poverty will continue to be a major source of conflict as the practice of *almajiranci* is undermining their potentials as youths and making them ready recruits for violence when conflicts erupt. For socio-economic development of Kano State, youths must be empowered. Thus, while *almajiri* is seeking for Islamic knowledge, human face must be given to the process and the human dignity of the *almajiranci* should always be a factor by designing programmes that ensure their rights, development, growth and protection. Side by side, *almajiranci* should be exposed to both Islamic as well as western education. This will empower them economically as they can be absorbed into private/public sector of the economy. Also, this will reduce their level of ignorance.

To achieve the above, a more conducive atmosphere for Islamic education should be provided. The *Mallams* should be absorbed formally into the educational system with adequate remuneration. In addition to providing accommodation and food for the children, they can be trained to acquire specialized skills side by side with Islamic education. This will empower them and make them useful to themselves and the society.

In the last twenty years, Nigeria has had thirty-seven poverty programmes implemented with the best of intentions by the Federal Government (See Tomlinson, 2002:34). Despite these programmes, the poverty level is on the increase to the extent that it has manifested its ugly face in frequent occurrence of ethno-religious crises across the country. The reasons for the failure of the poverty programmes is their insensitivity to the needs of the poor as they are conceived and implemented from the top without any membership at the community and local government levels. Therefore, to ensure sustainability of poverty programmes, the top-down approach should be discarded in favour of bottom-up approach. This approach to solving poverty involves interrogating the poor by asking them what they think they need to alleviate their situation.

For Nigeria to focus its attention on the fight against poverty and by implication, frequent occurrence of ethno-religious crises, there should be considerable improvement in the use of public resources more efficiently by all tiers of government. What obtains presently is that the economy is split into two instead of one. While 90% falls into the non-oil economy, the remaining 10% falls into the oil sector. Unfortunately, most of the resources of the country stay within the oil economy and have little benefit to the lives of the ninety percent (90%) of Nigerians living on the non-oil economy, meaning that most Nigerians within the 90% non-oil economy are very poor and live on subsistence activities.

The social problem in Nigeria is responsible for the problem of insecurity. Poverty, it can be argued, is responsible for the high level of corruption in all sectors of the economy. To control the level of poverty therefore, infrastructural facilities like electricity, potable water supply, good roads, public schools, health facilities should be made available. Unfortunately, these facilities were relatively better in the yester years when compared to the present situation. For example, electricity consumption which was 3500 mega watts in Nigeria in 1999 when Obasanjo became the Head of State has dropped to 1000 mega watts in 2007 when he quitted the stage. Ironically, between 1999-2007, N540 billion was spent on the sector without anything to show for it (AIT, Interview with Alhaji Habu Fari on 23/03/07). Many Nigerians whose businesses depend on electricity as a means of daily survival are rendered helpless. For instance, welding, printing, business centers, barbing saloons, technicians, fashion designing are all affected. Therefore, tackling poverty would be difficult if these basic facilities which are prerequisites for survival are lacking.

Human development should be the bedrock upon which all governmental policies, programmes and actions rest. Nigeria in general is an agrarian society with fertile land in all parts of the country. Therefore, the strategy of both social and economic empowerment for the people should be adopted. This will lead to mass food production where hunger, want and degradation will become a thing of the past. Government's policy on micro, small and medium scale enterprises should be encouraged as they play a significant role in economic development. In order to spearhead sustainable development in Kano State, micro, small and medium scale enterprises should mobilize local resources for growth, empowerment and poverty reduction. The administration of Alhaji Musa Yar'Adua has created a special ministry for Youth at the Federal level. This is a right step in the right direction which should be emulated by all the states and Local Government Areas of the Federation. This is because the spate of ethno-religious and communal clashes across the nation is a reflection of the socio-economic problem of the society resulting from the high level of poverty in the country.

Lastly, good governance is a good step to poverty reduction. Financial abuses like corruption, lack of transparency and accountability should be fought gallantly through reform measures. In this vein, institutions such as the Economic and Financial Crimes Commission (EFCC), the Independent Corrupt Practices Commission (ICPC) should be further be strengthened. This is because through their efforts, the looted public money has been recovered thereby enhancing funds availability for pro-poor growth strategy by government.

References

Adamu, A. (2005), "People of the North Think", in Bobboyi H. and Yakubu A.M. (eds.), *Peace Building and Conflict Resolution in Northern Nigeria*, Kaduna, Arewa House

AIT, (2007), "Face The Nation Programme: Interview with Alhaji Habu Fari, NDP Presidential Candidate" 23 March

Albert, I.O. (1999), "Ethnic and Religious Conflicts in Kano" in Otite,O and Albert,I.O.(eds) *Community Conflicts In Nigeria: Management, Resolution and Transformation* Ibadan, Spectrum Books Limited

Al-Sawy, S. (2002), *Post September 11 American's Questions About Islam,* Egypt: Umm Al-Qura

Bashir, I. (2005), In Search of Peace in the Heart of Nigeria: A Political Economy Analysis in Bobboyi, H. and Yakubu, A.M. (eds.), *Peace Building and Conflict Resolution in Northern Nigeria,* Kaduna, Arewa House

Ekoko, A.E. and Amadi, L. O.(1989), "Religion and Stability in Nigeria", in *Nigeria Since Independence: The First 25 Years,* Vol. ix, Ibadan, Heinemann.

Elaigwu, J.I. (2005), "The Management of Ethno-Religious Conflicts in Northern Nigeria: Towards a more peaceful and Harmonious Geo-polity" in Bobboyi H. and Yakubu, A.M. (eds.), *Peace Building and Conflict Resolution in Northern Nigeria,* Kaduna, Arewa House.

Federal Government of Nigeria (2003), *Strategic Conflict Assessment Consolidated and Zonal Reports.* March , Institute for Peace and Conflict Resolution: The Presidency, Abuja.

Federal Republic of Nigeria (2005), *Poverty Profile for Nigeria,* Abuja, National Bureau of Statistics.

Federal Republic of Nigeria (2006*) Annual Abstract of Statistics 2006,* Abuja National Bureau of Statistics.

Feierabend, I.K. and Feierabend, R.L. (1972), "Systemic Conditions of Political Aggression: An Application of Frustration – Aggression Theory" in Fierabend,I.K., Fierabend,R.L.and Ted, R.G.(eds.) *Anger, Violence and Politics: Theories and Research.* New Jersey; Prentice-Hall Inc., Englewood Cliffs

Ibrahim, F.O. (2003), "Poverty and Local Government Performance in Nigeria" in Dalhatu, S. and Umar M.A. (eds.), *Towards Improved Local Government Management,* Kano Munawar Books

Ibrahim, F.O. (2004), "State, Religion and Federalism within the Context of Nigeria: A case study of the 2001 ethno-religious crisis in Kano State", Msc. *Thesis* Submitted to The Department of Political Science, Bayero University, Kano.

Jalingo, A.U. (2001) ,"Poverty And Poverty Alleviation in Kano State: Some Preliminary Observations", in *ECPER Journal of Political and Economic Studies,* Kaduna: Emwai Centre For Political and Economic Research.

Jega, A. (2004), "Democracy, Economic Crisis and Conflicts: A Review of the Nigerian Situation", in *The Quarterly Journal of Administration* Vol. XXXII, No.1 March 2004 Ile-Ife; Obafemi Awolowo University.

Kwanashie, M. (2005), "Poverty, Underdevelopment and the Culture of Conflict in Northern Nigeria" in Bobboyi H. and Yakubu A.M. (eds.), *Peace Building and Conflict Resolution in Northern Nigeria,* Kaduna, Arewa House.

Lawan M.M. (2000). ,"The Threats of Ethno-Religious Conflicts to the Sustainability of Democracy in Nigeria, in *Journal of Social and Management Studies* Vol. 7 Kano; Bayero University.

Makarfi, M.A.(2005), "Peace-Building and Conflict Resolution: The Experience of Kaduna State in BobboyiH and Yakubu, A.M(eds.), *Peace Building and Conflict Resolution in Northern Nigeria* ,Kaduna: Arewa House.

Narayan, D., Patel, R., Schafft, K., Rademacher, A. and Koch-Schutte, S. (2000), *Voices of the Poor: Can Anyone Hear Us?* New York; Oxford University Press Inc.

Omorogbe S.K. and Omohan M.E. (2005), "Causes and Management of Ethno-Religious Conflicts: The Nigerian Experience" in Yakubu, A.A., Adegboye R.T., Uban, C.N. and Dogo, B. (eds.), *Crisis and Conflict Management in Nigeria Since 1980* Vol. 2, Kaduna: Nigerian Defense Academy Book Series No.1.

Schock, K. (1996), "A Conjunctural Model of Political Conflict: The impact of Political Opportunities on the Relationship between Inequality and Violent Political Conflict", in *The Journal of Conflict Resolution (JSTOR),* Vol. 40, No.1 March, 1996.

The Noble Quran (undated), English Translation of the Meanings and Commentary, Madinah Munawwarah, King Fahd Complex

Tomlinson, M.D. (2002), "Poverty Reduction Strategy in Nigeria: An Assessment" in Jega, A.M. and Wakili, H. (eds.), *The Poverty Eradication Programme in Nigeria: Problems and Prospects,* Nigeria: the Centre for Democratic Research and Training, Mambayya House, Bayero University, Kano

CHAPTER ELEVEN

THE PROLONGED MILITARY RULE AND POVERTY EXACERBATION IN NIGERIA, 1984-1999

Mahmoud Mohammed Lawan

Introduction

No one can say with any certainty whether Nigeria have seen the end of military rule in the country. This, however, is not to suggest that military rule is desirous, in spite of the rumblings and the inactions of our politicians under democracy in the last eight years, the worst form of democracy is still far better than the most benevolent military regime. Nigeria was several times in the military cage, in fact in the last forty seven (47) years of Nigeria's independence from the British colonialists, the country had been under military rule for nearly twenty nine (29) years. While it is difficult to commend the military in their management of the nation's socio-political and economic resources, but there are little areas of commendation, although even these areas are overshadowed by the reckless manner the military administered the Nigerian state, in the 29 years of their involvement in the process of governance.

In spite of the self-proclaimed mission of the military as the messiah in Nigeria's political development and the destructive impact of their prolonged involvement in politics, the military has acquired the image of an "evil empire" (Falola; 1994).

This chapter examines and assesses the impact whether positive or negative of the prolonged involvement of military rule on the vexed issue of poverty between 1984 and 1999. In this connection, the chapter is structured into six (6) sections. Section one is basically the introductory section. Section two reviews the concepts of military and poverty. Section three reviews Nigeria's political history, albeit in brief. Military intervention in Nigerian politics is addressed in section four, while section five assesses the impact of poverty under successive military regimes from 1984 to 1999. Section six concludes with general recommendations on the way forward in the task of poverty eradication.

Conceptual Review: Military Rule and Poverty:

In the recent time, one of the scholars who operationalize the concept of the military is Hutchful; he defines the military as:

A body of armed men and women practising the legitimate profession of arms under the authority of civilian leaders and the control of duly appointed commanders (1998:249).

From this definition, the military is considered as a highly professional body of armed personnel, with organized hierarchy and unity of command; and highly disciplined. The military as an institution is viewed to be apolitical, and possessing the requisite skills and training to perform some clearly defined constitutional responsibilities, which usually include defending the territorial integrity of a nation against external aggression and assisting the police in the maintenance of internal security, especially in suppressing insurrection (Jega: 2002; 30).

In his book, "Ground Work of Military Law and Military Rule in Nigeria", Achike traces the origin of the term military, from the Latin word, "miles", meaning a soldier. Military, according to him, means anything pertaining to members of the armed forces (1980: 28). The members of the armed forces comprises the army, the Navy, the air force and the police, and in Nigeria whenever the military control the government, these four arms of the military constitute themselves into the highest decision-making organ of the state, in the management of the state administration. In addition, appointments as state administrators or military governors are, in most cases shared among these four arms of the military, with high centralization of power and command, at both the federal and state levels; as obtained in the military formations. The excessive centralization of power negatively affected the federal status of the Nigerian state, as a result of the prolonged stay of the military in governance.

The literature on military in Nigerian government and politics seem to gravitate around three major positions. The first position which considers the Nigerian military as the most reliable managers of social change is often cited to explain the formulation of policy changes, which have considerably affected the process of national development. Scholars from this perspective cited the creation of states, local government re-organization and the massive infrastructural development witnessed under the Gowon and Murtala/Obasanjo administration as cases in point. A prominent scholar on Nigerian military, Adekanye has observed that, the task of "keeping Nigeria one" was one in which the military most distinguished itself (cited in Oyediran, 1988: VII). However, even this position is contestable with the experience of Nigeria under military rule within the period of 1984 to 1999, as successive military regimes reverse the gains of the 1970s and even desecrated some of the national institutions established during that period in the name of adjusting the Nigerian economy. Similarly, the creation of states in 1987, 1991 and 1996 was not conducted on the basis of fairness and equity for the people from whom these states were excised. Thus, the prolonged stay of the military in governance exposed the military as bad managers of social change, because the numerous policies introduced in the 1980s and

1990s become conduct pipe for the looting of public funds. For instance, programmes like the Directorate of Food, Roads and Rural Infrastructure (DFRRI), Better Life for Rural Women; Mass Mobilization for Social and Economic Reconstruction (MAMSER) etc. while being laudable in conception were destroyed because of poor implementation and misapplication of resources meant for the target beneficiaries.

The second position advanced by scholars on the military in Nigerian politics, is that the military is considered as an anti-revolutionary force, incapable of creating the necessary conditions for revolutionary transformation. In fact, the military even thwarted efforts by the civil society towards democratic change as evident in the conduct of the Babangida and Abacha military regimes in the 1980s and 1990s.

Cases of anti-democratic posture of the military is cited in the Nigerian Labour Congress(NLC) versus the military regime in the case of fuel subsidy removal; the students' anti-SAP protests of 1988 and the Numerous strikes by the Academic Staff Union of Universities (ASUU) for improvements in learning conditions in the universities. In the brushes with the military, these groups often considered as potentially revolutionary are in most cases smashed by the military and their leaders arrested, for standing on the side of the popular aspirations of the people.

The third category of military scholars view the military as essentially conservative, un-progressive force, incapable of building lasting institutions in Nigeria, they argued that the performance of the military in the first coming of the military from 1966 to 1979 have been abysmally poor. In fact, Olugbemi, Adekanye and Odetola assessed the performance of the military in the area of agricultural development, and concluded that the performance was mediocre (Oyediran, 1988: X). They further argued that this poor performance is reflected in the Gross Domestic Product which declined from 61 per cent in 1964 to 18 per cent in 1980, as well as the declining share in export earnings of agricultural production (Oyediran, 1988: XI).

Consequently, by 1988 at the height of the implementation of SAP, agriculture suffered serious decline and neglect as a consequence of the removal of subsidy on petroleum products and the basic under funding of the sector. For instance, the allocation for the agricultural sector in 1992 was 4.83 per cent of total expenditure; it dropped drastically in 1993 to 1.23 percent (Newswatch, 1993: 40).

On the whole the military is generally considered as bad managers of the economy, at least from the experience of Nigeria under the SAP regime of General Ibrahim Babangida. In fact, Dudley concludes that the military are destructive economic agents and highly conservative, because they are essentially resistant to change or always want to maintain the status quo.

It can therefore be concluded that, in the Nigerian case, there has been a general recognition that military involvement in governance in post-colonial countries had resulted in little, if any, development. In most cases, they generated tremendous political turmoil and conflicts, as well as profound squandering of the resources of these countries. Moreover, military rule had profoundly resulted in the emergence of authoritarian despots with terrible records of gross human rights violation, and who had not only personalized power, but the public treasury as well (Jega, 2002: 31).

Nigeria's Political History in Perspective

The greater part of Nigeria's political history is considered as Anglo-colonial history. However, Nigeria's history as a political entity can be divided into three phases. Firstly, the pre-colonial history which was dotted with the traditional political institutions organized according to the existential political and socio-economic formations. Under this phase, various kingdoms and empires existed such as the Sokoto caliphate; the Alafinate kingdom; the Tiv society; the Benin kingdom; the Kanem- Bornu Empire, the Igbo traditional system, the Urhobo gerontocratic system etc. These kingdoms had developed their own respective political institutions and ideas on governance. In fact, Walter Rodney, the famous Guyanese historian, attested to the fact that Africa, Nigeria inclusive developed at their pace, although the rate of development was slow and incomparable to the western notion of development. However, the colonial intervention in Africa obstructed this pace of development. In Nigeria, this period is also known as the period of British control which lasted for almost 100 years from the conquest of Lagos in 1860 to the independence of the country in 1960. Within this period, the social formation was restructured into the wider capitalist social formation, which became an appendage of British and western imperialism. The third period of Nigeria's post-colonial history can be described as the direct outcome of the crises and contradictions of a peripheral capitalist social formation. The political Bureau captured the situation in Nigeria's post-colonial history in the following words:

> Nigeria's political misfortunes in the past and the failure to evolve a united, prosperous and just nation can be blamed partly on inadequate and defective structures and orientation which British colonialism bequeathed to the young nation at independence and the reluctance of succeeding Nigerian governments to tackle these problems decisively (Political Bureau Report, 1987).

Under this period, successive military and civilian administrations in Nigeria misdirected, mismanaged and destroyed the basis of national development in the country. The military wasted the over 29 years of political governance, which only produced authoritarian disposition; human right violations on a massive scale; corruption; ethno-religious violence; economic downturn and an endless transition process that succeeded in breeding corrupt and arrogant politicians devoid of the basic principles of decency in democratic ethos and development.

In fact, the Babangida and Abacha military Juntas in the history of military in governance clearly demonstrate the folly; trauma and the political upheaval visited on the Nigerian people and society, as a consequence of the authoritarian disposition and the personalization of power under the two military regimes. The civilians in power especially in the first republic; 1959 – 1966 and the second republic; 1979 – 1983, were not better either. The country under the two republics drifted to the brink of a precipice. As at 1999, when the Abdulsalami Abubakar military Junta, finally handed-over power to the civilian administration there was no better way to explain the Nigerian tragedy under the military, other than the description given by Karl Mier, that " This House has Fallen; Nigeria in Crisis". Nigeria was truly in crisis and dangerously drifting towards anarchy, especially with the annulment of the June 12, 1993 elections by General Ibrahim Badamasi Babangida, which was believed and hailed locally and internationally, to be the fairest and freest elections in the history of Nigeria.

Military Intervention In Nigerian Politics

In the first place, the military is a product of colonial intervention in African history. In fact, the military in modern Africa is the product of colonialism, which manifested in the scramble and the eventual partition of Africa at the Berlin conference of 1884.This is because the process of colonial conquest and division of the African continent was specifically brought about by military conquest. Consequently, within the context of Africa, the military emerged from the rubbles of colonization and colonial imperialism. It is important to observe, that we use the word modern military to distinguish the present state and form of the military in Africa from the various traditional military systems in Africa that existed prior to colonialism (Igbuzor, 2005: 98 – 99).

However, Achike captured more aptly the origin of the Nigerian military:

> The origin of what is today recognized as the Nigerian Army is traceable to the diverse local forces raised in the second half of the 19th century by the British colonial government in Nigeria. These forces were raised primarily to subjugate local opposition to British penetration and rule in West Africa and in addition to serve as an auxiliary force for augmenting imperial forces as a counter against the French during the crucial period of the Anglo-French rivalry in Nigeria (1978: 6).

This, however, was one of the factors that led to the emergence of the Nigerian military. Again, the various local forces formed the nucleus of the "West African Frontier Force" which was raised by Sir Frederick Lugard in 1897 to subjugate the entire West African region under the supreme control of the colonial office in Britain (Igbuzor, 2005: 99). Achike further captured the motive and character of the West African Frontier Force (WAFF) by stating that:

> The formation of the West African Frontier Force was motivated by political considerations and by necessity. Its creation provided a standing army for dealing with issues which required military intervention in West Africa. Secondly, its formation provided an opportunity for establishing effective British presence in West Africa. The Berlin conference of 1884 – 1885 had provided that the occupation of parts of Africa by foreign powers could only be validly made if such occupation was effective. By necessary implication, this demanded the maintenance of a military force that would ensure obedience to the British administration in the area allegedly occupied by them (Achike, 1978: 8 – 9).

Since then, the military evolved into its current form and character to the extent that in the immediate post – independent period of the early 1960s, the military was kept at bay. However, in the late 1960s and 1970s, military incursion into politics and governance became the order of the day, not only in Nigeria, but in many parts of Africa, Latin America and the Caribbean.

The first direct military intervention in Africa leading to the overthrow of a civilian government took place in Sudan in November, 1958 when General Ibrahim Abboud seizes power (Igbuzor, 2005: 99). The second coup d'etat in 1965 in Algeria opened the floodgate of numerous coups in rapid succession in Africa such as Congo-Kinshasa (1965), Dahomey (1965); Central African Republic (1966); Upper Volta, now Burkina Faso (1966); Nigeria (January and July 1966); Ghana (1966); Burundi (1966); Togo (1967) and Sierra Leone (1967). According to Igbuzor, within the decades of the 1960s and 1970s, military intervention in Africa became a dominant feature. As a result, between 1960 and 1982, almost 90 percent of the 45 independent Black African states experienced a military coup, an attempted coup or a plot; and during the course of some 115 legal government change, the states experienced 52 successful coups, 56 attempted coups and 102 plots making military coup "the institutionalized mechanism for succession" in post – colonial Africa (2005: 100). Indeed, the rapid and frequent intervention of the military in the process of governance has led to militarism and militarization of African political process.

In the context of Nigeria, the first direct military intervention in governance occurred on the 15th January, 1966, which was led by Major Kaduna Nzeogwu, with four other Majors, which popularly came to be referred to as the five Majors. The first coup d' etat terminated the Balewa government and brought General J.T.U Aguiyi – Ironsi to power. From the independence of Nigeria in 1960 to 1999 when the military finally handed over power to the civilian administration of Chief Olusegun Obasanjo, the country had experienced a series of successful and unsuccessful coups as the table below indicates.

Table 1: The Number of Coups and the Tenure of Military Regimes in Nigeria's Political History

S/N	Date of coup d'etat	Name of military Head of State	Tenure of Office	Remark
1.	15th January, 1966	General J.T.U Aguiyi Ironsi	16th Jan.-29th July, 1996	Success-ful
2.	29th July, 1966	General Yakubu gown	30th July 1966-29th Aug, 1975	"
3.	29th Aug, 1975	General Murtala R. Mohd	30th Aug, 1975-13th Feb. 1976	"
4.	13th February, 1976	General Olusegun Obasanjo	14th Feb. 1976-1st Oct. 1979	"
5.	31st December 1983	General Muhammad Buhari	1st Jan. 1984-27th Aug. 1985	Success-ful
6.	27th Aug., 1985	General I.B. Ba-bangida	28th Aug. 1985-27th Aug. 1993	"
7.	17th November, 1993	General Sani Abacha	17th Nov. 1998-8th June 1998	"
8.	NA*	General A.A. Abu-bakar	9th June, 1998-29th May 1999	"

Source: Compiled by the Author, 2007.

*NA – Coup d'etat was not applicable in this case, since Abacha died and Abdulsalami was made head of state by the inner caucus of the military junta

It is clear from the table above that, Nigeria had experienced seven successful military coups d'etats, which produced seven different military leaders; however the eight military Head of State, General Abdulsalami Abubakar assumed power after the death of General Sani Abacha in mysterious circumstances on the 8th of June, 1998. It is equally important to observe that over the years there had been a series of unsuccessful and attempted coups plots, prominent of which are the Orkar and Mamman Vatsa's coups of April, 22 1990 and December, 1986 respectively. Again, as the direct danger and implications of prolonged military in governance, the internal organization of the military institution became prone to internal wrangling, politicking and political maneuvers largely because a clique of military officers wanted to remain in power and consolidate their hold to it. This brought into lime - light the era of fathom coup, orchestrated by some loyal military officers, in order to either clear the way for some officers and /or to eliminate some perceived enemies of the military Junta in power. Notable examples include the Fadile/Gwadabe coup plot and the Diya/Adisa coup plot under the Abacha military regime from 1993 to 1998.

In respect of the factors usually responsible for military intervention in Nigerian politics, there are both internal and external factors. Internal to the Nigerian Armed forces, such as personal ambitions of the military officers; politicization of the Army by (a) involving it in matters with strong socio-political underpinnings like the quelling of the Tiv riots in 1965 and the Maitatsine religious uprisings in Kano in 1980 (Falola: 1994; 2) and even involving the army in election matters. Other internal factors include the introduction of quota recruitment policy in the Army; as well as the attempt and desire to reverse unpopular government policies (e.g. demobilization within the Army) (Falola: 1994; 3).

There are equally external factors such as the corruption and mismanagement of the economy by the civilian administration; the contagious effect of coups in other countries.

Similarly, there is the involvement of foreign secret agencies in coup plots. For instance, there was the alleged C.I.A involvement in the abortive coup attempt of February, 1976, which led to the assassination of General Murtala Ramat Mohammed. Another factor that has not been given much prominence is what General David Jemibewon referred to as "psychological propaganda". Narrating his personal experience while undergoing military training in the United States of America, Jemibewon stated that not only was the American commandant bent on usually accompanying officers from the third world countries to public functions, but also that the "..commandant had the habit of introducing (us) at the place (we) went to as future heads of state and insisted, therefore, that (we) be treated with the dignity benefiting (our) future positions (cited in Falola, 1994: 3).

It is important to note that in the motivation, planning and execution of a military coup, a combination of these factors usually come into play and strongly influence the coup plot. However, no matter the heavy influence of the factors and the drives for military intervention, it is unanimously agreed that military rule is an aberration. In fact, coups and counter coups are illegal, because there has never been any provision for coups in any Nigerian constitution, past or present (Falola, 1994:16). Quite understandably as well, the military in the context of Nigerian experience with military rule is not a credible alternative for political leadership; economic management and overall national development.

Conceptual Overview of Poverty: The Problem of Definition

Poverty is a universal phenomenon. It is a feature of all societies whether developed, under – developed and, or developing. However, the depth and extent of poverty differs from one region of the world to the other, but it is typically higher in the less developed countries of the world. According to the United Nations Development Programme (UNDP), about 2.5 billion people are trying to survive on less than $2 a day (Awake, May, 2007: 3).

A substantial percentage of the world population is highly under-nourished; lack access to basic education and medical services; and cannot obtain clean drinking water for human purposes, while a small minority of the world population lives in affluence and prosperity. It is Ironic that, there is global prosperity in the world, but still people live in poverty in the midst of plenty of resources. It has been estimated that the 2005 gross world product, the total value of goods services produced in that year, exceeds $60 trillion (Awake, 2007: 3). Similarly, according to a recent United Nations publication, the wealth of the world's three richest individuals is greater than the combined gross domestic product of the 48 poorest nations in the world (cited in Lawan, 2007: 2-3). Thus, poverty is multi-dimensional and its effects devastating. Poverty also manifests itself in a variety of forms and contexts, and it is induced by a variety of causes and mechanisms (Dike, 1997: 57).

Any investigation into the concept and phenomenon of poverty has always been a problematic exercise. An overview into the abundant literature on poverty reveals that there is no general consensus on any acceptable definition of the concept of poverty. Fundamentally, poverty includes different dimensions of deprivations. In general, it is the inability of the people to meet economic, social and other standards of well – being (Egwuatu, 2002: 69). According to the World Bank, poverty is defined as an unacceptable human deprivation in terms of economic opportunity, education, health and Nutrition, as well as lack of empowerment and security (cited in Egwuatu, 2002: 69).

Similarly, the United Nations Development Programme (UNDP) has introduced two relevant concepts: human Development, defined as a process that enlarges peoples' choice including freedom, dignity, self – respect and social status, and Human poverty, which refers to the deprivation of essential capabilities such as a long and healthy life, knowledge, economic resources and community participation (cited in Egwuatu, 2002: 69).

On the other hand, Ajakaiye contends that poverty can be broadly conceptualized in four ways:

> Poverty as the lack of access to basic needs/goods is essentially economic or consumption oriented and conceives the poor as those individuals or house – holds in a particular society, incapable of purchasing a specified basket of basic goods and services such as nutrition, shelter, water and health care. Poverty can also be a result of lack of or impaired access to productive resources including education, working skills and tools and political as well as civil rights to participate in decisions concerning socio-economic conditions. Poverty can also be the outcome of inefficient use of common resources. This may result from weak policy environment, inadequate infrastructure, weak access to technology, credit, etc. finally, poverty can be due to certain groups using certain mechanisms in the system to exclude "problem groups" from participating in economic development, including the democratic process (2002: 8).

In the same vein, Oyemomi described poverty as simply a state of pronounced deprivations (2003: 41). This deprivation may be in the lack of basic needs of life as Ajakaiye pointed out. He, however, further submits that the deprivations may be those that keep the poor from leading the kind of life that everyone values. Poor people also face extreme vulnerability to ill – health, economic dislocation, natural disasters, violence and bad weather – all of which reinforce their sense of ill – being, exacerbate their material poverty and weaken their bargaining position. Invariably, wherever the people's security towards this end cannot be guaranteed, they are also considered as poor (Oyemomi, 2003: 41).

Most literature on poverty appears to be in unanimous agreement that poverty can be relative or absolute. Poverty is absolute when people or group of people are unable to satisfy their most basic and elementary requirements of human survival. In relative terms, poverty would be a comparative state of deprivation among individuals, groups and/or segments of the society. While absolute poverty can be eradicated, relative poverty can only be controlled to bridge the gap in the society as all human beings cannot possibly be put at the same level of well-being even in the communist society (Oyemomi, 2003: 41).

It is clear from the foregoing that poverty is a state of want and deprivation, it is equally a condition of vulnerability and exclusion, and this may be multi – dimensional involving economic, social and political deprivations. The condition of poverty in Nigeria under the military has been heavily depriving due to a combination of factors, as will be examined in the following section.

Causes and Incidence of Poverty under Military Rule in Nigeria

Though poverty is not peculiar to any regime in Nigeria, whether civilians or the military. It is prevalent and widespread in all the two regimes in Nigeria. The scope of this chapter is the period from 1984 to 1999, which covers the military regimes of General Buhari, Babangida, Abacha, and Abubakar. Several factors account for the growing incidence of poverty in Nigeria. Some of the factors reflect the poor management and performance of the Nigerian economy, since independence. It is often argued that the level of economic performance of any country depends primarily on at least two factors; the level of resources relative to population, and the level of productivity. Nigeria belongs to the group of poor countries with high level of resources, but low level of productivity (Ukwu, 2002: 92). The country is basically an import-dependent and consumer economy; as such, productivity and innovation are not the common features of the Nigerian economy. Closely related to the mismanagement of the economy, is the massive corruption that has come to characterize the Nigerian political history, particularly under successive military regimes. Corruption has heavily impacted and constrained the Nigerian development agenda, largely because huge amount of the nation's resources are prudently looted and embezzled by government functionaries to the detriment of the country's developmental priorities.

Another factor that is generally responsible for poverty in Nigeria is the devastation and abject neglect of the agricultural sector. Prior to the discovery of oil in the late 1950s and 1960s, agriculture served as the major foreign exchange earner for the economy. Agriculture which should have served the other sectors of the economy fell from 60 per cent of GDP in the 1960s to 31 per cent by the early 1980s (FOS, ND: 3). Consequently, agricultural production declined because of the expensive imports (given the highly appreciated exchange rate) and heavy demand for construction labour encouraged migration of farm workers to towns and cities (FOS, ND: 3).

In addition, the oil boom of the 1970s only succeeded in creating mixed blessings for the country, as Nigeria generated huge oil revenue that was essentially looted by the parasitic ruling class and also massively invested into unproductive investment such as FESTAC 77 etc. By the decade of the 1980s, Nigeria experienced economic recession, arising from the fall in the prices of oil which led to sharp increase in the level of poverty in the country. From 1980 to 1984, average per capita income dropped, as did private consumption per capita (FOS, ND: 3).

Another factor that has helped to accelerate the depth of poverty in Nigeria is the adoption of Structural Adjustment Programme (SAP) by the military I n 1986. The policies adopted by the government under SAP, such as devaluation, subsidy removal, retrenchment, price control and cuts in public expenditures, led to massive unemployment, marginalization and social deprivation. The massive depreciation of the national currency, the Naira, led to rising cost in the prices of essential commodities. Similarly, as a consequence of devaluation and the rising level of inflation, the real wages of the Nigerian workers were devalued by about 300 per cent in 1986 (Olukoshi, 1991: 231). As a result, this has led to the erosion of the living standard of workers in Nigeria. In fact, in a study covering the period 1986 to 1996 conducted in 2002, it was discovered that SAP and its conditionality has adversely impacted on the living and working conditions of lecturers in the universities, to the extent that many of the lecturers resorted to multiple means of survival, while a substantial number migrated to the west including Europe and America (Lawan, 2002: 253), in search of greener pastures. In real terms, as a consequence of SAP, unemployment, retrenchment and poor access to medical and educational opportunities has driven many Nigerians to mental illness, death and serious economic and political deprivation and exclusion.

Other causes of poverty in Nigeria during the period under review include inadequate access to means of fostering rural development in poor regions and strong urban bias in the design of development programmes (Ajakaiye, 2002: 13). In addition, the destruction of natural resource endowment, which has potential for enhanced productivity especially in the agricultural sector, is a major cause of ecological poverty (Ajakaiye, 2002: 13 – 14).

Given the causes responsible for poverty in Nigeria, it is clear that poverty is rising. Under the period of military rule, poverty rose to 65.6% in 1996 as the table 2 below indicates.

Table 2: National Poverty Level, 1980 – 2004.

Year	Poverty level (In %)	Pop. In Poverty In million	Urban in %	Rural in %
1980	27.2	18.3	17.2	28.3
1985	46.3	34.7	37.8	51.4
1992	42.7	39.1	37.5	46.0
1996	65.6	67.1	58.2	69.8
2004	54.4	*NA	NA	NA

Source: FOS; Nigerian Poverty Profile, 2004

*NA - Figures in respect of these years are not available.

The table above indicated that from 1980 to 1985, two years after the over-throw of Shehu Shagari, national poverty level rose from 27.2% to 46. 3%. Similarly, evidence has shown that there was downward decline of poverty in 1992 to 42.7%. But by 1996, under the Abacha's regime, poverty rose significantly to 65.6%. This could be due to a combination of economic and political factors such as the high level of inflation which stood at 72.8% in 1995. The fall–out of June 12, 1993 election crisis, the international isolation of Nigeria by the international community and the stagnation of the economy as well as the massive corruption witnessed during this era combined to increase the level of national poverty in Nigeria.

In respect of the population in poverty, the period of 1996 witnessed a phe-nomenal rise in the level to 67.1% from 34.7% in 1985. Similarly and in accor-dance with the arguments by scholars, that there appears to be severe poverty in the rural areas, the table above shows the high degree of poverty from 1980 to 1996, which stood at 69.8% in 1996.

Consequently, poverty has continued to rise with grave consequences for national development, political stability and economic growth. It is also evident that the highest level of poverty in the recent past was witnessed under the mili-tary in 1996.

The Rise in Poverty Under Military Rule

It is clear from the foregoing that several factors have combined to heighten the degree of poverty in Nigeria under military rule. It is equally important to contend that poverty is not synonymous with military rule, however, the pro-longed stay of the military in power coupled with poor management of the country's resources could lead to sharp decline in the living standard of people, thereby engendering deprivation of numerous varieties. In assessing the impact of prolonged military rule vis-à-vis the increase in the level of poverty, the chapter examines some of the factors that have increased poverty and how they impacted on the poor people in the country.

1.   The Cancer of Corruption

Corruption which is considered to be the abuse or misuse of public trust for personal or pecuniary benefit seems to have become the norm rather than the exception (Gboyega, 1996:3), especially under military rule. Generals Babangida and the Abacha military Junta could be considered as the worst and brazenly corrupt military regimes. General Babangida tolerated and promoted corruption, by allowing people to compromise themselves, so that they might be loyal or amenable to his political manoeuvres (Gboyega, 1996: 5).

Some of the highlights of Babangida regime's corrupt practices and mismanagement of the nation's resources under his eight years reign include the following:

- $2 billion Gulf crisis oil windfall in 1991
- 30 per cent of oil revenue annually may have been diverted to frivolous uses throughout the time (World Bank)
- Huge extra – Budgetary Spending in the following years.

Year	Amount Involved in Naira
1989	15.3 Billion
1990	23.4Billion
1991	35Billion
1992	44.2Billion
1993	59Billion
Total	166.9Billion

- $200 million siphoned from the Aluminum smelter project
- ₦400 million wasted on the Better life for Women project headed by Maryam Babangida
- Colossal Corruption at the NNPC (example, the questionable corruption contracts of $101 million for the purchases of the strategic storage facilities
- $4.5 million paid to lobbyists to influence American's position on June 12 in the regime's favour;
- $1 million paid to a Gregory Copley to write a 15-page paper on the need for Babangida to continue in power;
- ₦1.2 billion spent weekly between June 12 and August 26 to settle the political class and others in Abuja
- N615 million spent on the illegal Association for Better Nigeria (ABN), which fraudulently canvassed support for Babangida's continuation in office.
  (*Source:* Maduagwu, 1996: 13-14).

These are only part of the tip-in the iceberg, in the celebrated looting and massive corruption that characterized the Babangida regime. There are many more cases of corruption and mismanagement that have not been documented and made public under the Babangida military regime. Most of the funds looted by Babangida and his cronies would have been judiciously used to provide basic infrastructure and improve rural-urban migration in the economy. Under the Abacha military regime, massive corruption was also perpetrated at both the federal and state levels. According to Ibrahim:

> Shortly after Abacha's death state officials were reported to have identified $1.8 billion placed by the late dictator in Brazil, Lebanon, Britain and Switzerland (2001: 78).

Similarly, on the 9th November, 1998, Mohammed Haruna, Press Secretary to the then Head of State announced that $75.2 million, 75.3 million and ₦252 million of state funds had been recovered from the family of Sani Abacha. This amount in naira terms translated as ₦64.6 billion, one quarter of the 1998 budget of the federal government. In addition, ₦8.6 billion was recovered from his Security Adviser, Ismaila Gwarzo (Ibrahim, 2001:78-79).

The Abacha presidency clearly transformed Nigeria into a criminal state, to the extent that, that General Sani Abacha had to only issue orders and directives for his security operatives to move into the Central Bank of Nigeria to make cash withdrawals. The then Governor of the Central Bank, had to allude to the fact that Abacha's signature was law, that no one dare to disobey or disregard it (Ibrahim, 2001:79).This massive level of corruption generally retarded and drained huge resources that would have been invested into productive ventures, which could have provided employment, basic needs of life such as health and education and enhanced the living standard of the people, thereby reducing the level of poverty in the country.

Although, some scholars are of the view that poverty could lead people to corruption. At the same time, the theft of state funds could lead to massive poverty, because what could have been judiciously applied to cater for millions of people in the land is now looted and converted into the personal use of a single individual or group.

For instance, the report of International Press Centre, revealed that:

> The Unaccounted $3 billion revenue by the Nigerian National Petroleum Corporation (NNPC) in 1995 could pay for the then proposed $2 billion 667km Lagos-Abuja speed train project that was expected to cover the distance in two hours. It could also buy five million bullet proof vests for the nation's security forces. The unpaid $1.79 billion by shell could finance the construction of seven thermal power stations with a total installed capacity of 1,720 mega watts at the cost of $1.80 billion (Cost of Corruption, 2007:6).

These huge revenue which was lost through corrupt and fraudulent practices could have drastically reduced the current power-generation and distribution problem confronting the nation and also reduce the incessant accidents on our nation's highways through the construction of the train project. In the long run, this would have provided employment to teeming able-bodied Nigerians and also minimize economic deprivation.

2. Frequent Policy Shifts Under the Military Rule

Policies are meant to be planned and/or designed and executed. However, such policies need to be plan on a continuous and uninterrupted basis, so as to achieve the desired effects and also benefit the target group. But when policies are constantly changed, especially with the change in government, then such policies are not likely to have the required impact for development. This has been the case, with successive military regimes in Nigeria, where numerous policies were reviewed or completely changed with every military that came on board, without achieving the desired result. For instance, it has been argued that successive governments in Nigeria since independence have established about 37 Poverty Alleviation Programmes (PAP) without having the necessary impact on the eradication of poverty in the country.

Similarly, frequent shifts in policies, in some cases, as a result of the change in governmental machinery of governance, as well as the duplication of the policies, has often led to missed opportunities and misguided priorities. In the eight years of Babangida regime, various agencies such as Directorate of Food, Roads and Rural Infrastructure (DFRRI), Mass Mobilisation for Social and Economic Reconstruction (MAMSER), National Directorate of Employment (NDE), Federal Road Safety Commission (FRSC), National Agricultural and Land Development Authority(NALDA), People's Bank, Better Life for Rural Women, etc were established, though the motives and conceptions were welcomed however, they ended up being drain pipe by the managers of these programmes. For instance, from 1986 to 1992, the Directorate of Food, Roads and Rural Infrastructures received budgetary allocations of ₦2, 435,940,924.00, while the actual amount released to the directorate was ₦1, 925,848,083.68 (Olagunju et al, 1993: Addendum).

In spite of these huge allocations, there has been insignificant improvement in the conditions of the rural people, and the extent of poverty has remained very high. Again, in some way, the funds ended up in the private bank accounts of the top military brass and their cronies. These frequent changes in government policies and the duplication of the policies have generally stunted development in the country; heightened economic and political deprivation; frustrated and discouraged foreign investment in the economy, and facilitated corruption and fraud in the country.

3. Political Transition Programmes

Nigeria has witnessed several political transition programmes initiated and implemented by the military. The longest being Babangida and Abacha transition projects, these were manipulated to serve the selfish interest of the military leaders. In the blind desire to perpetuate himself in office, Babangida severally shifted the goal-posts of the transition, and in the process the political engineering programme suffered heavily. Twice, the hand-over date was shifted and when finally elections were conducted on the 12th June, 1993, the results were annulled on very flimsy, unacceptable and unconvincing arguments. Politicians were banned and unbanned and the political parties established and ran by government, as if they were government enterprises. Party headquarters and secretariats at states and local governments' levels were equally built and provided to the parties, all in the name of enthroning a completely new political and social order. The outcome of both the Babangida and Abacha political contraption led to imminent chaos, arising from the annulment of the June 12th, 1993 elections and the subsequent isolation of Nigeria in the international community.

The military transition programmes, particularly the Babangida transition became the most expensive and costly transition ever implemented in any African country. Although, Olagunju et al (1993) tried to justify the cost of the Babangida transition programme, however, it is clear that there was colossal waste of resources in the transition process and apparent embezzlement of the huge resources invested into the programme. The table below gives a total breakdown of the summary of allocation, to some of the transition agencies established by General Babangida from 1985 to 1993.

Table 3: Summary of Allocation to Transition Agencies

Agencies	Period of time	Amount Allocated in ₦
NEC	1987-1991	2,569,918,031.20
CDS	1990-1991	29,593,095.00
MAMSER	1987-1999	390,421,654.00
NPC	1989-1999	977,580,066.00

Source: Compiled by the Author, from Olagunju et al; 1993: (Addendum A, B, C, and E)

It is important to note that, these huge budgetary allocations also included the recurrent and capital grants to these agencies, but there were special grants and extra-budgetary allocations approved by the government to serve certain special and immediate transition needs. As Part of the allocations to NEC, grants were extended to political parties, and this included funds voted for elections, voters' registration and NEC LGA buildings. Ironically, all the huge allocations could not impact positively on electoral and political changes desired by the

Junta, as the money ended up being a waste and a drain on the nation's economy. Similarly, massive allocations were expended on the Abacha and Abdulsalami transition programmes. These would have been judiciously applied to alleviate poverty and reduce crime and unemployment in the country. In spite of this, a large segment of Nigeria citizens' remains excluded from the political process. Consequently, politics became a pastime for the rich and the wealthy, and as such politics became monetized and commoditized by the military and participatory politics was further eroded.

In effect, the impact of prolonged military involvement in governance, and on poverty in Nigeria has led to further pauperization and marginalization of the average Nigerian. It has also led to serious agitations and restiveness among and between ethnic groups and nationalities, to the extent that ethnic conflicts and outburst took the centre-stage in the immediate post-military rule.

The scandalous mismanagement of the nation's oil resources, by the military further aggravated poverty in the Niger Delta, due largely to environmental pollution and the apparent underdevelopment of the region. The years of neglect by the military of the agricultural and educational sectors has led to food shortages and lack of access to educational opportunities by the poor, and the complete collapse of the educational sector.

The grave impact of poverty has also led to many unethical and immoral practices such as prostitution, to the extent that even our universities have become celebrated centers of campus prostitution. Prostitution has grown into a lucrative business where networks and syndicates with powerful connections exist, which promotes and facilitates the business in schools, hotels etc. The prolonged years of the military in power has succeeded in aggravating poverty and have equally accentuated the culture of begging in virtually all Nigerian cities, with the attendant negative effects on the country's image. The high cost of living occasioned by the prevalence of poverty has further impoverished Nigerians, to the extent that many people has resorted to taking frog meat for meals, as well as the consumption of fried Grasshoppers, as alternatives to other nutritional foods.

In the final analysis, military prolonged involvement in governance has had a negative consequence on income distribution and this has affected the prevalence of poverty, due partly to the poor management of the economy and general poor governance. In this context, therefore, having identified and discussed the impact, it is imperative that we now propose recommendations on the way forward, which is the subject of the next section.

Conclusion

In recommending the way out of the military and poverty quagmire, we would adopt a two-pronged approach, in the sense that the recommendations would give emphasis on solving the military question and poverty phenomenon in Nigeria. In the first place, there is the need to put in place a well-designed and integrated approach of social mobilization and political education of the military. The political education programme should rest on the following two pillars:

> One is to make the members of the Armed forces realise that they do not have any more moral or superior claims to be the saviour of society. The other is to realise that intervention in politics tends to threaten both their professional competence and their institutional cohesion or unity (Onyeoziri, 1988, cited in Oyediran, 1988: Xii).

This is important, because the fifteen years of military rule covered in this chapter, have proved that the military managed the economy badly as well as the polity in general.

Secondly, the military should be constantly involved in the management of disasters such as natural calamities like earthquake, floods, etc as well as in the construction of bridges, highways etc, as this will generally keep them busy throughout the year and thus remove their thoughts from the business of coup-making,

Thirdly and more fundamentally, the military need to respond to the current realities of a knowledge-driven world, by providing opportunities and access to education for their members. As the members of the military expand their horizon through knowledge, it will certainly liberate their minds and make them understand the current realities on the ground where military rule has become outlived and ex communicated, and therefore learns to remain committed to their professional calling. The civilians in the current democratic dispensation should work towards enthroning good governance, respect for the rule of law and democracy dividends, as this will prevent the urge and agitations for military take over.

It is clear from the evidence in this chapter that between the period 1985 and 1992, poverty has magnified and the poor became poorer, as such government need to revitalize the national economy, so as to provide opportunities and access for empowerment and self-employment. Similarly, poverty alleviation programmes should essentially be pro-poor and targeted towards attacking poverty in all its ramifications. One of the panacea for reducing poverty is through education. Consequently, the government needs to give education the priority it deserves, by improving budgetary allocation to the sector; rehabilitating educational infrastructures and enhancing access to the educational opportunities. Through, education people would be empowered to develop and explore their potentials and skills for self-employment and productive activities. In addition, education should be reviewed to incorporate skills acquisition, as this will make people self-reliant and economically empowered.

Agriculture needs to be given the proper attention that it deserves, because it is the heart-beat of industrialization and national development. In effect, the largest segment of the poor live in rural areas, where agriculture is the main preoccupation, as such governments, civil society groups, communal groups and even individuals need to individually and collectively encourage capacity-building through agricultural productivity. This will greatly provide employment and ultimately minimize economic deprivation.

The development of an effective infrastructural system is a corner-stone in the drive towards alleviating poverty anywhere in the world. Thus, Nigeria needs to first develop an effective and functioning electricity generating and distribution system, which would accelerate economic development and industrialization, and thereby reduce poverty in the country. The provision of similar infrastructures such as roads, telecommunication, water, sanitation and health would equally and fundamentally assist in the reduction of poverty and the ultimate development of the nation's abundant resources.

In fact, the provision of water is central to the eradication of numerous deadly diseases that afflict the poor. Thus, water gives life to everything, and without water human beings could not exist and contribute meaningfully to their society. There is also the apparent need to strengthened poverty alleviation institutions such as the National Poverty Eradication Programme (NAPEP), and the National Directorate of Employment (NDE) etc, in order to achieve the target goals. In strengthening these institutions, obstacles to their effective functioning should be removed such as the provision of sufficient funding and proper coordination of efforts at both the federal, state and local levels. There is also the need to remove duplication of functions, as this will greatly reduce waste and cost in the execution of their functions.

Poverty alleviation programmes should be designed to reflect the aspirations of the poor, and in doing so the programme should emphasize the following key elements of acceptability and sustainability. The people should be originally and heavily involved in the conception and design of the programmes, so that it is acceptable to them, and reflect their immediate needs and aspirations. The greatest poverty that afflicts Nigeria and Nigerians is the poverty of the mind, as such concerted efforts must be built in the psyche of Nigerians so as to cleanse our minds of this dangerous and deadly poverty.

References

Achike, O. (1978), *Ground work of Military Law and Military Rule in Nigeria*, Enugu; Fourth Dimension Publishers.

Ajakaiye, O. (2002), "An Overview of the Current Poverty Eradication Programme in Nigeria", in A.M. Jega and H. Wakili (Eds.). *The Poverty Eradication Programme in Nigeria: Problems and Prospects*, Kano Benchmark publishers Limited.

Awake, (2007), Vol.88, No.5 A Monthly Journal of Watchtower Bible and tract society of New York.

Egwuatu, B. (2002), "Strategies towards strengthening the poverty eradication programme in Nigeria", in A.M. Jega and H. Wakili (eds.) *The Poverty Eradication Programme in Nigeria: Problems and Prospects,* Kano: Benchmark publishers limited.

Falola, T. et al. (1994), *The Military factor in Nigeria; 1966-1985,* New York and Canada; Edwin Mellen press.

FOS (Undated), *Poverty and Welfare in Nigeria,* National Planning Commission, Abuja

Gboyega, A. (1996), "Corruption and Democratization in Nigeria, 1983 – 1993: An overview", in Alex Gboyega (ed) *Corruption and Democratization in Nigeria,* Ibadan: Agbo Area Publishers.

Ibrahim, J. (2001), "Manifestations and impact of corruption on Nigerian Society and Sustainable Democracy", in Lame, I. And Odekunle, F. (ed.) *fighting corruption and organized crime in Nigeria: challenges for the New Millennium,* Ibadan Spectrum books limited.

Igbuzor, O. (2005), *Perspectives on Democracy and Development*, Lagos: Joe-Tolalu and Associates.

IPC (2007), "Cost of Corruption", Vol.1 No.3, A Monthly Publication of International Press Centre.

Jega, A.M. (2002), "The impact of Military Rule on Governance in Nigeria" in A.M. Jega et al (Eds) *Democracy and Democratisation in Nigeria,* Kano: Benchmark publishers limited.

Lawan, M.M. (2007), "Expanding the Frontiers of Poverty Alleviation in Nigeria: The Role of the Nigerian Accountants", being the text of a lecture delivered at the investiture of the Executives of Kano/Jigawa district of ICAN, on the 30th June.

Maduagwu, M.O. (1996), "Nigeria in Search of Political Culture: The Political Class, Corruption and Democratization", in Alex Gboyega (Ed) *Corruption and Democratization in Nigeria,* Ibadan: Agbo Areo Publishers

NBS (2005), The Nigerian Statistical fact sheets on Economic and Social Development, Abuja: Golden Islanders Nigeria limited.

Oyeleye, O. (1988), *Nigerian Government and Politics under Military Rule;* Lagos: The Macmillan Press Limited

Oyeleye, O. (1996), "Billy Dudley on the Military and Political Development in Nigeria", in O. Oyeleye (ed.) *Governance and Development in Nigeria: Essays in honour of Professor Billy J. Dudley,* Ibadan: Agbo Areo Publishers

Odetola, O. (1982), *Military regimes and development: A Comparative Analysis in African Societies,* London: George Allen and Unwin

Olagunju, T. et al. (1993), *Transition to Democracy in Nigeria,* Ibadan: Spectrum Books limited.

Oyemomi, E.O (2003), "Poverty Reduction, NAPEP and the NGOs", in the Nigerian Accountant, the official journal of the Institute of Chartered Accountants of Nigeria, Vol.36, No.2, April/June, 2003.

Ukwu, I.U. (2002), "Towards Effective Poverty Eradication strategies", in the NCEMA POLICY Analysis series, vol.8 No.1.

Newswatch, October 4, 1993.

CHAPTER TWELVE

ENVIRONMENT-POVERTY NEXUS: OIL EXPLORATION AND
EXPLOITATION IN THE NIGER DELTA REGION OF NIGERIA

Adamu I. Tanko

Introduction

The 'environment' rather than what many people understand it to be, *only* as
the physical state of their surrounding, needs to be understood as the *home* for a
range of biotic and abiotic processes operating in and between ecosystems. In
other words, it provides human beings, as well as other species, with
economically directly relevant resources and with sinks to absorb the wastes
humans dispose of as a result of their use of natural resources (Opschoor, 2007).
Beside the direct resources, environment stores other indirect assets in the forms
of systems and processes that enable the resources to work over time (e.g. to
regenerate resource stocks, or to absorb and recycle wastes etc). In the words of
the ecologists, environment is the base of a series of life-support systems, which
in a way represent ecological processes that shape climate, clean air and water,
regulate water flow, recycle essential elements, create and regenerate soils, and
keep the planet fit for life. In other words, the life support systems provide the
basis for sustaining the productivity, adaptability and capacity for renewal of
lands, water and/or the biosphere as a whole. More specifically, environment
offers a range of services to society. These services according to Opschoor (2004)
serve two functions: infrastructural functions and provider functions.

Infrastructural functions concern the capacity of the environment to develop
and maintain these functions, which it carries out in two distinctive (regulation
and carrier) ways (Dasgupta, 1992). The former is a way by which environment
regulates balances between ecological processes such as a regulation of the
climate system, while the carrier is a way through which environment provides
space and suitable medium for human activities. The provider functions of the
environment on the other hand deals with both production function and
information function (Chambers and Conway, 1992), and they relate to the
provision of goods, services (and information) directly relevant in societal
functions. In real day to day activities, the fulfilment of the infrastructural
functions enables a system to operate its provider functions.

The environmental utilisation space, according to Opschoor (2007) is to a
significant degree constrained at any point in time, in terms of the resource flow
it can provide sustainably due to the capacities of the underlying infrastructural
(regulatory and carrier) functions. Maintaining and enhancing provider

functions for the benefit of present and future human beings has been the key concern in national and international environmental policy as it is the basis to which poverty relates to the use and misuse of the environmental resources.

Although the World Bank shorthand chooses to define poverty as "pronounced deprivation in well-being" (World Resource Institute, 2005: 15), in an elaborate sense it could mean a social condition of chronic insecurity resulting from a malfunctioning of economic, ecological, cultural and social systems, causing groups of people to lose the capacity to adapt and survive and to live beyond minimum levels of satisfaction of their needs and aspirations. Of course, looking at poverty within the frame of conventional analyses mainly in terms of income and consumption, it is obvious that the dimension of poverty is given a very narrow spectrum. This Chapter chooses to open the dimension, to include the complex spatio-temporal realities that exist between and among regions, countries, communities etc, which might be in the forms of illiteracy, ill-health, environmental degradation, gender bias etc.

Environment and Poverty: The Framework

It is easy to trace the evolution of environment-development system through the application of range of theories. Prominent among these theories in early times were the Malthus and Ricardo's in the 19th century, both of which focussed on economy-land interactions and, in the case of Malthus, with specific interest in links between development and the poor through population dynamics. These theories, while they opened great debates in the early times gave ways with the new notions of development led by scientific discoveries, and technological innovations, and especially in the era of imperialism and colonialism (Opschoor, 2007). It was not until the 1960s emergence of the concerns over limits to growth that newer theories focussing on poverty began to come. Among these was the Wilkinson (1973) on how poverty in the form of resource scarcity drives societies into a search for adaptive and mitigative response options including technological change, migration, trade and warfare, or those of Boserup (1981 and 1995) on the impact of population growth on the prevailing patterns of agricultural utilisation by intensification.

The present 'grand theories' about population, land and development may be divided into optimistic ones (i.e. rejecting), pessimistic or neo-Malthusians as led by Ehrlich, or mixed (e.g. Club-of-Rome's concerns over limits and how only profound societal change would be able to overcome them, and Wilkinson who showed how, historically, many attempts at adaptations to natural resource scarcities failed whereas others succeeded).

It is against this background that this Chapter describes and analyses environmental exploration for oil resources in Nigeria and subsequent exploitations as well as the consequent devastation on the socioeconomic and cultural lives of the Niger-Delta people. Thus, the chapter looks deeply into the issues of insecurity of the peoples' traditional resource utilisation base and how, despite the immense wealth accruable to the Nigerian nation, the people are living in conditions of abject poverty and underdevelopment.

Environment and Economy in Nigeria

Nigeria is a country in West Africa with a total land area of 923,768 sq. km. (356,700 sq. mi.). The country's population figure of over 140 million has been recently released; this reaffirms the position of Nigeria as the most populous country in Africa. The current life expectancy in the country is 56 years. Variety of customs, languages, and traditions among Nigeria's 250 ethnic groups gives the country a rich diversity. The dominant ethnic group in the northern two-thirds of the country is the Hausa-Fulani. Other major ethnic groups of the north are the Nupe, Tiv, and Kanuri. The Yoruba people are predominant in the southwest. The Igbo are the largest ethnic group in the southeast, with the Efik, Ibibio, and Ijaw (the country's fourth-largest ethnic group) comprising a substantial segment of the population in that area. Persons of different language backgrounds most commonly communicate in English, although knowledge of two or more Nigerian languages is widespread. Hausa, Yoruba, and Igbo are the most widely used Nigerian languages.

Its ecological landscape ranges from southern coastal swamps to tropical forests, open woodlands, grasslands, and semi-desert in the far north. The highest regions are the Jos Plateau 1,200-2,000 meters above sea level and the mountains along the border with Cameroon. The country's climate shows annual rainfall ranges from 381 cm. along the coast to 64 cm. or less in the far north.

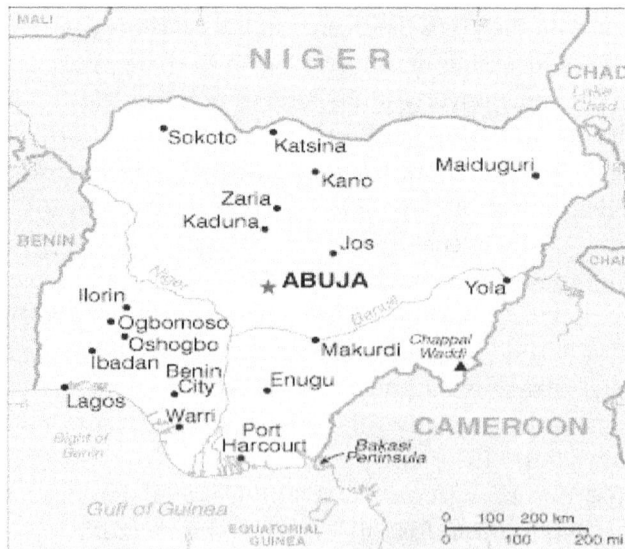

Fig. 1: Nigeria

Nigeria's economy has been dominated by the oil from the 1970s. The so called "oil-boom" led Nigeria to neglect its strong agricultural and light manufacturing bases in favour of crude oil. In 2002, oil and gas exports accounted for more than 98% of export earnings and about 83% of federal government revenue. Nigeria has crude oil reserves of some 25-30 billion barrels. Proven oil reserves are again expected to increase significantly as a result of the prolific potentials of Nigeria's deep and ultra-deep offshore environments where about 3.5 billion barrels of oil reserves have been discovered within the last few years.

In addition to the above, gas reserves of some 170 trillion standard cubic feet are available (Woodhill, 2007). These were established in the course of exploring and developing the nation's crude oil reserves. Significant gas reserves are expected to be proven when efforts are directed in the near future to searching specifically for gas deposits.

Current crude oil production stands at nearly 2 million barrels oil per day (bopd) with associated gas production of about 2 billion standard cubic feet per day (scf/d). Current LNG exports which commenced only in the last quarter of 1999 stands at 8.5 million tons per annum (Woodhill, 2007).

Oil Explorations and Exploitation in Nigeria: A Historical Review

Oil exploration activities in Nigeria began together with the exploration of other mineral resources in 1900 following Land Nationalization Act which vested all lands and mineral rights in the British Crown, the colonial administration mandated different survey committees to begin exploration activities. Exploitation of natural resources in British colonies was an integral part of British colonial policy which they justified as a way of not only making the colonies self sufficient but also economically profitable. According to Steyn (2003), an essential part of this economic approach to the British colonial territories was the mineral and geological surveying works carried out by various colonial administrations with the aim of discovering commercially viable mineral deposits.

While the surveys began with the discoveries of other (solid) minerals as the tin, columbite and coal, a particular emphasis on oil exploration began in January 1906 when the colonial government issued a number of prospecting licenses to the British Colonial Petroleum Corporation covering an area of 100 sq miles (256 Km^2) on the Rofutoro and Lafagbo Rivers in the Benin district (Steyn, 2003). This work continued up to 1914 without much success; discovering only traces of oil (together with bitumen) especially in areas near Lekki Lagoon, Abagana (21 km East of Onisha) and in the Awka district (in the present day Anambra state). Despite the very limited success, in 1914 a legislation; Mineral Oil Ordnance No. 17 on oil exploration was passed, with the implication of limiting oil exploration and exploitation in Nigeria only to British and British colonial companies. Thus, by the end of the First World War, two companies – Darcy Exploration and

Whitehall Petroleum began another phase of exploration between 1919 and 1922. This also proved unsuccessful, hence a suspension of all serious exploration operations in the country. Further operations which began after a joint application of Shell International and British Petroleum from 1937 to1951 – which gave a concession of exploration in the whole country, did not yield much. Thus, the concession area was later reduced to the southeast of the country and centered only to the Niger Delta area. Following this reduction, and especially with the Suez Canal crisis, more companies (Standard Oil and Gulf Oil from America) also showed interest. It was not until 1956 that first discovery of commercially viable oil reserves was made at Oloibiri (72 km East of Port Harcourt). Within two years about 12 locations around Oloibiri (especially at Afam and Bomu) were discovered to have oil at commercial quantities. Oil production started by 1958, first at Oloibiri and, then at Afam, each with 3,000bp/d. First shipment of Nigeria's crude oil (of 8,500 tons) arrived Rotterdam on March 8, 1958. At Independence in 1960, Nigeria had a small oil industry in which Shell-BP produced about 20,000 bopd. Following the advantages of proximity to industrial markets, quality of the oil (with low sulfur content) and the political instability in the Middle East, Nigeria oil sector grew very fast, that by 1966, production rose to 420,000 bopd.

The increases continued steadily that between 1987 and 1992, seventy-two new discoveries of oil fields were made in the Niger Delta. Recoverable oil reserves increased too from 16 billion barrels in 1989 to 20 billion barrels in 1992. By 2005, Nigerian crude oil production of 2.4 million bopd, put it as the largest oil producer in Africa and the tenth largest producer in the world (see Table 1). Plans are being made for the production to rise up to 4.0 million bopd by 2010.

Table 1: World Oil Reserves, Production and Export (2001)

Country	Total Oil Reserves (million barrels per day)	Total Oil Production (million barrels per day)	Net Oil Export (million barrels per day)
United States	22.0	9.02	0.9
Saudi Arabia	261.7	8.73	7.38
Russia	48.6	7.29	4.76
Iran	89.7	3.82	2.74
Mexico	28.3	3.59	1.65
Norway	9.4	3.41	3.22
China	24.0	3.30	0.10
Venezuela	76.9	3.07	2.60
Canada	6.6	2.80	1.80
United Kingdom	4.9	2.59	1.70
Iraq	112.5	2.45	2.00
United Arab Emirate	97.8	2.42	2.09
Nigeria	22.5	2.26	2.00
Kuwait	96.5	2.15	1.80

Source: Ross, M.L. (2003)

In Nigeria oil is sourced both at on-shore and off-shore locations. The major on-shore producing states are Abia, Akwa-Ibom, Delta, Edo, Ondo, Rivers, Bayelsa, Cross Rivers and Imo. These make up the Niger-Delta states of Nigeria, which has a reputation as one of the world's largest wetlands – of about 36,000 km² (14,000 sq. meters). It is an area of marshland, creeks, tributaries and lagoons that drain the Niger River into the Atlantic at the Bight of Biafra/Benin. A third of this area (about 12,000 km²) is fragile mangrove forest probably the largest mangrove forest in the world. The biodiversity of the Niger Delta is very high, as it contains diverse plant and animal species including many exotic and unique flowers and birds. Implied in this ecology is that it is an easily disequilibrated environment, with serious scarcity of arable land and freshwater. Additionally, transportation through the environment is very difficult; it is via rivers and creeks through dense forest. There is high incidence of malaria and other water borne diseases, and was notorious to early European visitors (including missionaries and colonialists) as the "Whiteman's grave yard" because of the high mortality rate they experienced. In short, the Niger Delta is a very sensitive ecosystem.

Chinese firms are also becoming increasingly involved in Nigerian oil sector. In December 2004, Sinopec and NNPC signed an agreement to develop the Niger-Delta's OML 64 and 66. Although not much success has been recorded in this area, in July 2005, China and Nigeria reached a trade agreement in which Nigeria will supply China with 30,000 bbl/d of crude oil over a five year period (Woodhill, 2006).

In recent times, Nigerian government has been working to promote local investment in the oil industry. Nigeria's Marginal Field Development Programme (MFDP) provides tax breaks and government incentives to encourage local involvement in the oil sector. In November 2004, 16 local companies acquired oil fields from the SPDC under the MFDP. The fields are estimated to hold 150-200 million barrels of oil. First oil from the fields has yet to come online. Nigeria also from 2006 had begun plans to increase local ownership in deep off-shore projects, calling for local ownership to be increased to 45 percent during 2006 and to 70 percent by 2010 (Woodhill, 2007).

Off-shore operations are mainly located in the Nigeria's deep waters. Following the high levels of insecurities at on-shore locations, most oil operations now come to concentrate in the deep water locations. By March 2005, of the 77 deepwater and inland blocks licensing approvals, 44 of them were for deepwater operations. For example, Chevron has, from October 2004 began an investment of US$2.5 billion to develop Agbami field which contains one billion barrels of recoverable hydrocarbons and located 70 miles from Nigeria's coast. In February 2005, the Nigeria National Petroleum Corporation (NNPC) awarded Chevron a US$1.1 billion contract for the construction of a Floating, Production, Storage and Offloading (FPSO) facility for the field. This work was being undertaken by

Daewoo Shipping and Maritime Engineering (South Korea).The FPSO is expected to export up to 250,000 bbl/d of oil and 450 million cubic feet per day (Mmcd/f) of natural gas.

Similarly, In October 2004, Total oil company announced the discovery of a major oil deposit in deepwater block OPL 222, followed by a January 2005 discovery of the deepwater Usan Field. The fifth successful appraisal well drilled in the Field is scheduled to begin in 2010; with initial output of 150,000 bbl/d. Block 222 is operated by Total (20 percent) in partnership with Chevron (30 percent), Exxon-Mobil (30 percent) and Nexem Petroleum (20 percent).

Oil Operations and Environmental Impact: A General Picture

Oil operations as a long life cycle begin with oil explorations, drilling and extraction. This is known as the "upstream phase". There are currently over 50,000 oil fields in the world and many exploration activities are continuing, with many licenses being applied for and awarded daily. These processes of exploration (locating oil deposits) in remote and inhospitable locations, bringing the oil to the surface (drilling) and then getting it to the market have major environmental, cultural and health impacts.

On- and off-shore operations are inherently invasive and affect ecosystems, human health and local cultures. Oil companies combine the use of remote sensing and satellite mapping technique with seismic testing to identify potential oil reserves. When reserves are identified remotely companies build roads, platforms and pipelines. Other related activities increase and test wells are drilled. Once oil is discovered, exploration activities are expanded for commercial scale extraction which requires more wells and infrastructure. Techniques for oil extraction include a range of drilling techniques and the use of sub-surface explosives (including in a few historical cases, the use of nuclear charges).

The physical alteration of environments from exploration, drilling and extraction can be greater than from a large oil spill. Major impacts include deforestation, ecosystem destruction, chemical contamination of land, water and air, long-term harm to animal population (particularly migratory birds and marine mammals), human health and safety risks for neighboring communities and oil industry workers and displacement of indigenous communities.

Exploration requires moving heavy equipment (mobile rigs for temporary drilling can weight over 2 million pounds) into remote environments. Clearing land for roads and platforms can lead to deforestation and erosion. Drilling during both exploration and extraction phases uses significant quantities of water, which are contaminated through drilling and then discharged along with cuttings into the environment. These discharges result in chemical contamination of land and water from petroleum waste, drilling fluids and by-products of drilling such as water, drill-cutting and mud. Epstein and Selber (2002) assert that "the general environmental effects of encroachment into natural habitats and the chronic effects of drilling and generating mud and discharge water on benthic (bottom-welling) population, migratory birds' population and marine mammals constitute serious environmental concerns for these ecosystems. Most of production waste from the industry is the hazardous and toxic effluent known as produced water.

Produced water is extracted from the ground along with oil and is often injected into wells under high pressure to force more oil to the surface. Produced water not injected is discharged into surface waters. As Doyle (1994) explains, this

"produced water is at least four times saltier than ocean water and often contains 'industrial strength' quantities of toxins such as benzene, xylene, toluene and ethylbenzene. Heavy metals such as barium, arsenic, cadmium, chromium and mercury have also been found in produced water. Produced water can also be radioactive – in some cases, as much as 100 times more radioactive than the discharge of nuclear power plant".

Water used in oil production can also be contaminated by chemicals used during extraction. For example, the oil industry uses millions of tons of barium (a toxic heavy metal) in drilling fluids each year. Common components of drilling fluids can solubilize the barium, creating hazardous waste, which is also often discharged into environment from leaks of re-injected materials.

Exploration and extraction also produce voluminous amounts of solid waste known as drilling wastes and associated waste. Although associated waste constitute a relatively small production of total wastes, they are most likely to contain a range of chemicals and naturally occurring materials that are of concern to health and safety. In oil fields, virtually every stage in production has a waste pit. As Doyle notes, during drilling

"various muds, oily fluids, lubricants and other chemicals are used to cool the drill bit, stabilize the walls of the boreholes, or liquefy earthen cuttings. These fluids and additives accumulate in large quantities during the drilling process, and are often stored or finally disposed in waste pits" (Doyle, 1994).

Exposed water pits pose a danger not only to aquifers but also to animals and birds that mistake the pits for water holes and become coated with toxic waste.

In addition to operational leaks, oil spills also occur during extraction. In 2002, the Natural Academy of Sciences (NAS) estimated that 38,000 tons of petroleum hydrocarbons were released into the world's oceans each year during the 1990s as a result of oil and gas operations (Natural Resource Council, 2002). On- and off-shore oil production can also create significant air pollution. Emissions from drilling equipment, hydrocarbons escaping from wells, flaring of natural gas and emissions from support vehicle can degrade local air quality (Caswell, 1993).

Oil exploration, drilling and extraction can also lead to a range of acute and chronic health impact. These risks occur through exposure to naturally occurring radioactive materials brought to the surface during drilling as well as through the bioaccumulation of oil, mercury and other products in mammals and fish that human consume (Epstein and Selber, 2002). Noise vibration and exposure to toxic chemicals are also issues in upstream and downstream operations. Many of the substances used in daily extraction works cause adverse dermatologic and pulmonary reactions among workers. The most common dermatologic conditions are contact dermatitis and acne, but other conditions include keratotic facial and neck lesions, neoplastic change from exposure to oil and sunlight, and acquired perforating disease and calcinosis of the hands and fingers. Adverse pulmonary reactions to hard metal (a mixture of tungsten carbide and cobalt used for oil well drilling bits) include asthma, hypersensitivity pneumonitis and interstitial pulmonary fibrosis (Epstein and Selber, 2002).

The risk of explosions, injuries and fatalities during exploration and extraction are also cases for concern. Virtually every segment of oil and gas production involves risks of fires and explosion, particularly off-shore drilling operations that are vulnerable to blowouts. The handling of heavy pipes and other equipment also creates safety risks. Thus oil workers around the world face significant occupational hazards. Oil production activities not only disrupt sensitive environments, but threaten the survival of indigenous population that lives in those ecosystems.

Environmental Impact of the Oil Industry in Niger-Delta

Socially the Nigerian oil producing area comprises diversity of ethic groups who account for nearly 20% of the Nigeria population. About 70% of the population lives in rural communities. They make a living from fishing or subsistence farming, supplementing both their diet and income with variety of forest products. Land, especially arable land, is very scarce in the densely populated Delta with land scarcity exacerbated by declining crop yields and soil pollution that render vast tracts of land unusable. The oil-producing regions of the Niger-Delta (ND) are mostly inhabited by ethnic minority groups such as Abriba, Andoni, Effiks, Isekiri, Kalabari and Ogoni, and these and other oil-producing communities have largely been excluded from the benefits of oil production in their traditional territories where poor infrastructure, poor housing and lack of water supply, electricity and sanitation prevail. Poverty levels in the ND are exacerbated by high levels of unemployment and high rates of male out-migration to the urban areas. As a result, women play key role in the ND communities. In addition to infant and child care, women are responsible for at least 50% of agricultural labour, operated most of the retail sector and process nearly all fish catches, while also providing the much needed continuity within the community and social structure.

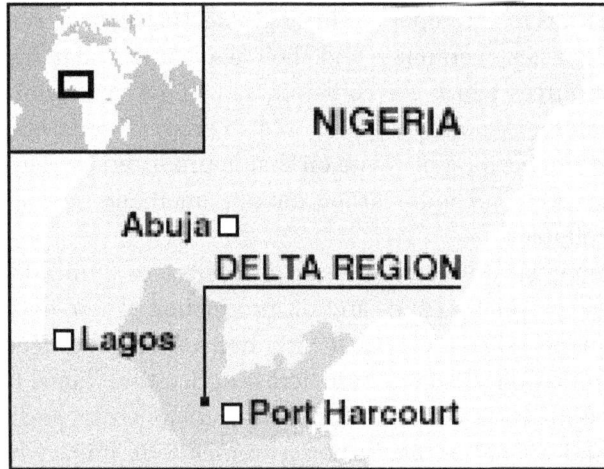

Fig 2: Nigeria's Niger-Delta Region

The environmental impact of oil industry in the ND has resulted in the clearing of vast tracts of land for surveying, laying of receiver cables, exploration base camps, heliports and seismogelite explosive shots in which explosives are detonated in holes that are generally 3 - 6 meters deep. The clearing of land result in deforestation in the immediate environment, destruction of crops where communities reside close to the exploration areas, soil erosion due to soil disturbances that alter drainage in the affected area, and negatively affects fauna across migration routes. Seismic explosions in the areas, and surveying aircrafts and helicopters further lead to high levels of noise pollution and scare both the indigenous communities and fauna in the region.

Oil exploration has also opened up vast areas by building of access roads and brides that connect previously isolated areas with the rural transportation network, thereby attracting civilians and colonists in search of land for both settlement and cultivation, this factor increased land scarcity in the area. Drilling operations immediately deny local inhabitants access to a specific piece of land as well as access to water courses in the vicinity. This situation in the ND has aggravated the existing problem of land scarcity. Drilling also generates loud noise well above safety standards and industrial wastes that include drilling muds, industrial cleaning solvents, cuttings from holes, crude oil, natural gas and formation/produced water. The content of drilling mud that serve as lubricant, coolant and pressurizes during drilling, varies from well to well, but in general is made up of clays, barite and chemical additives which can be very toxic.

Produced water on the other hand, is highly toxic and very hot and contains high levels of chlorides and heavy metals. In general each exploratory well generates about 157,920 litres of industrial waste that used to be discharged either into local waterways or into open, unlined waste pits (reserve pits). Either way, these industrial wastes eventually find their ways into water courses, soil and groundwater resources which are contaminated to the detriment of the people, fauna and flora in the region. Air pollution also occurs through the flaring of associated gas and the burning of waste oil that is produced by the testing process and which pollutes the air with carbon dioxide, methane, sulphur dioxide and other airborne pollutants.

Where commercially viable crude oil deposits are found, there are established permanent production sites and oil production. These entail land alienation when production sites are permanently demarcated and declared off-limits to local communities, oil pipelines built across agricultural lands to connect flow stations with the main oil terminals, road built to construct and maintain flow stations. The land alienation again has a tremendous impact on the densely populated ND. The oil production causes a new set of environmental problems, mainly owing to the separation of oil from formation/produced water at separation facilities and through flaring of gas, either at production sites or at the separation facilities. The separation process generates about 16,168 million litres of liquid waste everyday in some places, which is discharged untreated into unlined production pits. In the ND, in the past, the heavy hazardous sludge created during the separation process has generally been disposed of directly into water courses in the immediate environment without proper treatment of the effluent prior to discharge. Both processes result in major water and soil pollution of the immediate environment and pose major health risks to communities who make use of these resources, especially water resources in the absence of piped water (Aston-Jones, 1999).

Gas flaring during production and separation also poses a major health risk and sources of air pollution. Nigeria flared 95% of all associated gas during production up till the 1990s, when the percentage of gas flared dropped to around 75%. Despite the reduction, Nigeria is noted as a country with very high proportion of gas flaring. For example, Saudi Arabia flares only 20% of gas, Iran 19%, Mexico 5%, Britain 4.3%, Algeria 4% and Russia 1.5%. Thus, the country's high levels of gas concentration in production fields coupled with the densely populated characteristics of human settlement in the ND and the nature of the Delta environment in turn means that the immediate detrimental impact of gas flaring on oil-producing communities affects a greater number of people and the communities.

Environmental impacts of gas flaring include thermal air, water and soil pollution, destruction of vegetation and wildlife, damage to infrastructure by acid rain and damage to soil, crops and vegetation by the severe heat and the deposition of contaminants. Oil-producing communities subjected to continuous flaring are exposed to severe heat, noise and fumes which constitute serious health risks and the discomfort of 24 hours of synthetic bright, orange light. As one of the Ogoni songs reveals:

> "The flames of Shell are flames of Hell,
> We bask below the light
> Naught for us to serve the blight
> Of cursed neglect and cursed Shell"

Oil spills are major environmental problems and result from a variety of causes including oil well blowouts, oil pipeline leakages, human error, equipment failure and accidents during the loading of tankers. In Nigeria, Woodhill (2007) has reported the World Bank 1996 estimates of over 4,000 oil spills since production began in 1958. Between 1976 and 1996 for example, there were a total of 2,768 reported oil spills in which 3.8 million barrels of oil were spilled into the sensitive ND ecosystem. These include major oil spills such as the Fania oil well blowout (January 1980, 146,000 – 200,000 barrels of oil spilled), the Oyakama oil spill (1981, about 120,000 barrels of oil spilled), the Fantua oil spill (1984, about 200,000 barrels of oil spilled) and the Shell pipeline burst at Bagg-Jumbo (1995, 250,000 barrels of oil spilled).

While in other countries of the world no distinction is made about spills, in Nigeria there are three types of oil spills, namely: equipment failure, human error and sabotage oil spills. Equipment failure account for the majority of oil spills and no doubt, the result of variety of factors including overflow at loading terminal, vale failure that leads to pressure problems and rapture and/or corroded pipes. Oil spills at Shell operations, in particular, result from equipment failure mainly because the company set up its oil infrastructure in the 1960s and 1970s and has failed to maintain and replace aged equipments and pipelines properly, thereby making it more prone to rapture and corrosion. Human error oil spills result mainly from negligence and personnel failure to perform tasks properly. Sabotage oil spills are regarded as deliberate and malicious damage to oil pipelines and equipment by disgruntled people who either regard compensation paid for damage as inadequate or who want increase in compensation for damage already inflicted, or oil producing communities who want to force oil companies to provide amenities for them. Oil companies normally attribute spills in the past to sabotage since they are never compelled to pay compensation where the spill is caused by sabotage. In fact, the government is made to pay the oil companies.

Oil spills damage crops, pollute water and soil and kill marine resources within the immediate vicinity of the spill, while flooding during the rainy season can and does transport the oil to other locations thereby enlarging the geographical impact of the oil spill. Due to lack of scientific data on the spills, both government and industry downplay impacts, arguing that the ability of tropical environment through weathering and microbial processes can rapidly degrade acutely toxic substances. The reality of it is that despite the natural rehabilitation ability of the tropical climates, it still takes a long time for the natural environment to recover fully from oil spill. Soil polluted in a major oil spill, for instance, takes about 10 years to recover to such a level where peasant farmer can consider cultivation again – and this is with human assisted rehabilitation. Sam Badilo Bako (quoted by Steyn, 2003) summarizes the plight of the people of the ND in the following words:

"We in [ND] are facing a situation which can only be compared with our experiences during the civil war.... ocean of crude oil had emerged, moving swiftly like a great river in flood ... swallowing up everything ... cassava farms, yams, palms, streams, animals etc for miles.... There is no pipe borne water and yet the streams, the only source of drinking water are coated with oil. You cannot collect a bucket of rain water for the roofs, trees and grass are all covered with oil. Anything spread outside... is soaked with oil as the wind carries the oil miles away.... Nor can you enter a bush without being soaked to the skin. But men and women forced by hunger 'steal' occasionally into the 'ocean', some have to dive deep in oil to uproot already rotten yams and cassava .... We are thus faced with a situation where we have no food to eat, no water to drink, no homes to live in, and worst of it all, no air to breath".

The State and the Niger Delta Question

Several efforts to draw the attention of the country were made by the ND people. These were, seemingly not heeded by the state. In most cases, their actions were confronted with punitive military attacks. However, counter-operations by the Ogoni groups against the Federal Government and Shell (Nigeria) drew international attention to their plights. Through their efforts, Shell (Nigeria) was forced out of the Ogoni territories. This was viewed by the government as unacceptable, and in 1995 some nine Ogoni leaders (including their leader Ken Saro Wiwa) were executed. This drew international attention to the county and hence, international media campaign began. The campaign made public the devastations of oil production activities, and Shell (International) was made the culprit, as the cases in other oil producing areas around the world also came into limelight.

Nigeria, having been presented as collaborator of major oil corporations, conniving especially with Shell (Nigeria) against local communities, and also accused of human right abuser, the country was suspended from the Commonwealth in 1995. Moreover, some diplomatic representatives from the European Union, Canada and South Africa were withdrawn from Nigeria. In 1996, the United Nations (UN) and Commonwealth instituted formal inquiries into human right abuses in the country, and restrictions were placed on weapon sales to it.

By the late 1990s, the country (and many other countries of the world where oil operation is important were) forced to begin to appreciate the environment-poverty nexus, and to focus mitigation activities. Lack of effective legislation and articulate/comprehensive programmes to deal with the activities of major corporations in the country were identified. For these, the Federal Environmental Protection Agency (FEPA) was established in 1988 was mandated to review the 1988 National Policy on Environment and to initiate legal apparatus to deal with environmental pollution problems.

The review activities led to the establishments of key ministries and parastatals to deal with environmental matters as well as to focus health and poverty issues especially in the Niger-Delta area. For instance, in addition to the Federal Ministries of Environment (FMEnv) and Petroleum Resources (FMPR), the Department of Petroleum Resources (DPR) was created and charged with the responsibilities of regulating environment activities of the oil sector. Moreover, in order to encourage grassroots participation of local communities in decision making, Oil-Mineral Producing Areas Development Commissions (OMPADEC) and Niger-Delta Development Commission (NDDC) were created (at different times). The major plans were that the Commissions could serve to catalyze economic and social development in the oil-producing areas (Tanko, 2007).

One key positive element of the new "reform" was the fact that oil industry was now made to appreciate the level of devastation it causes to the environment and the consequent human element of poverty issues. Thus, in addition to the main concern and respect for all national (and international laws and conventions against environmental damages of oil operations, they are made to institute various Corporate Social Responsibility (CSR) programmes with the aims of ameliorating the socioeconomic hardship caused by their environmental activities to the people (Tanko, 2007).

Conclusion

There is no doubt that oil, a vital environmental resource, is the backbone of the economies of many nations. In Nigeria, it is the major source of the country's foreign reserve, accounting for over 90%. Its production in the Niger-Delta since 1958 no doubt led to severe changes in the economic activities of the people. The activities of oil from exploration to full exploitation lead to landlessness and/or scarce agricultural land through denial to the people access to traditional economic modes of production, and also right to live in safe and healthy environment due to severe pollution. Therefore, the federal and states governments in the ND should as matter of urgency consider the long felt plight of the people of the ND and their environment. Aggressive means of resolving conflict in the face of poverty aggravate rather than redress the debilitating position of the poor in the region. Oil Multinational Corporations (OMC) operating in the region must also be made by the federal government to redirect their efforts towards ensuring that the average people in the oil reach ND are free from oil spillage, killings, and organized state terrorism in the name of peace making.

References

Aston-Jones, N. (1998), *The Human Ecosystems of the Niger-Delta:* ERA Handbook, Benin City: ERA, 1998

Boserup, E. (1981), *Population and Technology:* Oxford: Blackwell.

Boserup, E. (1995), *The Conditions of Agricultural Growth.* London: Allen and Unwin

Caswell, M.F. (1993), Balancing Energy and the Environment: in *The Environment of Oil,* R.J. Gilbert (ed.), pp. 179 – 214. Boston, Kluwer Acad.

Chambers, R. and Conway, G.R.(1992), "Sustainable Rural Livelihoods: Practical Concepts for the 21st Century", *Institute of Development Studies (IDS) Discussion Paper* No. 296, University of Sussex, Brighton: IDS

Dasgupta, P. (1992), "Population, Resources and Poverty", in *AMBIO, 21* (1)

Doyle, J. (1994), *Crude Awakenings: The Oil Mess in America: wasting energy jobs and the environment.* Washington D.C. Friends Earth

Epstein, P.R. and J. Selber, (2002), *Oil: A life Cycle Analysis of its Health and Environmental Impacts:* Boston: Centre of Health Globe, Environ., Harv. Med. Sch.

Natural Resource Council (2002), *Oil in the Sea III: Inputs, Fates and Effects*: Washigton D.C., National Acad.

Opschoor, (Hans) J.B. (2007), *Environment and Poverty: Perspectives, Propositions Policies.* Institute of Social Studies, The Hague, Netherlands, Working Paper 437, Electronic format: www.iss.nl/workingpapers.

Opschoor, (Hans) J.B. (2004), Biodiversity, sustainable Economic Analysis, CDS Public Lecture, Centre for Development Studies, Trivandrum, India

Ross, M.L. (2003), Nigeria's Oil Sector and the Poor, prepared for the UK Department for International Development: Nigeria, Drivers of Change Programme, May 23, 2003.

Steyn, Maria S. (2003), "Oil Politics in Ecuador and Nigeria: A perspective from Environmental History on the Struggle between Ethnic Minority Groups, Multinational Oil Companies and National Governments". PhD Thesis, Faculty of Humanities, Department of History, University of Free State, Bloemfontein, South Africa.

Tanko, A.I. (2007), Environmental Concerns, Assessment and Protection Procedures for Nigeria's Oil Industry, Paper Presented at the Department of Geography, University of Canterbury, Christchurch and Centre for Development Studies, University of Auckland, New Zealand (on May 8 and May 23, 2007 respectively).

Woodhill, (2006), Environmental Evaluation Studies (EES) on Obe Field (OML) carried out for Tuskar Resources Nigeria Limited, September 2006

Woodhill, (2007), Environmental Impact Assessment (EIA) for Obe Field (OML 110) Additional Oil Wells at Nigeria's Offshore Location: An EIA Report submitted on behalf of Tuskar Resource Nigeria Limited, March 2007.

World Resource Institute, WRI(2005), The Wealth of the Poor: Managing Ecosystems to Fight Poverty. Washington, D.C: WRI

CHAPTER THIRTEEN

ENVIRONMENT, CONFLICT, AND POVERTY IN THE NIGER DELTA REGION

Kabiru Ahmed

Introduction

Conflict is a "contradiction arising from differences in interests, ideas, orientations, perceptions and tendencies" (Nnoli, 1998: 6). Crises are also said to arise from crisis of justice or crisis of nature (Sachs, 1999). It is often difficult to distinguish the two types because 'crisis of native e.g. drought may be accentuated by injustice as conflict is politicized, as is the case in Dafur region of Sudan.

Crisis of justice include exploitation of African natural resource endowment by colonialists, and contradictions arising from structural adjustment and mismanagement. Examples of conflicts arising from the exploitation of African natural resources endowments by colonialist are the land reform programme in Zimbabwe where minority white farmers occupied more than half of the land, which is also the best land. In Democratic Republic of Congo, there was the fear by the west of the spread of communism and Russian control of the mineral resources including copper, uranium, cobalt, and diamonds. This explains the conflict in DRC from independence to date.

The contradiction arising from structural adjustment and mismanagement leads to discontent as governments fail to meet the basic needs of the people, who in turn may demand for justice and change as is the case in most African countries. The crisis in the Niger Delta region arises from the production of petroleum resources and the communities requesting for more benefits through resource control.

Agitation for Resource Control in the Niger Delta Region

The Niger Delta Region

The region is Nigeria's oil producing area, it is the largest delta and largest oil producing region in Africa. The region is a sedimentary deposit covering some 20,000km^2 and has a population of about 30.5m people.

The region consists of three morphological units including the barrier islands, the tidal plats, and the flood plain. The vegetation comprises of mangrove, fresh water swamp forest, and lowland rainforest. Population distribution is controlled by relief and availability of dry land. This is because of the flooding recorded for 2-5 months, and the floods occupy potential areas.

Crops produced are cassava, yam, cocoyam, sweet potatoes, maize, rice, cowpea, melon, and groundnuts. Tree products include banana, sugarcane, plantain, citrus, pineapple, mango, guava, cashew, and palm oil. Wildlife is supported. The morphological units supporting agriculture are the lowland rain front zone, the floodplain and the barrier islands with alluvial soils. Agricultural intensification is required to produce more to support the increasing population. This calls for increased fertilization and agricultural subsidy. Otherwise farmers may have to switch to low nutrient demanding crops such as cassava instead of high level crops as pepper, groundnuts and yam.

Some industrial development has been achieved with refineries, petrochemical industries, fertilizer industry, power station, and a steel complex. Others are textiles, food processing, glass and paint industries. The agricultural and industrial development constitute formidable challenges of fertility decline and erosion, costal erosion, subsiding geosynclines, see level rise, annual flooding and industrial pollution from petrochemical activities and as spills and acid rain from gas flaring. These problems affect the livelihood of the ethnic groups who depend on the natural resource endowment. These groups include Ijaw, Urhobo, Itsekiri, Efik, Etche, Ibibio, Andoni, Ikweri, Isoko, Edo, Ogoni, and Kwale Igbo.

The huge revenue generated from oil production is accompanied with environmental and livelihood degradation. The degradation has been the cause of social discontent, communal tension, and violent complict. The challenge now is resource management and the agitation for resource control.

Resource Control

Despite the huge revenue generated from oil production, the basic needs of Nigerians are not met and there is frustration from lack of adequate food and poor nutrition, safe water supply, health care, and education. The much desired electricity for domestic use and industrial growth is unreliable. The citizens are experiencing a vicious cycle of poverty and corruption.

Obasanjo stated in his inaugural speech as Present of the Federal Republic in 1999, that "no society can achieve anything near its full potential if it allows corruption to become the full-blown cancer that it has become in Nigeria". The new President, Alhaji Shehu Musa Yar'aduwa identified corruption, in his inaugural speech, as an important obstacle to achieving national development and requested Nigerians to join forces to fight the evil of corruption in our midst. This suggests that corruption has eaten so deep into our consciousness that special type of therapy is needed to root it out.

Corruption is related to poverty, while poverty breeds frustration and conflict. In his address at the Kennedy School of Government, Harvard University (1999), Obasanjo observed that "poverty breeds frustration, and frustration frequently breeds aggression both domestic and external". As far as the Niger Delta is concerned, the explanation is that, inequities experienced in distributing the wealth of the region, particularly as it affects the immediate producing areas, has been a source of social discontent, generating conflicts and communal tension (Onosode, 2003: 2). It is the discontent and conflicts which gave birth to the demand for 'resource control'.

The reaction of communities in the oil producing areas to deprivation and poverty started with appeals for improved livelihood, and then followed by vandalisation and destruction of oil installations, and later the kidnapping of expatriate staff of oil companies by militant groups. The Movement for the Survival of Ogoni People (MOSOP) was formed in 1990, and the movement issued the Ogoni Bill of Right, which demanded to control and use Ogoni resources for Ogoni development, and the right to protect Ogoni environment from further degradation. Other movements are the Nigeria Delta Peoples Volunteer Force (NDPVF), whose leader Mujahid Asari Dokubo issued a warning and threatened international oil companies to withdraw their nationals, from the Niger Delta oilfields before 1st October, 2004. He declared that, they wanted a sovereign national conference that will lead to self-determination and resource control for the Ijaw and other nationalities in the Niger Delta. The Ijaw ethnic group, which he represents, is spread across the Rivers, Bayelsa, Delta and Ondo States. He was later detained and charged for treason. The Movement for the Emancipation of Niger Delta (MEND) was formed later.

Former Bayelsa State Governor, Chief Diepreye Alamieyesigha delivered a lecture entitled,"The Niger Delta Youth Restiveness: The Way Forward," during the commissioning of the information technology training centre of the Abuja Council of the Nigerian Union of Journalist in Abuja, in which he stated that youth restiveness stern from the fact that the youth are aware how the petronaira is used to develop other parts of Nigeria without commensurate projects in their region. He called for resource control and self-determination of the region in order to promote prosperity and peace rather than conflict (*New Nigeria*, Sept. 23, 2004). A year later, the Governor presented another paper titled, "The Niger Delta Crisis: Yesterday, Today and Tomorrow" at the Institute of African Studies, University of Ibadan. He stated that the security of Nigeria in the next thirty years depends on how we can manage the inequality in the Delta Region, and demonstrate genuine interest in developing this region by recognizing communal property rights, environmental justice, and corporate accountability. He urged that the ongoing National Political Reform Conference must address the issue of revenue control and national integrity (*New Nigerian*, March 23, 2005). The Governor of Delta State, James Ibori, addressed the Urhobo Community in Lagos in Jan. 2006 and advised the people of Niger Delta Region to demand for resource control, and increased autonomy for the federating units (NN, Nov. 24, 2005).

The pressure from various political groups, vandalisation and oil bunkering increased, while the people become more militant and resorted to kidnapping of oil workers.

Vandalisation

Groups vandalize oil pipelines to cause 'sabotage spills' from the desire to attract relief materials or community projects by oil companies. The flat topography and floods help to spread oil spillage, from vandalized pipeline, over a wide area to cause devastating environmental effects. Vandalisation also cuts oil supply to electricity generating stations leading to interrupted power supply. The oil companies reported cases of sabotage of facilities and theft, resulting in losses of several thousand barrels of crude oil. In April 2003, vandalisation of two major oil pipelines that convey oil from Escravos to Warri and Kaduna refineries led to the shut down of the refineries. Similarly in May 2003, the pipeline to Egbin and Delta iv generating stations was vandalized and the power supply interrupted.

The Federal Task Force on Petroleum pipeline vandalisation, whose members are armed, failed to control vandalisation because it is well coordinated, financially rewarding and more sophisticated despite the risks. The General Secretary of the Trade Union Congress of Nigeria (TUG) observed that the Task Force has failed to control vandalisation because vandalisation is more frequent and has spread to all parts of the country. He advised government to establish effective poverty eradication programme because poverty pushes school leavers to take such risks (New Nigeria, March 2, 2006). Vandalisation spreads outside the Delta region and a Lagos traditional ruler was arrested by Police and believed to be a leader of an illegal pipeline vandalisation group (*New Nigerian*, Oct. 27, 2004). Vandalisation was reported, for the first time, in the North in July 2003, when pipeline supplying fuel from Kaduna refinery to Jos, and from Warri refinery to Suleija deport was blown up at Kukameke village, Rigachukwu, Kaduna State and at Koton Karfe, Niger State respectively.

The *New Nigerian* Editorial (May 22, 2006) observed that:

> We are, however, surprised that people continue to indulge in the dangerous habit of vandalizing NNPC pipelines in order to siphon petroleum products in spite of the risk it entails. While the general belief is that poverty and joblessness contribute, to a large extent, we do not believe that it is an excuse for anybody to be involved in such wicked act

Kidnapping

The struggle for resource control metamorphosed into militant struggle as waves of kidnappings were reported. In January 2005, Niger Delta militants kidnapped four men including an American, Briton, Bulgarian, and Honduras. The kidnapped workers of Shell Petroleum were held by armed gunmen of the MEND at an offshore oil rig. The hostages were held for 19 days before their release and handing over to the President at the State House, Abuja. MEND demanded a ransom of 2.5bn and the release of their leader, Dokubo. The handing over of the hostages to the President was considered the first recognition of the authority of MEND.

The President later observed, that no self-respecting government would allow hostage taking to become the order of the day, and he promised to put a stop to hostage taking (New Nigerian, Jan. 31, 2005). However, kidnapping continued and nine oilmen comprising of three Americans, a Briton, two Egyptians, a Filipino, and two Thais were kidnapped on February 18, 2006 around Shell- Forcadors oil export terminal. The excuse given by MEND for their action was that Joint Task Force set up by the government attacked their communities in February 2006. However, six of the hostages were released on March 1, 2006. The three not released were workers of US oil service company, Wilbros. They restated a demand of 1.5bn to be paid by Shell for environmental pollution as well as the release of Ijaw leaders. However, the three hostages (two Americans and a Briton) were released on March 27, 2006 after about one month in captivity.

Kidnapping became widespread as others joined MEND in the illegal activity. Youth said to be representing the Ogboinbiri community in Southern –Ijaw Aga, Balyelsa State captured 16 staff of Agip Oil Company, an Italian firm, and 8 soldiers attached to the company. They demanded Agip to implement a MOU signed by the firm and the community. The MOU signed promised a number of projects including employment, scholarships, and shore protection to check erosion. The hostages were released after one week in captivity (*New Nigerian*, August, 1 2006). This is similar to the case where Ijaw Youth kidnapped 8 expatriate workers of Peak Oil drilling company for not implementing an MOU signed with the community in Ekeremor LGA of Bayelsa State (*New Nigerian*, June 5, 2006).

President Obasanjo inaugurated a government committee on the physical and social development of the Niger Delta Region in an attempt to achieve peace and stability. The committee was set up in April 2006 to produce a road map on the sustainable development of the region through employment, education, health, transportation, power supply, communication and environmental management. About five months after this goodwill gesture, the President observed at a stakeholders' meeting in Abuja that the situation in the region is totally unacceptable and hostage takers or terrorists were to be hunted by a combined team of soldiers and the police, "force for force" (*New Nigerian*, August, 16, 2006). Three months later, the Joint Revolutionary Council (JRC) comprising NDPVF, MEND, and the Martyrs Brigade, issued a statement warning the Federal government to release Dokubo or be prepared for war.

We demand once again, the unconditional release from the gallows" of the Nigerian State, the flag bearer and leading light of the Ijaw and Niger Delta struggle, Alhaji Mujahid Dokubo Asari. If the demand is not met in goodtime, we will roll out the drums of war and our heroic and patriotic combatants will begin a revolution against all interests and agents of the Nigerian State as well as its imperialist collaborators (*Newswatch*, Nov. 6, 2006 :13).

Dokubo, who was arrested for treason in 2005, was released on bail in June 2007 on health grounds. For this gesture, 10 Indians abducted by MEND were released while JRC spokes person, Cynthia Whyte, declared complete cessation of hostilities against the Nigerian State. She observed that JRC was prepared to listen to leaders who understand the anguish and pain of the people, and are committed to improve their livelihoods. (*Sunday Trust*, June 176, 2007).

Dialogue

The Minister of Information and National Orientation observed that the criminal activities of hostage takers should be condemned by all because it retards the development of the region (NN, February 18, 2006). Similarly, the Minister of State for Petroleum Resources said to the Offshore West Africa (OWA) conference in Abuja in March 2006 that stakeholders in the Niger Delta should enhance dialogue and denounce militancy in order to achieve development of the region. Commander of the Joint Military Task Force (JTF) whose five solders were murdered by MEND militants, remarked that his men were in the region to create enabling environment for dialogue to hold as violence would not solve the problem of the region (*Leadership Weekend*, Feb. 25, 2006).

The political Reform Conference was inaugurated on February 21, 2005 by the President, and the delegates deliberated for five months up to July 2005.The South-South (Akwa Ibom, Bayelsa, Edo, Cross-River, Rivers, and Delta) went to the conference and insisted on an increase of the derivation from 13% to 50%. After lengthy deliberations, the committee on Revenue Allocation and Fiscal Federalism recommended that the country's resource should remain under the control of the federal government, thereby throwing out the demand for resource control and confederal arrangement. However, the National Political Reforms Conference announced a review of the derivation from 13% to 17%, this was as the delegates from south-South walked-out against the decision. The delegates insisted on a demand of 25% derivation. The Chairman of South-South Dr. Edwin Clerk mentioned that the decision was irreversible because it was arrived at after consultations with the grassroots in the region.

The chairman, media and strategy committee, Northern Delegates Forum issued a press release after the conference that the increase to 17% was acceptable it we are to avoid gross in balance in the development of various regions of the nation. At 25% derivation the Federal Government gets 46.9%, South-South States 28.61, while all other states and FCT get only 24.3% which is less than the

South-South States. At 50% derivation the federal government gets only 32.06% less than the South-South at 49.0%; while all the states get less than 20% (*Leadership*, August. 14, 2005). It is also noted that the Federal government funds NNDC, and ecological funds from its own share of derivation. It has been argued that the investment by the federal government does not make much impact on the well-being of the environment and people of the South-South because the money is not judiciously spent. The governors of the South-South, who agitate for resource control and increased derivation, were alleged to buy air crafts, television stations and newspaper houses, and buying personal shares in private refineries instead of using the funds to the benefit of the masses (*Leadership August*, 21, 2005).

A communiqué released at the end of a National Conference on Peaceful Co-existence, Pluralism and Nation-building organized by Usman Danfodio University Sokoto in December, 2004 observed that the failure of government is an important factor in the recurrence of conflicts in Nigeria:

> Pervasive and persistent poverty as well as other forms of deprivations amidst widespread corruption and embezzlement of funds by public officers, have reinforced or created social exclusion" and precipitated conflicts (Conference Communiqué).

Transparency International (TI) estimated the corruption perception index in 2000 and placed Nigeria in last position i.e. most corrupt out of 159 countries. Nigeria was ranked at second to the last position in 2003, and lowest position together with Chad in 2005. The strong advocate of resource control, Governor Deprieye Alamieyesigha was arrested in London Heathrow Airport in Sept., 2005 for money laundering. Before his arrest in Britain, ICPC preliminary investigation revealed that he awarded multimillion Naira contract and payments for Niger Delta University to non- existent companies (The News, 26th Sept., 2005). In 2006, the government of UK returned to the government of Nigeria, the sum of nearly 1m pounds being money recovered from former Governor of Bayelsa State.

The former Governor of Bayelsa between May 1999 and December, 2005, was charged with possessing bank accounts in London, Cyprus, Denmark and the United States (*New Nigerian*, November, 18, 2006). In another development the Chief of Nigerian Police, Inspector General, was held on corruption charges and retired for misuse of police welfare funds. One billion was found in his Nigeria bank accounts, while he had other foreign bank accounts.

Jega (2006:10) observed that, "not only does 'grand corruption' i.e. by high public officials, demoralize workers and citizens, it also brings about ineffectiveness in governance and generalized inability to satisfy the basic needs and aspirations of the citizens".

To avoid diversion of public funds for private use, it was suggested by Mr. George Timinimi, a two time facilitator and negotiator for the release of kidnapped oil workers, that derivation funds be directly disbursed to communities in the Delta Region for the execution of their identified projects and not through state government (*New Nigerian*, April 4, 2006). The Imo State government, wanted oil producing communities to propose projects for implementation but the communities (Ohaji snd Egbene) demanded to be given 60% of the fund for their area (*New Nigerian,* July 2, 2002).

Conflict Management

The struggle for resource control in the Niger Delta, is manifested inform of vandalisation, kidnapping and call for resource control. The struggle involve three stake holders i.e. the federal government, international oil companies, and the communities. The federal government owns the oil and gas, and all revenue from the sales of oil and gas goes to the government. The oil companies, on the other hand acquire land to produce the oil and to pollute part of the land. The oil companies partner with government, they also pay rate to the government. Finally, the communities are compensated by the government and by the oil companies by implementing development projects including providing employment, infrastructure, and environmental management projects. However, the economic incentive is considered to be inadequate and has unsatisfactory impact. The communities are demanding for participatory approach to development. Another approach is to control conflict through military force and to this effect, European countries and USA have offered to support the government achieve this objective. In this section the three approaches to conflict resolution are discussed including economic incentives by government agencies and oil companies, participatory approach, and the military option.

Economic Incentive

The Oil Minerals Producing Areas Development Commission (OMPADEC) was set up by a Decree in 1988 to administer the 3% derivation in order to provide infrastructure and control environmental degradation. More than 23bn Naira was spent between 1988 and 1998 giving out contracts for job not eventually completed, and the organization left the Delta Region littered with abandoned projects. It was accepted that the organization was under funded and there was mismanagement of public resources. The 1999 constitution reviewed the situation and the Niger Delta Development Commission (NNDC) was established by an Act, to achieve a more effective utilization of the revised 13% derivation revenue. NNDC received over 43bn naira from government and oil companies between 2001 and 2004 but this was considered inadequate and proposed an annual subvention of 300bn naira to be fully effective.

In 2004, the President proposed to the National Assembly to amend the Act establishing NDDC, and Senate Committee on the Niger Delta visited Bayelsa

State for public hearing on the proposed amendment bill. The various stakeholders were given a chance to amend the laws in the interest of the region. The stakeholders objected to the states contributing 10% of their monthly statutory allocation to the commission, and they objected to the reduction of governments' contribution from 13% to 10%; and wanted contributions from oil companies to be increased from 3 to 5%. A representative of the Niger Delta Youth Volunteers for Development requested that 5% of the annual budget of oil companies operating in the region should be paid to NNDC while a representative of the South-South Youth Leaders Coalition wanted state to pay 10% of their monthly statutory allocations as well as 30% of the 13% derivation to be paid to NNDC in order to make more funds available to NNDC for projects.

Stakeholders blamed poor funding for the low performance of the commission, while others attribute the failure to mismanagement of the funds by the management of NNDC. The commission introduced a master plan for sustainable development of the region up to 2015. The projects to be executed are road construction, and rehabilitation, education, health, electricity and water supply.

In 2006, the President inaugurated a committee on physical and social development of the Niger Delta Region, with membership drawn mainly from ethnic groups within the region. The committee was to workout a road map for the sustainable development of the region. The road map covers the areas of employment, education, health, transportation, power supply, communications, and empowerment. The president indicated that youth from the region would be employed as teachers, army, navy and airmen. A federal University of Petroleum Resources to be built in Port-Harcourt and Federal Polytechnic in Bayelsa State. Road projects to be executed are the dualizing of the East-West road, and construction of coastal road to link all the oil producing states. Environmental projects will continue including erosion and flood control projects, rehabilitation of oil spill sites, and enforcement of a reduction of gas flaring to zero by 2008. Power plants will be located within the region. It is hoped that the projects proposed will have an impact to end the violence in the region. In July 2007, the new administration under President Yar'Adua set up Peace and Reconciliation Committee at federal level and requested affected states to follow suit.

Oil companies are not left out of the struggle to assist communities with development projects in an attempt to end the violence in the region. Chevron Texaco was reported in 2002 to have spent some $90m in ten years for community projects on access roads, water supply, education, electricity, and credit scheme. In 2002, an MOU was signed between Chevron and the communities to implement projects on healthcare, transport, education, communications, agriculture, and recreation. In 2004, Mobil Nigeria was reported to have commissioned projects on water supply and schools worth N90m in Akwa Ibom State.

Shell (SPDC) reported in the 2002 annual report on "people and environment" that $67m was spent to reduce poverty and empower communities. The report noted that Shell moved from community assistance to community development in 1997. In 2004, the annual report on sustainable development indicated that Shell invested $30m on community projects in agriculture, health, education, water, infrastructure, micro credit, and business development. This is in addition to a partnership with USAID on a five-year agreement to spend over $20m to build capacity in agriculture, healthcare, ad business enterprise. There was a second partnership with Africa for three years to spend $4.5m on reducing death from malaria. There was also contribution of $54.5m to NNDC.

The 2006 sustainable development report showed that Shell spent $32m on community projects, and signed partnership with NNDC to construct the Ogbia – Nembe road at $73m with Shell paying 70% of the cost. There was another partnership with Globacom to set up 225 telephone kiosks in remote communities in the region. This was in addition to continued implementation of older partnerships, as is the case with Africare, on controlling malaria. Today, in spite of the huge annual community development budget by the oil producing companies, "the oil producing communities remain socio-economically impoverished. The peace and social stability that are a minimum condition for operations remain elusive"(Onosode, 2003: .83). While government and oil companies interventions are considered inadequate, accountability and transparency remain the watch words for conflict management.

A World Bank report entitled "Breaking the Conflict Trap; Civil War and Development Policy" stated that the root cause of violence is endemic poverty rather than ethnic differences and effective management of such conflicts lie in judicious spending of revenue derived from natural resources. In Nigeria accountability is very much in question as the Irekefe Judicial Tribunal on Crude Oil Sales discovered that NNPC was cheated of millions of dollars through inappropriate agreements with Shell, and Mobil. The tribunal discovered that NNPC used to give one to two months grace period for buyers of crude oil to pay, and this gave them enough time to deposit and yield enough interest with which to settle NNPC (Abba et al., 1985).

In 2003, the Managing Director NNPC was relieved of his job for ignoring the maintenance of the nations refineries in favour of the monopoly of imports by independent marketers (*African Business*, December, 2003), who were reported by the Department of Petroleum Resources to have imported low quality products. (*New Nigerian*, December 17, 2003). The Federal Ministry of Finance was forced to set up an oil and gas account unit in December, 2003 to control fraud inform of the considerable losses in revenue due to the discrepancies discovered in the records of lifting of oil by NNPC and by the joint venture partners, and NNPC account was never rendered to the Auditor General for scrutiny. Corruption is a crisis and so is conflict and we need to struggle against both. The struggle against corruption is a challenge to federal and state government agencies, as well as to the committees in the Delta region.

Partnership and Participation

It has been argued that oil companies acquire land to produce oil; their operations also take away more land because of degradation resulting from erosion, oil spill, and gas flaring. Mismanagement through corruption is also believed to make ineffective the economic intervention by governments and oil companies, which means communities remain trapped in the vicious cycle of poverty. It is believed possible to break this vicious cycle i.e. achieves improved livelihood and environmental management through partnership and participation.

Government partners with international community to get more funds for the development of the delta region such as the $81m to be disbursed over a period of 8 years for rural development and environmental management, with contributions coming from the international fund for agricultural development ($15m), local governments ($32m), NNDC ($14.4m), States (8.2m), communities ($4.4m), and federal government ($3.8m). NGO's also form coalitions such as the South-South coalition of about 40 NGO's from the Delta region which visited the President in 2003 and pledged that they were for development and not violence, and supported the unity and corporate existence of Nigeria. They requested for $30m to be distributed through NNDC for community projects in the Delta region. South-South coalition is also a member of a larger forum, the Partnership for Indigenous Peoples Environment (PIPE) which is recognized by the UN. PIPE organized an Indigenous Peoples Caucus on Sustainable Development in 2003, to which South-South coalition made a submission. The oil companies operating in the region also partner with international organizations to execute community projects, as well as forging partnership with communities by signing MOU on community projects. All partnerships should be seen to focus on infrastructural development such as provision of roads, water, electricity, schools, and health care centers.

Infrastructural development should be carried out side-by-side with capacity development aimed to eradicate poverty through income generating activities. The income generating activities should be in the form of community projects or micro projects aimed to provide employment, and environmental management. Micro projects include agro projects, forestry, livestock fisheries, and small-medium scale industrial projects. Micro projects are identified on the basis of needs and communities should be consulted to choose projects they need. They should be consulted on how projects are implemented and by whom. It should start with pilot projects and are later replicated if found successful. Replication of projects should be facilitated though media, education, and extension services. Participatory projects are recommended for the increased accountability, a higher sense of ownership, and sustainability.

Military Option

A New Nigerian editorial observed that,

"no responsible and self-respecting government can sit idly and allow the creation of armed military groups in this country, much less their use to blow up economic installations and seize hostages, foreign ones at that. This amounts to terrorism and at worst a declaration of war against the state. Waging war and resorting to terrorism cannot be a solution, the federal government is then required to rise up to its constitutional duties and crush such a rebellion (*New Nigerian*, March 7, 2007)".

The militants are better guided to follow the path of dialogue.

The Director of Operations at Defense Headquarters recommended that the government should intensify military action to combat the activities of militants in the Niger Delta Region. He observed before the House Committee on Defense that criminal activities of the militants has exceeded oil bunkering and vandalisation to an armed struggle for self-determination using machine guns, grenades, rocket propellers, and AK-4 ripple (*New Nigerian*, March 8, 2006).

There are three actors in this option, the federal government wants to eliminate conflicts in order to ensure the production of oil and sustained revenue needed to conduct the affairs of government. Secondly, the oil companies have invested billions of dollars to establish production lines, which are destroyed by militants, who also kidnap their foreign workers. Thirdly, the US and European governments want to ensure continued supply of oil and gas and seem to be competing with Asia and South American countries for the commodity.

The Gulf of Guinea supplies 15% of US's oil import and could in future supply up to 25% of US exports because US is increasingly turning to Africa for its oil due to the increased tension in the Middle East. Nigeria is the largest producer in the region supplying more than 10% of US imports. That is why the US energy strategy considers establishing an African Command (AFRICOM) to safeguard African supplies. Today USA, UK and France have military advisers and training bases in Africa. The US set up a military base in Africa to station personnel, weapons and supplies to save transporting them from distant bases when needed. Sao Tome and Principe is considered to be the home of AFRICOM.

As far as the Niger Delta is concerned, the US government directed two refitted Second World War warships to be deployed to protect oil industry in the Delta region. The British government also offered a naval ship to be used to protect oil installations in the Delta region; government rejected the offer and preferred smaller past boats managed by the Nigerian Navy (*New Nigerian*, August 13, 2003). The Delta State government also turned down an offer for Scotland Yard detectives to investigate the kidnapping of expatriate oil workers. These offers by foreign governments are to ensure that multinational companies are not put out of business and their governments deprived of vital sources of fuel.

The multinational oil companies are deeply involved since 1992 when MO-SOP demanded payment of $6bn from Shell as oil royalties due from 1958 when oil production started, in addition to $4bn as compensations for damages resulting from pollution. Shell did not yield to the demand and was declared "person non grata" in Ogoni land from January 1993. Shell had to stop production, and lobbied for reconciliations through the Christian Association of Nigeria with the assistance of the Council of Churches of Great Britain and Ireland (*Africa Today*, March, 2001). The federal government appointed a facilitator to reconcile Ogoni community and Shell (SPDC). The facilitator, Reverend Father Mathew Hassan Kukah, began the reconciliation by a dialogue on the demands made by MOSOP, and later on environmental degradation and the need to clean up. Representatives of UNDP were invited to assess the clean up required; the team visited Ogoni land and held town hall meetings. The team recommended for Shell to pay for the cost of technical study as well as the clean up under the concept of "Polluter Pays Principle (PPP)". Kukah also inaugurated a committee chaired by the Vice chancellor of University of Port Harcourt to harmonize the various requests for development projects. He also invited Archbishop Tutu and Professor Wangan to advise and pray for the success of the initiatives started (*Sunday Trust*, June 10, 2007).

American oil companies demanded for security from the US government in order to protect their investment in the gulp region. In 2006 Shell led a group of oil companies to approach the US military for protection because of Nigeria government inability to control the violence in the delta region. It is also known that American navy is patrolling the offshore oil fields of international companies in the Delta Region (Lubeck, et al., 2007). African countries object to such developments and there was public outcry against the presence of American solders in Nigeria as trainers, and a General in the army lost his job for objecting to too much nosing in the affairs of the military by US military advisers.

Thus, it can be said that Nigeria is capable of controlling the situation in the Niger Delta and this should be done through dialogue and the control of corruption in the Region's states in particular and the country in general. Secondly, Nigeria should strive not to bring religion into this issue and to avoid militarization of the problem out of scale by allowing the US and European allied forces to establish military bases. We must avoid what is happening in Iraq where American Intervention has failed to control insurgency but guaranteed the US of its oil supply from Iraq oil fields. We should also be mindful of the conflicts in Zimbabwe and Democratic Republic of Congo and not to allow the allied forces to be party to the conflict in the Delta Region.

Conclusion

Spokes person to the Joint Revolutionary Council reported, after the release of Dokubo, that they declared complete cessation of hostilities against the Nigerian State. Dokubo himself surrendered his arsenal to the government and opted to work with government agents to secure peace through dialogue with the militants. He even urged the militants to lay down their arms and work for peace.

However, a few weeks later, the kidnapping took a new turn as nursery students were kidnapped on their way to school. This suggests that the kidnappers kidnap not for resource control objectives but to extort money from their victims. It is a money making venture as is oil bunkering. This means the only dialogue the kidnappers understand is making money and kidnapping is criminal, barbaric and a destabilizing business enterprise which needed to be stopped through participatory development, dialogue, and forgiveness.

References

Abba A., et al (1985), The *Nigerian Economic Crisis: Causes and Solutions*, Zaria: ASSU &Gaskiya Corporation Ltd. Zaria.

Africa Today (2001), March.

African Business (2003), December.

Jega A.M. (2004), "Democracy, Economic Crisis and Conflicts: A review of the Nigerian Situation", *The Quarterly Journal of Administration*, Vol. XXXII, No. 1

Leadership (2005), August, 14

Leadership Weekend (2006), February

Lubeck, P.M. Watts M.J., and Lipschultz (2007), "Convergent Interests: U.S. Energy Security and the "Security" of Nigerian Democracy", *International Policy Report*. A publication of The Centre for International Policy.

New Nigerian (2002), July, 2

New Nigerian (2003), August, 13,

New Nigerian (2003), December, 17

New Nigeria, (2004), September, 23

New Nigerian (2004), October, 27

New Nigerian (2005), March, 23

New Nigerian (2006), March, 8

New Nigerian (2005), September, 26

New Nigerian (2006), "Editorial", May, 22

New Nigerian (2005), January, 31

New Nigerian (2005), November, 24.

New Nigerian (2005), March 23

New Nigerian (2006), April, 4

New Nigerian (2006), August, 1

New Nigerian (2006), June, 5

New Nigerian (2006), July, 2

New Nigerian (2007), March, 7

Newswatch (2006), November, 6.

Nnoli O. (1998), "Ethnic Conflicts in Africa: A comparative Analysis", in Nnoli O. (ed.), *Ethnic Conflicts in Africa*, CODESRIA, Basford.

Onosode G.O. (2003), *Environmental Issues and Challenges of the Niger Delta*: The CIBN Press Limited, Yaba, Lagos

Sachs W. (1999), "Social Jusitice and Sustainability in Post-Development Era", in Suleiman M. (ed.), Ecology, *Politics, and Violent Conflict.* Zed Book, London.

Sunday Trust, (2007), June, 10

CHAPTER FOURTEEN

THE IMF/WORLD BANK STRUCTURAL ADJUSTMENT PROGRAMME
(SAP) AND POVERTY GENERATION: THE EXPERIENCE OF PUBLIC
SECTOR WORKERS IN NIGERIA

Habu Mohammed

Introduction

There has been considerable literature on poverty, its manifestation, dimension and consequences in Africa and the world over. The plethora of literature on poverty characteristically emphasize, among other things, whether the phenomenon is absolute or relative, transient or permanent without theoretically and empirically examining the exogenous factors that generate, and in some cases, exacerbate poverty among the already existing poor population. Where such attempts are made by bourgeois economists and policy experts they tend to mischievously down play, if not completely ignore, the political and economic content of the global economy and the manner in which global economic institutions torpedo the process of self-reliant and independent local policies that would turn around the economy and provide the much needed multiplier effect of reducing the scourge of poverty. The result is that, by a simple design orchestrated by policy experts who are ideologically the architect of neo-liberalism purportedly propagating the gospel of poverty reduction, prescription on how to reduce global and national poverty rate is 'given' rather than initiated in local economies. With the introduction of the IMF/World Bank inspired Structural Adjustment Programme (SAP) in many African countries hit by the structural, cyclical and systemic crises of global capitalism, the already existing gap between rich and poor widened, thereby providing another dimension of externally induced poverty, particular among the middle class and other social groups.

This chapter examines the extent to which the IMF/World Bank policy as contained in SAP pauperized workers in Nigeria's biggest employment sector, i.e. the public sector. This is not to suggest that the policy, which was embraced and vigorously implemented by the Military government in 1986, only affected the middle class found in the public sector employment. Rather, the various sectors of the Nigerian economy, including informal sector and various social groups as well as institutions have been negatively affected by the implementation of SAP. However, various literature on SAP in Nigeria emphasize the performance of one sector of the economy or the other with little work on the impact of the programme on workers in the public sector. Since the sector occupies a unique position in the country's labour force due to its size, its examination within the context of IMF/World Bank reform measures on labour and capital, informs the class character of neo-liberalism in Nigeria. The central thesis of this chapter is that SAP is archetypical of how the Bank and the Fund's externally packaged economic measures explain the dynamics of poverty and inequality in the country.

The chapter is, therefore, divided into four sections. The first section reviews, albeit in brief, the existing body of literature on SAP and workers. In the second section, a general framework for the understanding of the IMF/ World Bank SAP is examined, while the third section examines how SAP pauperized workers in the public sector. Finally, the fourth section concludes the chapter.

Review of the Existing Literature on SAP and Workers in Nigeria

A number of scholarly works have been written on Africa's experience under SAP in general and Nigeria's version of the programme in particular. Though scholars researched and examined the subject critically, particularly in the mid-1980s and the tail end of the 1990s, literature on the IMF/World Bank SAP as noted earlier concentrated on sectoral performance of the economy. Our focus in this review is to bridge the existing gap by examining scholarly works on SAP and workers from the political economy standpoint.

In his assessment of the IMF/World Bank SAP, Olukoshi (1989) examines the extent to which the programme affected workers living conditions. His central argument is that the monetary thrust of the programme, particularly the devaluation of the Naira in comparison with the real wage, resulted in hardship and deterioration in the living conditions of workers in Nigeria. This is because the attendant rise in the prices of goods and services was accompanied by reduction in wages and salaries (1989:229).

In his paper titled "Structural Adjustment and Multiple Modes of Livelihood in Nigeria", Mustapha (1991) gives an exposition on the impact of SAP on middle class and the extent to which those who were hit by the adjustment measures, particularly workers, resorted to different modes of sustaining their livelihood in the informal sector. Mustapha's argument is that due to the growing poverty and the vulnerability of the general population to hardships in the period of SAP implementation, fixed salary earners, faced with the dwindling value of their 'take-home' pay intensified the process of multiple modes of livelihood. Prominent among the survival strategies of workers identified by Mustapha were conversion of motorcycles into "express taxis" or "kabu-kabu", cars into taxis, and commercialization of private assets, farming and sometimes corruption (Mustapha, 1991:10-11).

Mustapha's argument on SAP and multiple modes of social livelihood among workers has been further developed by Odah (1993). While agreeing with

Mustapha that workers, particularly civil servants, resorted to conversion of their motorcycles into "express taxis", "Okada", or "Achaba" in order to supplement their income, his analysis went a little further by identifying some negative social practices such as prostitution and drug trafficking engaged in by some female clerks as a result of the difficult situation workers found themselves in under SAP. These forms of 'economic activities' engaged by workers as a way of cushioning the hardship of SAP, Odah argues, have no prospects "for meaningful accumulation or even economic survival" (1993:12).

In contrast to Mustapha and Odah's multiple modes of livelihood thesis, Kusa (1994:80) emphasizes on what she described as "cost recovery measures" in the public sector that drastically reduced the real income of workers. According to her, these measures include, among others, the introduction of fees and other levies in schools, hospitals, etc. In view of the deplorable condition of people in the period of the implementation of SAP, Kusa (1994:87) agrees with Mustapha on the informalization of economic activities among the workers. Therefore, like Onimode (1988), Amale (1991) and Ihonvbere (1991), Kusa concludes that the implementation of SAP in Nigeria had a class character. She points out that only the government, speculators and the compradors supported its introduction and implementation in the country (1994:91).

In Amale's view, while it is true that SAP negatively affected the different sectors of the economy, Nigerian workers were the most badly hit by the programme and, therefore, felt the pains of adjustment more than any other social groups (1991:123). His position is predicated on his contention, also shared by Bangura and Beckman (1991), that the monetarist inclination of the IMF/World Bank adjustment policies in the country ensured the extraction of surplus value from the workers' labour to the propertied class, while the state acted as protector of the interests of the latter. Under this arrangement, Amale (1991:126) strongly affirms that "the impact of the adjustment programmes on Nigerian workers should, thus, be located within the context of this bias for capital and the class that controls the same in the society".

Aremu (1990) and Toyo (1990) also share the argument of Amale that the state served as an agent of the propertied class and subordinated the workers in the process. Looking at Second Tier Foreign Exchange Market (SFEM) in particular, Aremu points out that the 'market' increased profits to government, but the 'gains' were not geared towards the improvement of wages and salaries of workers. In this regard, he states the contradictions of the adjustment programme in the following words: "to regulate wages, but allow profits and prices of goods to rise shows the partisan and class character of SAP" (1990:144).

While analyzing the dynamics of capitalist development in Nigeria and how SAP reinforces its processes, Toyo pointed out that the programme facilitated uneven development not only among the various sectors of the economy, but also between the propertied class and the working people (1990:67). According to him, the already existing gap between the capitalist class and the working people became more pronounced as several measures introduced turned out to curtail the purchasing power of workers. Corroborating Toyo's thesis is the work of Ihonbvere (1991) who examined beneficiaries of SAP. According to him, only the post-colonial state and their agents, local and international, benefited from the implementation of the IMF World bank SAP in Nigeria (Ihonbvere, 1991: 82-84).

The review of literature above shows that SAP incapacitated the ability of workers to enjoy a better standard of living thereby promoting the ideals of capitalist bias on labour. It created a gap between the propertied class and bourgeois technocrats on the one hand, and workers on the other. The central discourse is that measures introduced under SAP made it difficult, if not impossible, for public sector workers to afford basic necessities of life, particularly against the background of wage freeze and incessant rise in the prices of goods and services hitherto subsidized by the government.

Framework for the Understanding of the IMF/World Bank SAP and Poverty Among Workers

The Structural Adjustment Programme is a policy designed to achieve a viable balance of payments (BOP) in the medium term, if not the short term. The adjustment package is often referred to as stabilization and, or adjustment measures (Harris, 1986:84). In their modern technical uses, the words 'stabilization' and 'adjustment' are often associated not only with particular measures and instruments of economic recovery, but with the international institutions which recommend these measures (Green and Faber, 1994: 2). The institutions are the International Monetary Fund (IMF), which approves a standby facility and, the International Bank for Reconstruction and Development (IBRD).

In other words, while on one hand, stabilization programme technically refers to adjustment programmes by the IMF standby credit or extended arrangements for a reasonable period of time, on the other hand, World Bank supported programmes entail extensive institutional and policy reform measures. The aim of these measures is to, apart from strengthening the market forces in the determination of world prices, extend "the scope of operations of the private sector and the strengthening of the administrative and technical capacities of the public sector" (Loxley, 1986:100). Furthermore, since the second half of the 1980s when the two Bretton Woods institutions (the IMF and World Bank) started operating a joint adjustment programme, the design and implementation of SAP has remained in their hands. Therefore, the questions to ask are: What are the propositions of these two financial institutions, especially within the context of the Nigerian economy? And how do these propositions been applied to ultimately pauperize the public sector workers? These questions bring us to the philosophy of the IMF and the World Bank, especially in their interaction with Nigeria and indeed other developing countries that have implemented in the 1980s or are still implementing the economic package of the institutions.

For the purpose of our discussion, the philosophy of both the Fund and the Bank means their theoretical underpinnings which are implicitly or explicitly contained in their adjustment package to developing countries. Within the context of the general economic crisis in the Third World countries and Nigeria's experience of the crisis in particular, the philosophy of adjustment programs makes no dividing line among countries. The philosophy of 'adjustment' has an objective character; it arises as a result of the expansion of neo-liberal paradigm of liberalism in the economic processes of developing societies. This is because wherever the programme was implemented, the elements of neo-classical economic principles with the dominant monetarists variant, have been the underlying practice. Hence, a brief focus on some of the essential tenets of monetarists approach to balance of payments crisis can help us understand the IMF/World Bank philosophy of and framework for adjustment in the public sector, with particular emphasis on workers in that sector of the economy.

The monetarist approach came into prominence in the course of the 1970s, particularly after the collapse of the Bretton Woods system which saw the demise of global Keynesianism. Hitherto, Keynesian analysis perceived the solution to the problems of world economy from the notion of state's intervention in the determination and allocation of resources. In addition to this, Keynesian scholars believed that state intervention sought to regulate demand through fiscal and monetary policies so that market failure can be averted (Osadchaya, 1983:9); and also to fight unemployment as opposed to inflation (Olukoshi and Nwoke, 1994:12-13). However, against the background of the inflationary spiral that bedeviled western economies in the late 1960s and 1970s, monetarists not only questioned the failure of governments to regulate the supply of money in their economies, but also "accuse the Keynesians of allowing workers to grow strong through the expansion of government expenditure" (Olukoshi and Nwoke, 1994:14). Similarly, the failure of the Keynesian theory to solve the problems faced by the economies of Western Europe was compounded by the collapse of Bretton Wood's system, a system which had been founded on the basis of Keynes's theoretical conception of addressing economic crisis emanating from BOP disequilibrium (Osadchaya, 1983:14).

The objectives of monetarists are essentially geared towards achieving what they called 'market perfection' or Pareto optimality. This can be achieved by addressing the problem of the world economy, particularly inflation, through the use of policy measures that are geared towards the reduction of the state's involvement in macro-economic policies. Other measures include: putting a check or ceiling on the number of wage employment and, the determination of resources and prices through the market mechanism (Usoskin, 1981:127). It is imperative to note that this idea was also embraced by the leading capitalist countries in the 1980s, particularly with the coming into power of conservative governments in the United States, Britain, West Germany, and Canada. Basically, these forces combined to reaffirm the ascendancy of monetarism in both the Western liberal thinking of macroeconomic goals as well as the IMF/ World Bank conception of world economic crisis. Bangura (1987:98) noted that:

> During the first two decades of post-war period, the IMF was guided by the Keynesian principles of fixed, but adjustable exchange rates and was not unduly worried about state intervention, which in any case, helped in generating a long period of boom. But the high inflation rates which accompanied the boom, the prolonged United State's balance of payments crisis leading to the devaluation of dollar rates in the early 1970s allowed for a radical shift in IMF/World Bank ideology, forcing them to attach strict monetarist conditions to their credit facilities.

Indeed, as a result of internationalization of the monetary principles by the leading capitalists countries, the theoretical construct of the IMF/ World Bank SAP has come to be associated with the "invisible hand" as its moving force. Added to this is the growing bias against both the public and the private sector workers. The bias is predicated on the fact that under adjustment programme wages are regulated, but profits and prices of goods and services are allowed to enjoy free movements. Invariably, therefore, the sole aim of the IMF/World Bank inspired SAP is to widen the scope of capitalism in developing countries through tight deregulated economic policies (Harris, 1986:87), and by extension, the widening of income gap between the rich and poor.

IMF/ World Bank SAP and the Exacerbation of Poverty among the Public Sector Workers in Nigeria

The term 'poverty' is not a concept that can be defined with all the exactness that other concepts carry. Many definitions have been given to the concept of poverty, depending on one's perception or indices of a poor state of mind, condition or environment (See Bellu, 2005). In short, poverty, like other sociological, political and economic concepts, is a relative term. Generally, the various definitions of poverty point to the fact that the phenomenon of poverty has to do with the inability of an individual or a group to satisfy certain minimum standards of living. According to World Development Report (1990), poverty can be defined as "the inability to achieve a minimum standard of living" (in Elumilade et al, 2006:67).

Thus, a poor man as defined by Elumilade et al is "considered as one without job, who cannot help himself or cater for his family, who has no money, farm or business" (2006:68).Though a good definition that describes who is a poor man in relation with who, our conception of a poor man goes beyond this definition to include economic vulnerability and the inability to secure the basic necessities of lives without much pains. In other words, in the context of the structural adjustment measures, poverty manifests itself in different ways and at different location in the country, cutting across the various class strata in society. To be specific, public sector workers, variously described as middle class have been wiped out as a result of SAP. Generally, the Nigerian society under SAP has been stratified into two - the rich and the poor, and in some cases, the rich get richer with the poor becoming poorer by the day. The poverty level in the country in 1985 (one year before SAP) was 38%, in the period of the implementation of the programme it increased to 43% in 1992 and 47% in 1996 (Aigbokhan, 2000:2).

The middle class, to which many public servants belong to, were pushed by the austere conditions of SAP to undergo a vulnerable life without some basic necessities of life, and in most cases, found it very difficult to maintain their pre-SAP barest minimum standard of living. Unemployment and rises in the prices of goods and services rendered them poor and incapacitated in various facets of human existence. Thus, with the deregulation of the economy against the back-drop of reduction in the size of the public service, SAP engendered various socio-economic deplorability and vulnerability which further pauperized the poor and semi-poor in the Nigerian society.

In the public sector, the idea of an economy regulated by market forces apparently means the disengagement of the state from its traditional role of regulating the economy and, of course, pruning down the size of the sector, including the size of its labour force (Havnevik, 1987:85). Not surprisingly, therefore, the IMF insisted that deviation from the market forces and lack of demand restraint policies dealing with reduction in government expenditure on social services, increase in taxation and wage restraint, among others, are the major reasons behind distortion in African economies (Harris, 1986).

From this framework we can argue that elements and measures of the Nigerian adjustment programme in the public sector, as in all other sectors of the economy, were premised to attain the basic tenets of monetarism. One of these tenets as pointed out earlier was to roll back the state's role in the economy by trimming the size of the public sector institutions in Nigeria. The institutions were set up primarily to provide defined essential services to members of the public (Omole, 1987:150). The public sector was, therefore, the dominant sector of the Nigerian economy and it constituted, by the beginning of the 1980s, nearly half of GDP and two third of the formal sector employment (World Bank, 1994:121). Consequently, a major short-term objective of the IMF/World Bank Structural Adjustment was to create a hospitable climate for private sector participation. This is largely because as the Bank always maintains, the public sector lies at the core of stagnation and decline in growth in African economies (World Bank, 1994:99).

In line with the above assumptions, the implementation of SAP in Nigeria entailed measures to achieve private sector participation, both local and foreign, through adjustments in public expenditures; lessening the dominance of unproductive investments in public sector; adoption of appropriate pricing policies for public enterprises and rationalization of public sector enterprises (Mbanefoh, 1992:98).

It was within this context of public sector reform that we can understand the social dimension of SAP on public sector workers. Thus, in a system where the economy is said to be "mixed", as in the case of Nigeria, a substantial part of nation's resources is supposed to be channeled to social service sector in order to satisfy the general public. This involves a large capital outlay and expenditure on social services such as health, education, transportation facilities etc. On the contrary, adjustment reforms in the public sector meant a reduction in government spending on these vital social services. Consequently, the cost of social services under the period of adjustment became additional expenses on the income of workers, especially the low income earning groups. For example, as a result of reduction in public health expenditure, highly recommended drugs disappeared in the clinics, hospitals and dispensaries. In some sub-sectors of the public sector like the states civil service, hardly could one find a situation where workers were reimbursed for their medical services. Reimbursements for medical expenses became very erratic as very few top civil servants were able to get their application approved (Mohammed, 1998).

Therefore, substantial amount of workers' salary was spent on medical charges, high school fees, transportation fares etc. In 1994, for example, public servants in Kano found it difficult to contain the charges imposed by the Nassarawa Specialist Hospital (now Abdullahi Wase Specialist Hospital) as hospital room charges ranged from N1200.00 to N1400:00, depending on the type of room and facilities in each room; special consultation fees, N50.00; general consultation, N3000.00; deposit on drugs, N1500.00, dressing, N100.00, to mention but a few (Nassarawa Specialist Hospital, 1994). These charges were subject to review depending on the rate of inflation in the country. The same trend was the case in highly populated cities like Lagos and Ibadan where there were high concentration of public servants.

Similarly, with the subsequent increase in the price of petroleum from N3.25 per litre to N11.00 per litre in 1994, the condition of living of workers was seriously affected. Civil/public servants who did not have personal vehicles to transport themselves from home to their places of work spent more than N1, 000.00-N2, 000.00 for transportation monthly. Workers who were fortunate enough to own personal cars before SAP found it difficult to fuel their cars to their satisfaction. Some of these workers had to either sell their cars or convert them into commercial taxis or "Kabu-Kabu". The latter, as Mustapha (1991:8) rightly pointed out, is new means of earning a social livelihood in Nigeria, fueled by crisis and adjustment, especially among the workers in the public sector. These activities were more pronounced beginning from 1989 and the early years of the1990s when, as a result of deregulatory measures introduced in the public sector, senior civil and public servants below GL.17 were asked to surrender official vehicles attached to their offices (see Editorial, Triumph. 1989.1). Also, while loans and advances were suspended, traveling allowances enjoyed by all categories of workers were reduced by 50%, and meal subsidy to officers on GL.09 and above was cancelled (Daily Times, 1989.3).

In essence, while the allowances of some public sector workers were being cancelled or reduced from time-to-time as a result of deregulatory policies of government or what the World Bank (1994.121) called "control of the payroll systems", prices of goods and service were enjoying an unstoppable increase. Since the implementation of SAP in 1986, the fuel price per liter had risen by over 400 percent; milk by 1000 percent and bus fare by 500 percent (CDHR, 1991:38). Also, tariffs on services provided by the then National Electric Power Authority (NEPA) and the Nigerian Telecommunications (NITEL) were increased by over 500 percent. With the introduction of the Second Tier Foreign Exchange Market in 1986 and later, the Foreign Exchange Market (FEM) in 1988, the value of local currency to the U.S. dollar depreciated and this systematically eroded the living standards of the middle class, to which many public servants belonged before SAP, and the poor, while it increased the riches of those engaged in the foreign exchange businesses (Adejumobi and Momoh, 1998:211).

In other highly placed agencies in the public sector like the Nigerian National Petroleum Corporation (NNPC), Central Bank of Nigeria (CBN), Nigerian National Development Company (NNDC), etc, workers enjoyed palatable reviews in their salaries and emoluments. In fact, these categories of workers in the public institutions were better off under SAP, and their standard of living was by far above that of other public servants like teachers, including university lecturers, employees of Nigerian Railway Corporation (NRC), etc. For example, the fat salary and allowances to workers in the CBN under SAP might be largely due to their role in the smooth implementation of SAP, particularly their role in the speculative exchange rate activities which made possible easy primitive accumulation of capital.

Salary differential in the public sector accentuated inequality in the distribution of income. The inequality in income confirms Thomas and Canagaraja's findings that between 1985 and 1997 the extremely poor in Nigeria became poorer, while the standard of living for other groups improved (in Ross, 3003:8). Hence, we can argue that instead of directing resources for equitable distribution of economic well being, SAP did not provide or entrench the principle of equity in the distribution of income amongst the public sector employees. Little wonder then that after one year of SAP in Nigeria, the Pay Research Unit of the Office of the Head of Civil Service of the Federation observed with dismay that the minimum wage structure of civil servants in Nigeria had become obsolete and inhuman (NLC, 1987).

Furthermore, with the implementation of Privatization and Commercialization, prices of several public services increased beyond the reach of a majority of workers, especially some section of the so-called middle-class. The class had enjoyed unstoppable high consumption habits and better living conditions in the period of oil boom. However, the period of adjustment programme changed their life styles and consumption habits. Some of them had to abandon the use of telephone lines in their houses or traveling by air as commercialization ensured an arbitrary hike in the rates and fares of these public services from 50% to 800% (Nnoli, 1993:166).

Similarly, as some of the parastatals were either fully or partially privatized, fully or partially commercialized, the number of unemployed labour in the country increased. For example, in August 1989, about 3,393 workers of the Nigerian Port Authority were sacked; and 3,000 workers from the National Electric Power Authority (NEPA) were believed to have lost their jobs (Nnoli, 1993:161). A similar trend could be found in various states in the federation as massive retrenchment in the public sector continued. This was evident in the lay off of 2,282 workers in Delta Steel and 7,000 civil servants from Edo state in 1995 (CLO,1996:166). In fact, some of the serious social problems in Nigeria in recent years like armed robbery, 419 syndicate, drug addiction, etc. may not be unconnected with retrenchment of workers. Capped with the persistent inflationary trend which stood at 8.75% at the end of 1996, the household income of both the wage and non wage earners declined and this had negatively affected the purchasing power of the ordinary Nigerian.

At another level, one of the social costs of market reform policies as contained in the Nigerian version of SAP was the strengthening of the already existing contradictions of labour relations in the public sector. This was because public sector workers, particularly those from the public corporations, were sacked for various other reasons such as merger of companies, as in the case of Nigerian National Supply Company (NNSC) or reorganization of public enterprises, as in the case of Nigeria Railways Corporation (NRC) and the Nigerian Airport Authority (NAA).With particular reference to the latter, for example, commercialization led to the retrenchment of 8,000 workers in the NRC, while 2,500 workers were retrenched in the NAA in 1988, respectively (Nnoli, 1993.163). It should be noted that the retrenchment exercise under SAP was a continuous process and its magnitude was real and apparent.

Basically, the anti-worker logic of SAP can be located within the context of bias for capital in the capitalist process of accumulation (Amale, 1991:126). The reason for labour subordination under SAP regime can be found in two ways. First, the domestic capitalist class was of the view that either through direct government legislation or the generalization of public wage awards, the state had imposed increase in wages in the private sector leading to a reduction in the profit margin of various firms (Bangura and Beckman, 1991: 142). As such, government should stop any arbitrary wage increase that would affect wage structure and industrial relations in the private sector. Second, the IMF and the World Bank, through adjustment policy, maintained that workers should be reduced to a manageable proportion because they were "too many" and "too costly" for the state to maintain (Bangura and Beckman, 1991:141). Therefore, it can be said that the combined pressure by the domestic and international agents of capital necessitated the marginalization of labour in the realm of public sector employment.

This explains why the Federal Government did not want any workers reaction to the stagnant or fixed emoluments or simply the demand by workers for better wages and salaries from the state. However, in order to keep workers under submissive control and subordination, government in Nigeria decided to weaken collective bargaining in the public sector, especially in the civil service where the emphasis in the period of SAP implementation was placed on the use of the National Public Service Negotiating Councils I, II and III system as opposed to centralized wage determination through ad-hoc commissions (Alkali, 1993:137).

Conclusion

It can be seen from the above discussion that the SAP had a double standard approach to Nigeria's public sector institutions. Indeed, with particular reference to workers in that sector of the economy, the theoretical aim of adjustment can best be described as anti-workers. More importantly, the principle of economic growth rather than redistribution had been the objective of the programme. Therefore, it is the contention of this chapter that unless relations of production which owe their dialectic motion historically are structured objectively and independent of the IMF/World Bank crisis management and economic policy (SAP), the social condition of workers cannot be improved. The Nigerian state should, as a matter of urgency, pay attention to the plight of workers and their dependents who have been forced into excruciating poverty. The state needs to understand that workers have a greater role to play in the development efforts of their country than the IMF or the World Bank. The best step to move the country beyond SAP and its manifestation since 1999 in what is called deregulation of the economy under civilian rule is further democratization of policy. This will help in the proper allocation of resources that will turn around the economy towards auto-centric development in which the input of workers is needed alongside other available resources in the country. The alternative development strategy should focus on the satisfaction of human basic needs for sustained growth and self-reliance, the empowerment of the people by access to basic factors of production, especially land and capital, creation of employment opportunities and improving the pattern of distribution of national wealth.

References

Adejumobi, S. and Momoh, A. (eds.) (1998), The Nigerian Military and the Crisis of Democratic Transition: A Case Study in the Monopoly of Power, Lagos: CLO Publication.

Aigbokhan, B.E. (2000), "Poverty, Growth and Inequality in Nigeria: A Case Study", in African Economic Research Consortium (AERC) Publication.

Alkali, R.A. (1993), "Nigeria: Federation and Wage Differentials in a Mono-Cultural Economy", Journal for Political and Economic Studies, Vol. 1, No-3.

Amale, S. (1991), "The Impact of the Structural Adjustment Programme on Nigerian Workers, in Olukoshi, A. (ed.), Crisis and Adjustment in the Nigerian Economy, Lagos: JAD Publishers.

Aremu, I. (1990), "The Structural Adjustment Programme and Nigerian Labour", in Olaniyan, C.O. et.al (eds.), Structural Adjustment in Nigeria: The Impact of SFEM on the Economy, Lagos: NIIA Press.

Bangura, Y. and Beckman, B.(1991), "African Workers and Structural Adjustment: The Nigerian case", in Ghai, D. (ed.), The IMF and the South: The Social Impact of Crisis and Adjustment. London: Zed Books Ltd.

Bangura, Y. (1987), "Crisis and Adjustment: The Experience of Nigerian Workers", Paper Presented to the Conference on Africa:The IMF and the World Bank, Organized by the Institute of African Alternatives, London, September 7-10.

Beckman, B. (1991), "The Politics of Labour and Adjustment: The Experience of the Nigerian Labour Congress". Paper presented to conference on the politics of adjustment, organized by CODESRIA, Dakar, Senegal, September 9-12.

Bellu, L. G. (2005), " Impacts of Policies on Poverty – The Definition of Poverty", in On-line Resource Material for Policy making, EASYPol , Italy: Policy Assistance Division, FAO.

Committee for the Defense of Human Rights (CDHR) (1991), Annual Report on Human Rights in Nigeria

Civil Liberties Organization (CLO), Annual Report on Human Rights in Nigeria, 1996.

Daily Times, January 26, 1989.

Elumilade, D.O. et.al (2006), "The Institutional Framework for Poverty Alleviation Programmes in Nigeria", in International Research Journal of Finance and Economics, ISSN 1450-2887 Issue 3

Green, R.H. & Faber, G.M. (1994), "The Structural Adjustment of Structural Sub-Saharan Africa, 1980-1993", Editorial of International Development Studies (IDS) Bulletin, Brighton: Institute of International Studies, Vol. 25, No. 3 July.

Harris, L. (1986), "Conceptions of the IMF's Role in Africa", in P. Lawrence (ed.) World Recession and the Food Crisis in Africa. London: James Curry.

Havnevik, J.K. (1987), "Introduction" to Seminar Proceedings No.18 Havnevik, K.J. (ed.). The IMF and the World Bank in Africa. Uppsala: Scandinavian Institute of African Alternatives.

Ihonbvere, J.O. (1991), "Structural Adjustment in Nigeria", in Turok, B (ed.), Debt and Democracy: Alternative Strategies for Africa, London: Institute of African Alternatives (IFAA)

Kusa, A.O. (1994), "The Structural Adjustment Programme of the Nigerian State", in Olukoshi, et.al (eds.), Nigeria's International Economic Relations, Lagos: NIIA Press.

Loxley, J. (1986), "IMF and World Bank Conditionality and Sub-Saharan Africa", in T. Lawrence (ed), World Rrecession and the Food Crisis in Africa. London: James Curry.

Mbanefoh, G.F. (1992), "The Public Sector and the SAP", in O.P. Adeotun & E.C. Nigeria. Ibadan: Nigerian Institute of Social and Economic Research.

Mohammed, H. (1998), "The SAP and Workers in the Public Sector: A case Study of Kano civil Servants, 1986-1994". Unpublished M.Sc. Dissertation, Department of Political Science, Bayero University, Kano.

Mustapha, A.R. (1991), "Adjustment and Multiple Modes of Social Livelihood in Nigeria", in United Nations Research Institute for Social Development (UNRISD), Discussion Paper, No 26.

Nassarawa Specialist Hospital, (1994), "New Hospital Charges", Ref. No. NSMC/SUB/155/1/72, with effect from October 1, 1994, dated September 2.

Nnoli, O. (1993), "Nigeria: The Failure of a Neo-colonial Society", in Nnoli, O. (ed.), Dead-End to Nigerian Development: An Investigation on the Social, Economic and Political Crisis in Nigeria, Oxford: CODESRIA

Nigerian Labour Congress (NLC), (1987), "Wage Freeze, freezing workers to death", in NLC Bulletin III, April 10.

Odah, J.E. (1993), " Labour Response to Structural Adjustment Programme in Nigeria", Paper presented at a Workshop on Structural Adjustment Programme and Workers' Health in Nigeria, Organized by the Department of Sociology, University of Jos, Jos April 22-24.

Olukoshi, A. (1989), "The Impact of IMF-World Bank Programme on Nigeria", in Onimode (ed.), The IMF, The World bank and the African Debt: The Economic Impact, London: Zed Books and IFAA

Olukoshi, A. (1991), "The Origins, Dimension and Consequences of the Nigerian Economic Crisis, 1982-1985", in Olukoshi, A. (ed.) Crisis and Adjustment in the Nigerian Economy, Lagos: JAD Publishers.

Olukoshi, A. and Nwoke, C.N. (1994), "The theoretical and Conceptual Underpinnings of Structural Adjustment Programmes", in Olukoshi, A.O, Olaniyan, R.O. and Aribisala, F (eds.), Structural Adjustment in West Africa, Lagos: Punmark Nigeria Ltd.

Omole, M.A.L. (1987), "The Collective Bargaining in the Public Sector', IN Otobo, D. and Omole, M. (ed.), Readings in Industrial Relations in Nigeria, Oxford: Malthouse Press

Onimode, B. (1988), A Political Economy of the African Crisis, London: Zed Books Ltd.

Osadchaya, I. (1987), "Keynesianism Today", A Critique of theory and Economic Policy, Moscow: Progress Publishers.

Ross, M.L. (2003), " Nigeria's Oil Sector and the Poor", in a paper Prepared for the U.K. Department for International Development, May 23.

Triumph Newspaper, Editorial, January 27, 1989

Toyo, E. (1990), The Impact of SFEM on the Economic Development of the Population in Town and Country", in Olaniyan, et.al (eds.), Structural Adjustment in Nigeria: The Impact of SFEM on the Economy, Lagos: NIIA Press.

Usoskin, M. (1981), "The Stability Problem: Monetarism Vs. Keynesianism", in Meleikonvasky, A.G. (ed.), Present Day Non-Marxist Political Economy" A critical Analysis, Moscow: Progress Publishers.

U.S Department of State (1998), " Nigeria: Country Report on Human Rights Practices for 1998", Released by the Bureau of Democracy, Human Rights, and Labor, January, February 26, 1999.

World Bank, (1994), Adjustment in Africa: Reforms, Results and the Road Ahead, A World bank Policy Research, New York: University Press.

CHAPTER FIFTEEN

THE MILLENNIUM DEVELOPMENT GOALS (MDGS) AND POVERTY IN NIGERIA: AN APPRAISAL

Sadiq Isah Radda

Introduction

Nigeria became politically independent on 1st October 1960. Since then, successive governments have been battling with the problem of poverty in the country. Available evidence indicates that there were numerous government programmes and policies related to poverty eradication or reduction prior to the advent of Obasanjo's second administration in Nigeria. The introduction of the Structural Adjustment Programme in Nigeria by Ibrahim Babangida's in 1986 indicated the need for safety-valves for the poor via policies and programmes that would alleviate poverty. The negative effects of structural adjustment policies on the vulnerable groups in the society were many: income inequality due to unemployment; and unequal access to food, shelter, education, health and other necessities of life.

It was the continuous deterioration in the living conditions of the people in the late 1980s that saw the emergence of poverty alleviation programmes. They included National Directorate of Employment (NDE) which consisted of four main programmes: the Vocational Skills Development Programme, the Special Public Works Programme, the Small Scale Enterprises Programme, and the Agriculture Employment Programme; the Directorate of Food, Roads and Rural Infrastructure (DFRRI), which supported a multitude of programmes targeted at rural communities, women, agricultural sector and extension services, education and vocational training, cottage industries and food processing, primary health care delivery and enlightenment/awareness and cooperatives. There was the Family Support Programme and Family Economic Advancement Programme by Maryam Babangida and Maryam Abacha respectively.

There is no gainsaying that poverty reduction is one of the most difficult challenges facing Nigeria and its people; and it is one of the major obstacles to the nation's pursuit of sustainable socio-economic growth and eventual development. This chapter attempts a critique of yet another variant of poverty reduction strategies that have implication for Nigeria. These methods are encapsulated in the much-celebrated Millennium Development Goals and the National Economic Empowerment Strategy (henceforth referred to as MDGS and NEEDS respectively).

Accordingly, the paper is divided into five sections, after this introduction. Firstly, we examine the concept of poverty. Secondly, a look at poverty-reduction methods (MDGS and NEEDS) will be done. Thirdly, a critical examination of the MDGS and NEEDS respectively will follow. Fourthly, efforts will be made to offer pathways to halt the aggravation of poverty in Nigeria; and the final section, the fifth, gives a concluding remark.

Poverty as a Social Problem

Social problems can be considered as pervasive conditions that affect and afflict a majority of the population. This notion of social problems makes the record of poverty as a social problem impeccable. According to Bradshaw (2006), regardless of how we look at the "science" of poverty, or what O' Conner calls the "knowledge of Poverty," it is essential to retain focus on the fact that the definition of poverty and the policies addressing it are all shaped by political biases and values. According to Valentine (1986), "the essence of poverty is inequality. In slightly different words, the basic meaning of poverty is relative deprivation." A social (relative) definition of poverty allows community flexibility in addressing pressing local concerns, while objective definitions allow tracking progress and comparing one area to another. In its general sense poverty refers to the lack of necessities of life: food, clothing, shelter, medical care, and security. Even though needs may be relative to what is possible and are based on social definition and past experience (Asen, 2002; Alcock), these are normally considered necessary for decent human existence based on globally shared values.

Furthermore, Aliu, (2001:14; 2002) says that poverty can be defined in absolute or relative terms. Absolute poverty is a condition where a person or group of persons are unable to satisfy their most basic and elementary requirements for human survival in terms of food, clothing, shelter, health, transport, education and recreation. Relative poverty is a comparative state of deprivation among individuals, or groups.

In Nigeria, when poverty is viewed qualitatively, it is seen to have many manifestations and dimensions: joblessness; over-indebtedness; destitution; begging; economic dependence; lack of freedom; inability to provide the basic needs of life for self and family; lack of access to land and credit; inability to save or own assets; and unforeseen generalized powerlessness. However, lack of food is the most critical angle of poverty, a reason why a popular slogan says "when hunger is excised from poverty, the burden of poverty is light" (Blakely and Bradshaw, 2002).

The description of Nigeria as a paradox by the World Bank (1996) is confirmed by events and official statistics in the country. The paradox is that the poverty level in Nigeria contradicts the country's immense wealth. Among other things, the country is enormously endowed with human, agricultural, petroleum, gas and large untapped solid mineral resources. Despite these enormous advantages, the extent of poverty in Nigeria is baffling. For example, the poverty rate in Nigeria increased from 27 percent in 1980 to 66 percent in 1996. By 1999 it was estimated that more than 70 percent of Nigerians lived in poverty. Life expectancy is a mere 54 years, and infant mortality (77 per 1,000) and maternal mortality (704 per 100,000 live births) are among the highest in the world. Unemployment, especially youth unemployment), with all its associated vices is unusually high in Nigeria.

There is an estimated 1.2 billion poor people in the world out of which over two thirds are women. In Nigeria, like in nearly all parts of the world, women are worst affected by poverty. The impact of poverty on women shows not only on material shortages but also in lack of opportunities for self-actualization in such vital fields as education, health, enjoyment of cultural, political and social rights.

Additionally, they face abject poverty with its consequences: inadequacy food, clean water, sanitation, and health care; lack of access to the critical resources of credit, land and in some cultures inheritance; denial of opportunities, choices, access to information, education, and skills; extending their working hours inordinately at home and outside; and limited decision-making both at home and in the society at large. while there is nagging poverty in Nigeria, people with disabilities are left without special consideration further exposing them to the negative impacts of poverty over and above those that are able-bodied. Disabled people in Nigeria have little or no access to health and counseling services, educational opportunities, vocational training or access to national economic resources.

It can be reasonably asserted that there are many causes of poverty that cut-across economic, social, cultural, demographic, educational and political variables. In sum, these variables exacerbate poverty in Nigeria, resulting in unequal distribution of societal resources, unfair power structures, bad governance, lack of gender empowerment, destitution and poor educational structures and opportunities.

Poverty-Reduction Methods: MDGs and NEEDS in Perspectives

In this Section, efforts are made to examine the recently-introduced and pursued poverty-reduction methods, namely, MDGS and NEEDS.

The Millennium Development Goals

The eight Millennium Development Goals (MDGs) – which range from halving extreme poverty to halting the spread of HIV/AIDS and providing universal primary education, all by the target date of 2015 – form a blueprint agreed to by all the world's countries and the entire world's leading development institutions representing efforts to meet the needs of the world's poorest. The immediate past Secretary General of the United Nations Organization says:

We will have time to reach the Millennium Development Goals – worldwide and in most, or even all, individual countries – but only if we break with business as usual. We cannot win overnight. Success will require sustained action across the entire decade between now and the deadline. It takes time to train the teachers, nurses and engineers; to build the roads, schools and hospitals; to grow the small and large businesses able to create the jobs and income needed. So we must start now. And we must more than double global development assistance over the next few years. Nothing less will help to achieve the Goals. (Former United Nations Organization Secretary General, Kofi Anan, 2006.)

The Eight Goals

The United Nations Millennium Declaration, signed in September 2000, commits the states to the following goals:

1. Eradicate Extreme Poverty and Hunger

- •Reduce by half the proportion of people living on less than one U.S. dollar a day.
- •Reduce by half the proportion of people who suffer from hunger.
- •Increase the amount of food for those who suffer from hunger.

2. Achieve Universal Primary Education

- •Ensure that all boys and girls complete a full course of primary schooling.
- •Increased enrollment must be accompanied by efforts to ensure that all children remain in school and receive a high-quality education

3. Promote Gender Equality and Empower Women

- •Eliminate gender disparity in primary and secondary education preferably by 2005, and at all levels by 2015.

4. Reduce Child Mortality

- •Reduce the mortality rate among children under five by two thirds.

5. Improve Maternal Health

- •Reduce by three quarters the maternal mortality ratio.

6. Combat HIV/AIDS, Malaria, and Other Diseases

- •Halt and begin to reverse the spread of HIV/AIDS.
- •Halt and begin to reverse the incidence of malaria and other major diseases.

7. Ensure Environmental Sustainability

•Integrate the principles of sustainable development into country policies and programmes; reverse loss of environmental resources.

•Reduce by half the proportion of people without sustainable access to safe drinking water (for more information see the entry on water supply).

•Achieve significant improvement in lives of at least 100 million slum dwellers, by 2020.

8. Develop a Global Partnership for Development

•Develop further an open trading and financial system that is rule-based, predictable and non-discriminatory, including a commitment to good governance, development and poverty reduction-nationally and internationally.

_Address the least developed countries' special needs. This includes tariff- and quota-free access for their exports; enhanced debt relief for heavily indebted poor countries; cancellation of official bilateral debt; and more generous official development assistance for countries committed to poverty reduction.

•Address the special needs of landlocked and small island developing States.

•Deal comprehensively with developing countries' debt problems through national and international measures to make debt sustainable in the long term.

•In cooperation with the developing countries, develop decent and productive work for youth.

•In cooperation with pharmaceutical companies, provide access to affordable essential drugs in developing countries.

•In cooperation with the private sector, make available the benefits of new technologies—especially information and communications technologies. (Source: Wikipedia: The Free Encyclopedia).

National Economic Empowerment Development Strategy

In 2001 the National Economic Empowerment Development Strategy (NEEDS), was introduced. NEEDS is Nigeria's current poverty reduction measure to which the international community has expressed support for being, in theory, Nigeria's home-grown programme. NEEDS recognizes that poverty has many faces requiring attack from several different directions at once. It recognizes that the government must work not only to improve incomes but to tackle the many other social and political factors that contribute to poverty. These factors are very difficult to separate and are often considered as factors that result in social exclusion. For example, a poorly educated farmer is less likely to know how to keep his family healthy and less able to find alternative employment. As a result, he is more vulnerable to external shocks, such as drought or falling market prices. NEEDS intends to empower the poor by decisively tackling social exclusion and paying particular attention to generating jobs to improve incomes, housing, health care, education, political powers and physical security.

To improve the lives of the Nigerian people, NEEDS includes plans for creating jobs, creating affordable housing, improving health care services, strengthening the skill base, protecting the vulnerable and promoting peace and security.

An Appraisal of MDGs and NEEDS

In this Section, an appraisal of the MDGS & NEEDS is done in order show the loopholes of the strategies. One can say that the two strategies share certain common loopholes: they are foreign-induced; they are based on IMF/World Bank's naïve philosophy of one-size-fits all; they are elitist in nature; they are full of high-sounding slogans that are bogus and within the realms of monotonous political rhetoric; and they are not a product of research and scientific knowledge on the peculiarities of communities, societies, cultures, religions and nations. Moreover, insistence on the fight against certain non-deadly diseases (polio) to the neglect of more deadly ones (malaria) leaves the average Nigerian suspicious of foreign-oriented and elitist packages and programmes.

In general terms, the MDGs appear bogus. They could have been categorized into four. This is because MDGs 4, 5 & 6 meant to reduce child mortality, improve maternal health, combat HIV/AIDS, malaria, and other diseases can be subsumed into one goal: Enhanced Health Services. Apart from these common loopholes, each strategy is beset with some specific problems that are examined below:

MDGS: A Critical Examination

It is commendable that in the year 2000, the world symbolically, at a special session of the United Nations Organization (UNO), in New York, agreed to an Action Plan of halving poverty by the year 2015. Unfortunately, many crucial reasons (apart from the above mentioned) are impediments to the realization of the goals of MDGs. For example, there is apparent absence of genuine and action-matched political will on the side of the Nigerian government to the realization of the goals of MDGs. Clearly, it is business-as-usual encapsulated in verbal official rhetoric by politicians. Since, 1999-to-date, there does not seem to be enough commitment by governments (at various levels) to evolve, pursue and faithfully implement policies and programmes that favour human development in Nigeria; after all, MDGs are about human development.

The stark reality is that governments (at various levels) in Nigeria have no commitment to education. This is shown in the callous proliferation of education providers at all levels in the private sector culminating in the official neglect of public schools that suffer from gross under-funding. The annual budgetary allocation by the Federal Government has been plummeting since the inception of the Obasanjo government in 1999. Hence, the attempt at providing Universal Primary Education in the face of government ineptitude and certain societal cultural factors like hawking, begging, delinquency, etc would render the MDG on Universal Primary Education illusory.

Goal eight seeks to complement other goals to realize the aspirations of the MDGs through *increased development aid.* Since many nations of the world are poor (naturally or artificially) this component of the MDGs is crucial to the actualization of other MDGs. However, there are many snags: the rich countries and other donor agencies do not give aid without very harsh conditionalities and the aid they give is grossly insufficient in tackling the poverty of the world. Furthermore, the little aid given is siphoned by Nigeria's corrupt leaders and deposited into foreign accounts in the same rich countries.

Over the years, the health sector has suffered from neglect and underfunding. This may be why Maternal and Infant Mortalities are very high in Nigeria; currently, Nigeria is ranked second highest in maternal mortality with just 2% of the world's population but accounting for 55,000 out of 500,000 maternal mortalities (Obinna, 2007:35). In an embarrassing report captioned *Nigeria's Malnourished Throng to Niger's Feeding Centers* of 13th June 2007, Foot, who is the Nigeria Programme Manager for *Save the Children,* discovered that emergency feeding centers for malnourished children in Niger Republic, the poorest country in the world, are drawing a growing number of mothers with malnourished children from oil-rich Nigeria who cross the border in search of medical help not available at home. Ben Foot said: "In Nigeria, the government health infrastructure has completely collapsed in rural areas....Even when there are drugs and equipment available people have to pay and they can't afford them" (See: www.gamji.com, June, 2007).
It is safe to assert that the Nigeria's current reality will not allow for the realization of halving Maternal Mortality. And on the HIV matter, poverty, risky sexual practices, failed social /health infrastructure, pilferage/commercialization of antiretroviral drugs coupled with international conspiracy and the political economy of the HIV/AIDS pandemic will hinder any vicious attack on the scourge of the disease.

The goal of promoting gender equality can be elusive and utopian unless an operational meaning of the term is provided. Is gender equality connoting *equality in everything* and in all spheres? If this is the connotation, then realizing this aspect of the MDG will not be feasible due to religious and cultural prescriptions and proscriptions. However, the other aspect of the MDGs that touches on women empowerment is desirable and achievable especially if we consider the contributions women make in terms of physical labour, brilliant ideas on socialization; and women are, for a fact, more accountable and better managers of resources than men

The goals of MDGs will not be realized since rich countries assist in suffocating Nigeria's evolving democracy by recognizing illegitimate political leaders that are in power through election rigging; it is these leaders that will eventually become puppets of the rich countries. Hence, the rich countries will deny Nigeria many opportunities since local leaders cannot bargain with them. For example, Nigeria is denied tariff and quota-free access for export; the country is denied technological transfer that would usher-in industrialization; the nation is enmeshed in very obfuscating debt trap that the rich countries do not want settled; and Official Development Assistance (ODA) is very *dubious* as the bulk of the money is spent abroad on officials or foreign equipment.

There is no gainsaying the fact that corruption (which is the most debilitating and lingering evil that hinders the success of any development initiative whether local or foreign) is widespread in Nigeria. To buttress this point, Nuhu Ribadu of the Economic and Financial Crimes Commission said:

> Nigerian leaders have stolen about $500 billion (N85 Trillion) within the past 40 years. This amount represented six times in financial terms that funded U.S Marshal Plan for rebuilding Europe at the end of the Second World War…the money could have recreated the beauty and glory of Western Europe six times over (quoted in Sheyin, 2007:56).

The quest for environmental sustainability in Nigeria will continue to be a mirage since there is no reliable alternative source of energy for the people; the continuous hike in the prices of petroleum products makes matters worse! Furthermore, there is insufficient government effort aimed at halting desert encroachment, erosion and indiscriminate felling of trees in Nigeria. There can *never* be sustainable development, adequate environmental resources and sustainable access to safe drinking water where the government is a disinterested party.

NEEDS: A Critical Examination

National Economic Empowerment and Development Strategy (NEEDS) like New Partnership for Development in Africa (NEPAD) is no more than a foreign concocted and imposed development strategy; its contents are not anything new to social scientists. In implementation, the programme appears to be ad-hoc in orientation with little attention paid to the policy framework. Furthermore, the programme is hamstrung by political bias, official corruption and bureaucratic bottlenecks.

Mitigatory Pathways to Poverty Reduction in Nigeria

There is no doubt that the nature and extent of poverty in countries and in the entire world have political undertones. It remains in existence and is spreading because those in power (locally and internationally) do not want it eradicated. Thus, the fight against poverty is a long term political struggle (Obadan, (2002).

To know a problem could be half the solution. From the discourse above, it is clear that certain drastic measures have to be taken to offer pathways to tackling Nigeria's devastating poverty. For example, there has to be enough political will on the part of Nigerian leaders in conjunction with their foreign counterparts to recognize poverty as a social problem that needs vicious attack beyond the rhetorical level; the civil society has to be actively involved; and the financial and technical potential of the private sector need to be humanized and mobilized for general decent living in the country. Also, there must be covert and overt fight against corruption so that resources can get to their intended targets.

Furthermore, if government policies are to be cherished, embraced and promoted, the political process has to be free, fair and credible. Where illegitimate and inept political leadership are foisted on the citizenry, there will be no goodwill, sympathy, appreciation and popular acceptance of government initiatives.

It must be understood that the West's naïve philosophy of universalism encapsulated in the dictum of 'one-size-fits all' doctrine will make some aspects of the MDGs a complete mirage due to religious and cultural considerations. For example, to suggest gender equality on inheritance, divorce, polygamy, giving witness, etc would be offensive to Moslems.

If development programmes are to be acceptable to locals, they need to be de-linked from their foreign and elitist nature in practice and not in verbal terms; or, it should be substantially home-based. Furthermore, realizing any development programme in Nigeria requires a compassionate and reasonable examination of Nigeria's debt burden. With the ever-changing and escalating debt portfolio, hard currency that would assist in actualizing the goals of the MDGs will go to debt servicing.

There is a need for heavy dosage Official Development Assistance whose utilization should be carefully monitored by the givers. Also, the bulk of the money should not be expended on foreign technical partners and expertise thereby leaving a very meager sum for the actual project. If the ODAs are to make desirable impact, they should be devoid of harsh conditionalities. Additionally, anybody concerned with eradicating poverty *must* realize the importance of technology. Therefore, countries endowed with current modern technology (not obsolete) should be able to assist in transferring such technology to Nigeria to facilitate its industrialization and eventual positive transformation.

Conclusion

The chapter dwelled on the issue of poverty eradication in Nigeria keeping in view the MDGS. Clearly, poverty is very pervasive in Nigeria, Africa and the world in general. The poverty in Nigeria is ironical given the nation's abundant human and material resources; Nigeria's is an artificial kind of poverty engendered by corruption, waste and embezzlement.

Irrespective of the source of Nigerian's poverty, it has to be fought so that there will be respite for a majority of the people. Thus, the MDGs as visualized in the year 2000 with its eight goals (which can be regrouped into four) are desirable and worthy of pursuit as they offer hope for the world community that is dominated by poor people, Nigerians inclusive.

Unfortunately, available evidence indicates that realizing the MDGs in Nigeria could be a difficult task due to many factors: lack of political will; corrupt, illegitimate and inept nature of the country's political leadership; religious and cultural barriers; foreign and elitist nature of the programmes; Nigeria's dubious debt profile/trap; very meager condition-infested foreign aid; rich countries' hoarding of technology that could promote industrialization.

References

Alcock, P. (1993), *Understanding Poverty*, London: Macmillan.

Aliu, A. (2001), (NAPEP), "Conception, Implementation, Coordination and Monitoring" NAPEP Secretariat, Abuja, April.

Aliu, A. (2002), (NAPEP), "Implementation Progress Report: Background, Structure, Achievements and Problems", NAPEP Secretariat Abuja. February.

Asen, R. (2002), *Visions of Poverty: Welfare Policy and Political Imagination,* East Lansing: Michigan State University Press.

Blakely, E.J., & Bradshaw, T.K. (2002), *Planning Local Economic Development,* Thousand Oaks: Sage

Bradshaw, T. K. (2006), *Theories of Poverty and Anti-Poverty Programs in Community-Development,* Published by Human and Community Development

Central Bank of Nigeria (CBN), (1999), *Nigeria's Development Prospects: Poverty Assessment and Alleviation Study,* By Research Department (CBN, Abuja).

FRN (2001), *National Poverty Eradication Programme (NAPEP): A Blueprint for the Schemes,* NAPEP Secretariat, Abuja, June.

National Planning Commission, (2005), *National Economic Empowerment and Development Strategy, NEEDS,* Central Bank of Nigeria (CBN), Abuja. Nigeria.

Obinna, C. (2007), "Nigeria May not Meet MDGs 4 & 5", in *Vanguard* Tuesday, June 12,

Obadan, M. I. (2002), *Poverty Reduction in Nigeria and the Way Forward*, Published by Ibadan: National Centre for Economic Management and Administration (NCEMA)

Sheyin, E. (2007), "Nigeria and the Challenges of MDGs", in *Leadership*, Sunday, January 28, 2007)

Valentine, T. (1986), *Understanding the Impacts of Poverty*, London: Macmillan.

Wikepaedia: The Free Encyclopaedia

CHAPTER SIXTEEN

POVERTY ALLEVIATION AS A MACHINERY FOR ECONOMIC
RECONSTRUCTION IN NIGERIA

Mustapha Muktar

Introduction

Poverty alleviation is one of the most difficult challenges facing any country
in the developing world where, on the average, majority of the population is
considered poor. Statistics in Nigeria show that the number of those in poverty
has continued to increase. For example the number of those in poverty increased
from 27% in 1980 to 46% in 1985 and to 67% in 1996. By 1999, the percentage of
the poor population in Nigeria increased to more than 70% (Ogwumike, 2001).
Poverty alleviation programmes in Nigeria are means through which the government aims to revamp and reconstruct the economy. The high incidence of
poverty in the country has made poverty alleviation strategies important policy
options over the years with varying results. Poverty alleviation strategies ranging from Operation Feed the Nation of 1978, the Green Revolution of 1982, the
Directorate of Foods Roads and Rural Infrastructures (DFFRI), the National Directorate for Employment (NDE), Poverty Alleviation Programme (PAP) and the
National Poverty Eradication Programme (NAPEP), were all attempts made by
various governments in the country to curb the menace.

This chapter is aimed at appraising the performance of poverty alleviation
measures undertaken within the period 1999 – 2006, specifically the Poverty Alleviation Programme (PAP) and the National Poverty Eradication Programme
(NAPEP). The next section contains the literature review and theoretical issues.
Section three appraises the poverty reduction strategies in Nigeria from 1999 to
2006 and the last section is the conclusion.

The methodology employed in this chapter is the use of secondary source of
data. Information was gathered through reports, publications, the internet and
other secondary sources of data. Specifically data were collected from the Central
Bank of Nigeria and the National Poverty Eradication Council (NAPEC). The
collected data were analyzed using simple content analysis.

Literature Review and Theoretical Issues

Concept of Poverty

There is no standard definition of poverty because of its multi-dimensional nature. Poverty is commonly defined as a situation of low income or low consumption. It can also be defined as a situation in which individuals are unable to meet the basic necessities of life such as food, clothing, shelter, education, security and health. Ajakaiye and Adeyeye (2000) conceptualize poverty as a function of education, health, child mortality and other demographic variables. Poverty to them is the availability or otherwise of the above parameters. In a nut shell poverty can be seen as a situation in which an individual is unable, because of economic, social, political and psychological incapacitation, to provide himself and his family the barest basic necessities of life.

Classification of Poverty

Poverty can be classified based on different criteria, as absolute poverty, relative poverty, rural poverty and urban poverty. Absolute poverty refers to lack of minimum physical requirements for existence; relative poverty on the other hand refers to a situation in which a persons' or households' provision of goods is lower than that of others. Rural poverty is characterized by poor material condition, low level of education, lack of infrastructure, poor health condition, underemployment, low investment and high out- migration. Urban poverty on the other hand is characterized by environmental degradation, overcrowded accommodation, low per capita income, and other problems associated with urban areas such as slums, ghettos and shanties (Galbraith, 1969; Rogers et al, 1988).

Causes and Consequences of Poverty

Obadan (1997) identified some factors as the causes of poverty among which are; inadequate access to employment opportunities, inadequate physical assets, inadequate access to markets, destruction of natural resources, lack of power to participate in the design of development programmes and inadequate access to assistance for those living at the margin of existence. On the consequences of poverty, Aku et al. (1997) opined that there is general loss of confidence in a society stricken by poverty and this renders government policies ineffective. Poverty also results in increasing the fragility and vulnerability of members of society to external influences. Furthermore, poverty makes production remain largely subsistence due to lack of capital needed for expansion. Labour becomes intensive and marginal productivity remains low.

Approaches to Poverty Alleviation

There are many approaches to poverty alleviation, some of which are:

Economic Growth Approach

Given the low labour absorption capacity of the industrial sector, broad based economic growth should be encouraged. This should focus on capital formation as it relates to capital stock, and human capital. Human capital formation has to do with education, health, nutrition and housing needs of labour. This is obvious because of the fact that investment in these aspects of human capital improves the quality of labour and, thus, its productivity. Thus to ensure growth that takes care of poverty, the share of human capital as a source of growth in output has to be accorded the rightful place.

Basic Needs Approach

This calls for the provision of basic needs such as food, shelter, water, sanitation, health care, basic education, transportation etc. Unless there is proper targeting, this approach may not directly impact on the poor because of their inherent disadvantage in terms of political power and the ability to influence the choice and location of government programmes and projects.

Rural Development Approach

This approach sees the rural sector as a unique sector in terms of poverty reduction. This is because majority of the poor in developing countries live in this sector. In addition, the level of paid employment in this sector is very low and this means that traditional measures of alleviating poverty may not easily work in the rural sector without radical changes in the assets ownership structure, credit structure, etc. Emphasis in this approach to development has focused on the Integrated Approach to rural development. This approach recognizes that poverty is multi – dimensional and therefore, requires a multi – pronged approach. The approach aims at the provision of basic necessities of life such as food, shelter, safe drinking water, education, health care, employment and income generating opportunities to the rural dwellers in general and the poor in particular. One basic problem with this approach to poverty reduction is that it is difficult to focus attention on the real poor given that poverty in the rural area is pervasive. In other words it makes targeting of poverty reduction programmes very difficult.

Target Approach

This approach favors directing poverty alleviation programmes at specific groups within the country. It includes such programmes as Social Safety Nets, Micro Credits, and School Meal programme.

Poverty Reduction Strategies in Nigeria

In Nigeria, the poverty alleviation measures implemented so far have focused more on growth, basic needs and rural development approaches. They can be looked at from two perspectives; that is those in the pre SAP era and those in the SAP era.

The Pre-SAP Era

During this era, poverty reduction was never the direct focus of development planning and management. Government only showed concern for poverty reduction indirectly. For example, the objectives of the first National Development Plan in Nigeria included the development of opportunities in health, employment and education as well as improvement of access to these opportunities. These objectives, if achieved could no doubt lead to poverty alleviation. Similarly, the Fourth National Development Plan, which appeared to be more precise in the specification of objectives that are associated with poverty reduction, emphasized increase in real income of the average citizen as well as reduction of income inequality, among other things (see Ogwumike, 1987 and 1998). During the periods of the national development plans, many of the programmes which were put in place in Nigeria by the government (either wholly or in association with international agencies) had positive effects on poverty reduction although the target populations for some of the programmes were not specified explicitly as poor people or communities (Ogwumike, 1995 and 1998). Some of such programmes are the River Basin Development Authorities (RBDA), the Agricultural Development Programmes (ADP), the Agricultural Credit Guarantee Scheme (ACGS), the Rural Electrification Scheme (RES), and the Rural Banking Programme (RBP). Most of these programmes were designed to take care of such objectives as employment generation, enhancing agricultural output and income, and stemming the tide of rural – urban migration, which no doubt affected poverty reduction.

Despite some significant degree of success made by some of these programmes, most of them could not be sustained. In fact, with time, many of them failed as a result of diversion from the original focus. For instance, the Rural Banking and the Agricultural Credit Guarantee Scheme at many stages failed to deliver the desired credit for agricultural and rural transformation because a lot of savings were mobilized in the rural areas only to be diverted to urban areas in form of credits/investments. Other notable poverty reduction related programmes that were put in place in Nigeria before the advent of the Structural Adjustment Programme (SAP) include Operation Feed the Nation (OFN) set up in 1977, Free and Compulsory primary Education (FCPE) set up also in 1977, Green Revolution established in 1980, and Low-Cost Housing Scheme. Both OFN and Green Revolution were set up to boost agricultural production and improve the general performance of the agricultural sector among other things. These programmes made some laudable impacts; they enhanced the quality of life of many Nigerians. But the programmes could not be sustained due to lack of political will and commitment, policy instability and insufficient involvement of the beneficiaries in these programmes.

The SAP Era

Conscious policy effort by government towards poverty alleviation began in Nigeria during the era of the Structural Adjustment Programme (SAP). The severe economic crisis in Nigeria in the early 1980s worsened the quality of life of most Nigerians. The government made a determined effort to check the crisis through the adoption of SAP. However, the implementation of SAP further worsened the living conditions of many Nigerians especially the poor who were the most vulnerable group. This made the government to design and implement many poverty alleviation programmes between 1986 and 1993. Also, under the guided deregulation that spanned the period 1993 to 1998, more poverty reduction programmes were put in place by government. Oladeji and Abiola (1998) identified them as: The Directorate for Foods Roads and Rural Infrastructures (DFFRI), the National Directorate for Employment (NDE), Better Life Programme (BLP), People's Bank of Nigeria (PBN), Community Banks (CB), Family Support Programme (FSP) and the Family Economic Advancement Programme (FEAP).

Theoretical issues

Most studies of poverty alleviation have adopted different theoretical underpinnings in order to find a workable solution to their subject matter. These theories include the underdevelopment/dependency theories, the vent for surplus theory, the theory of basic needs and the individual deficiencies theory. These theories were more concerned with alleviating poverty without giving due attention to its root cause. This work adopts the theory of cumulative and cyclical interdependencies as its framework because the theory looks at individuals and their community as caught in a spiral of opportunity and problems, hence individual and community resources are mutually dependent.

Cumulative and cyclical interdependencies theory originated from the works of Myrdal (1957) who coined it as "interlocking, circular, interdependence within a process of cumulative causation" Myrdal argued that personal and community well being are closely linked in a cascade of negative consequences, and that closure of a factory or other crises can lead to a cascade of personal and community problems including migration of people from a community. Thus the interdependence of factors creating poverty actually accelerates once a cycle of decline starts. For example, at the community level, a lack of employment opportunities leads to out migration, closing retail stores and declining local tax revenue which lead to deterioration of schools and lead to poorly trained workers, resulting in firms not being able to utilize technology fully, which in turn leads back to a greater lack of employment. This cycle also repeats itself at the individual level. The lack of employment leads to lack of consumption and spending due to inadequate incomes, and to in adequate savings, which means that individuals can not invest in training, and individuals also lacks the ability to invest in businesses, or to start their own businesses, which leads to lack of expansion, erosion of market and disinvestment, all of which feed back to inadequate opportunities. Health problems and the inability to afford preventive medicine, a good diet, and a healthy living environments become reasons the poor fall further behind.

The complexity of the cycle of poverty means that anti-poverty programmes or solutions need to be equally complex, since poverty is not just from one cause but many. There is the need to follow steps in order to break the cycle. The following programmes were identified by Brandshaw (2006) as cycle-breaking efforts for alleviating poverty:

- Income and economic assets.
- Education and skills.
- Housing and surrounding (safe, attractive)
- Access to health care and other needed services.
- Close personal ties, as well as network to others.
- Personal resourcefulness and leadership abilities.

A key piece of this comprehensive approach to helping individuals from poverty is that there is no way the government can do all of this for every person without first increasing social capital among communities or subcultures of the poor. Strong interpersonal ties as in villages or organized groups can provide shared assistance that professionals can not. The key is helping groups of poor people build supportive communities with shared trust and mutuality. This program consciously seeks the benefits of building social capital (following Putman 2000) based on 'affinity groups' where people share common interests from their ethnicity, religion, family history, living area, or other sources of friendship.

Poverty alleviation programmes should structure their efforts around three focal points for breaking the cycle of poverty. These programme structures, like the cyclical theory itself, combine strategies and tools from response to the other theories of poverty.

1. **Comprehensiveness.** The first strategy to breaking the cycle of poverty is to develop comprehensive programmes. Comprehensive programmes are ones that include a variety of services and that try to bridge the individual and community needs.

2. **Collaboration**. The key to executing extensive programmes without becoming too uncontrolled is collaboration among different organizations to provide complementary services so that by their combination of efforts, the output is greater than could be done by each one alone. Collaboration involves networks among participants, though the coordination can vary from formal to informal.

3. **Community Organizing.** Finally, community organizing is a tool by which local people can participate to understand how their personal lives and the community well being are intertwined. Breaking the cycle of poverty must include individuals to participate as a community in the process, just like individuals create the spiral downward when they and their community interact in a cycle of failure. For the poor, empowerment is central to this issue.

It is interesting that this is the approach to poverty alleviation that is the least commonly described in the poverty literature, but community based examples are what are brought out whenever successes are discussed. There are no comprehensive community based self-sufficiency programmes from the federal government or most states.

Appraisal of the Poverty Alleviation Programmes (1999 – 2006)

In 1999 when the Obasanjo administration came to power, it was estimated that more than 70% of Nigerians lived in poverty. That was why, in November 1999, the N470 billion Budget for the year 2000 was to relieve poverty. Before the National Assembly even passed the 2000 Budget the government got an approval to commit N10 billion to poverty alleviation programme (Ogwumike, 2001). Poverty alleviation was seen as a means through which the government could reconstruct the economy and rebuild self esteem in majority of Nigerians. Among the poverty alleviation programmes were; the launching of Universal Basic Education (UBE) Programme, the Poverty Alleviation Programme (PAP) and the National Poverty Eradication Programme (NAPEP).

The Poverty Alleviation Programme (PAP)

This programme was introduced in 2000 to address the problems of rising unemployment and crime rates especially among the youth. The primary objectives of PAP are as follows:

- Reduce the problem of unemployment and hence raise effective demand in the economy.
- Increase the productiveness of the economy and

- Drastically reduce the embarrassing crime wave in the society.

The targets/components of PAP as identified by Obadan (2001) include the following:

- Provide jobs for 200,000 unemployed,
- Create a credit delivery system from which farmers will have access to credit facilities
- Increase the adult literacy rate from 51% to 70% by 2003
- Shoot up health care delivery system from its present 40% to 70% by year 2003
- Increase the immunization of children from 40% to 100%
- Raise rural water supply from 30% to 60% and same for rural electrification.
- Embark on training and attainment of at least 60% of tertiary institutions' graduates and
- Development of simple processes and small scale industries.

Several measures were put forward in order to achieve the above objectives and they include among others; increase in the salary of public workers, rationalization of organizations and methods within the system, particularly that of the existing poverty alleviation institutions, encouraging and rewarding all deserving Nigerians for industry and enterprise, substantial reduction of avenues for easy and illegitimate acquisition of wealth and the launching of the Universal Basic Education Programme (UBEP).

Appraisal of Poverty Alleviation Programme (PAP)

Looking carefully at the objectives of PAP, one can deduce that it was designed to touch almost all aspect of poverty ranging from absolute to regional poverty. It was however more specific in curbing unemployment hence raising the income of individuals so that their spending would increase and hence their needs be satisfied. However like in most programmes, PAP was hindered by poor implementation and being short term in nature it lacked continuity. The aim of the programme was defeated as credits given to finance micro enterprises were not utilized by the beneficiaries in such enterprises meaning that the target for employment generation was missed. PAP was also perceived as initiative of the ruling party's programme and therefore was not given much attention and, in some cases, resisted by chief executives of states controlled by the opposition parties. For example, Obadan (2001) observed that in the year 2000, "there were reports that the Alliance for Democracy (AD) governors of south west zone of the country were apprehensive that the peoples Democratic Party (PDP) at the centre might have conceived of the PAP for strategic political gains. Indeed there were allegations of AD governors working against the PAP in order to frustrate the PDP federal government. Despite the problems encountered in the course of implementation of PAP, Oyiza (2003) noted that it has succeeded in providing 82,000 jobs to different kinds of people across the country.

National Poverty Eradication Programme (NAPEP)

The programme was introduced in 2001. It was aimed at the provision of "strategies for the eradication of absolute poverty in Nigeria" (FRN, 2001) It was complemented by the National Poverty Eradication Council (NAPEC) which was to coordinate the poverty reduction related activities of all the relevant Ministries, Parastatals and Agencies. The council had the mandate to ensure that the wide range of activities were centrally planned, coordinated and complement one another so that the objectives of policy continuity and sustainability were achieved. The poverty reduction related activities of the relevant institutions under NAPEP have been classified into four, namely;

- Youth Empowerment Scheme (YES) which deals with capacity acquisition, mandatory attachment, productivity improvement, credit delivery, technology and development and enterprise promotion.
- Rural Infrastructure Development Scheme (RIDS) this deals with the provision of potable and irrigation water, transport (rural and urban), rural energy and power support
- Social Welfare Service Scheme (SOWESS) this deals with special education, primary healthcare services, establishment and maintenance of recreational centers, public awareness facilities, youth and students hostels development, environmental protection facilities, food security provisions, micro and macro credits delivery, rural telecommunications facilities, provision of mass transit, and maintenance culture.
- Natural Resource Development and Conservation Scheme (NRDCS) this deals with harnessing of agricultural, water, solid mineral resources, conservation of land and space particularly for convenient and effective utilization by small scale operators and the immediate community.

Appraisal of the National Poverty Eradication Programme (NAPEP)

NAPEP was centered on youth empowerment, provision of infrastructures, social welfare scheme and natural resource development/conservation. It was however broad based and encompassing. It tried to adopt the participatory, bottom-up approach in programme implementation and monitoring. However, a critical assessment of NAPEP revealed that it concentrated more on the youth empowerment scheme (YES) neglecting the other mandates; even the YES itself focused more on the disbursement and administration of NAPEP's vehicle popularly called "KEKE NAPEP" On the issue of natural resource development and conservation scheme, Abdu (2005) observed that less than 20% of the target beneficiaries have benefited through this scheme. This means that NAPEP has not made much impact in harnessing agricultural, water and solid minerals resources and conservation efforts especially in the rural areas where the main occupation is agriculture.

It has also been observed that most of the poor people have not participated in NAPEP's programmes due to lack of access to social and economic infrastructures provided to improve human capital. By and large the local people were not included in the identification of projects meaning that the ones identified were in most cases, inappropriate and unsustainable. Abdu (2005) also observed that in most localities, the credit facilities and other infrastructures provided by NAPEP were enjoyed by members of the ruling party while those identified as opposition were denied access and did not benefit from the programme thereby remaining in poverty. To crown it all, even where the ruling party loyalist were given the credit facilities, the funds were in many cases utilized for other purposes the result of which was that, in the long run the intended beneficiaries remained poor.

One of the greatest achievements of both PAP and NAPEP was the success of the programmes in providing jobs to a number of youth across the country. Through NAPEP's Youth Empowerment Scheme, a lot of unemployed youth acquired entrepreneurial and business skills in many areas resulting in the relative increase in their income levels. The Universal Basic Education which is a strategy employed by PAP in increasing literacy rate also made an impact in many communities where classrooms were constructed and learning materials provided for the benefit of the citizens. However a lot of problems have been encountered in the process of implementing the programmes. These problems includes: lack of involvement (in most cases) of the local people in the identification of projects, administrative and operational problems and above all, the failure in the selection of the target beneficiaries due to political reasons.

Conclusion

Considering the current poverty incidence in the country, one can conclude that the past poverty alleviation programmes have not achieved much. This is perhaps due to the problems identified as hindering the effective implementation of the programmes. The objectives and mandate of both PAP and NAPEP were aimed at provision of employment and income generation through various activities; however lack of involvement of the target beneficiaries in identifying the right projects coupled with administrative and operational failures were among the problems identified as hindering the achievement of the objectives of the programmes.

There is thus the need for involvement of the local people in the identification and design of projects so that sufficient participation can be achieved. Poverty alleviation programmes should also be designed I such a way as to be sustainable and should be geared towards provision of sustainable employment so that in the long run, their impacts trickle down to the grassroots. In addition, to alleviate poverty effectively, there is the need for the government to supply necessary inputs that can improve people's livelihood, productivity and increase in their wealth (income). These inputs can be in form of fertilizers, farming machines, seeds, training programmes, skill acquisition programmes, credit facilities and others.

References

Abdu, H. (2005), "Impact of National Poverty Eradication Programme (NAPEP) on Income Changes in Rural Areas" Unpublished Seminar Paper, Abuja.

Ajaikaye, D. and Adeyeye, V.(2001), "Concepts, Measurements and Causes of Poverty", CBN Executive Seminar, Ibadan.

Aku P.S. and Oladeji, S.I.(1997),"Perspective on Poverty and Poverty Alleviation Strategies in Nigeria" NES Annual Conference.

Aliu, A.(2001),"National Poverty Eradication Programme: Completion, Implementation, Coordination and Monitoring" NAPEP Abuja.

Bradshaw, T.K. (2006), "Theories of Poverty and Anti- Poverty Programs in

Community Development" http//:www.rprconline.org/

Federal Republic of Nigeria. (2001). *A Blueprint for the Schema of National Poverty Eradication Program* (NAPEP), Abuja

Galbraith, J.K. (1969), "A Schema for Monitoring Poverty Alleviation", in *Journal of Economics and Finance* VOL 6 No2 Portland.

Myrdal, G. (1957), *Economic Theory and Underdeveloped Regions*, London Gerald Duckworth and Co.

Obadan, M.I.(1997),"Analytical Framework for Poverty Reduction: Issues of Economic Growth versus Other Strategies," NES Annual Conference.

Obadan, M.I. (2001), "Poverty Reduction in Nigeria: The way Forward" *CBN Economic and Financial Review* Vol. 39 No. 4Ogwumike, F.O. (1995), "The Effect of Micro level Government Policies on Rural Development and Poverty Alleviation in Nigeria", in Journal *Of Social Sciences*, Vol. 1 No 1

Ogwumike, F.O. (1998), "Poverty Alleviation Strategies in Nigeria", Proceedings of 7th Annual Conference of the Zonal Research Unit of CBN

Ogwumike, F.O. (2001), "An appraisal of Poverty and Poverty Reduction Strategies in Nigeria", *CBN Economic and Financial Review* Vol. 39 No. 4

Oladeji, S.I. & Abiola, A.G. (1998), "Poverty Alleviation with Growth Strategy: Prospects and Challenges in Contemporary Nigeria", in Nigerian *Journal of Economic and Social Sciences NJESS* Vol. 40 No. 1 Oyiza, M.(2003),"Poverty Alleviation Programs and Rural Development: Which Way?" Unpublished Seminar paper UNIBEN, Nigeria.

Putman, R.D. (2000), *Bowling Alone*, New York: Simon Schuster.

Rogers, E.M. (1998), Social Change in Rural Societies: An Introduction to Rural Sociology. Prentice Hall, New Jersey

CHAPTER SEVENTEEN

TOWARDS A VIABLE POLICY FOR POVERTY ALLEVIATION BY THE YEAR 2015

Emmanuel Ajayi Olofin

Introduction

One of the problems the world tackles today is poverty which has adversely affected sustainable development. As far back as 1944, the International Labour Organization (ILO) in its Philadelphia Declaration stated that "poverty constitutes a danger to prosperity everywhere" and in 2005 ILO expressed its concern on the slow progress in poverty reduction, particularly on what it called the "feminization" of poverty. Indeed, poverty is now accepted as one of the factors that encourages environmental degradation and economic deprivation (See Agenda 21 of Rio Summit). Laudable as the Millennium Development Goals' (MDGs) objectives are, without reducing (eliminating if possible) the world's level of poverty substantially, they cannot be realized. It is for this reason that poverty alleviation, reduction, or eradication programmes have been recommended for all the nations of the world, particularly in the least developed economies such as Nigeria where 70% of the inhabitants are feared to be living below the poverty threshold. However, in a similar manner that the world's numerous summits on environmental degradation have not done much to restore the environment, a number of conferences, seminars and workshops held globally, regionally, and nationally to formulate policies and establish plausible programmes for poverty alleviation have not yielded desired results.

Nigeria has not lagged far behind in addressing the issues related to poverty alleviation at conferences, seminars and workshops. It is also not short of programmes aimed at reducing the level of poverty in the country that have spanned some four decades. Such programmes have included those anchored on agriculture such as Operation Feed the Nation under the military regime of General Obasanjo in 1976, followed by the Green Revolution under the regime of Alhaji Shehu Shagari, through Back to Land and Accelerated Wheat Production Programme under General Ibrahim Babangida and a host of others to the current Cassava production initiatives. Other programmes have been anchored on financial imperatives and they include the establishment of Community Banks, Agricultural Banks, Farmers' Loan schemes, Small-Scale Enterprises Support Schemes, micro-financing to the current financial sector reforms. Other poverty alleviation programmes have been targeted at the economic empowerment of certain vulnerable groups. Among these have been Better life for Rural Women, FEAP and the contemporary NAPEP and NEEDS (with its state and local government variants).

The Problem

Notwithstanding all the conferences and seminars held and despite the programmes established to achieve poverty alleviation in the country, poverty remains virtually untouched. Even though the Central Bank governor stated that the poverty index improved from 70% of Nigerians in 1999 to 54% in 2006 (Soludo, 2007), to the ordinary Nigerian poverty has worsened over the years. These people consider indices such as the fact that over half of the graduates of the universities, polytechnics and other tertiary institutions are jobless while another quarter are not fully employed. These are in addition to school drop-outs who lose out right from the start. The result is a steep poverty gradient in the country.

Daily one encounters "scavengers" who rampage through dustbins and refuse dumps in search of anything that can help to sustain their lives. Armed bandits have multiplied in number to terrorize every locality. Members of such gangs and other frustrated and jobless youth have become easy weapons in the hands of selfish politicians and wealthy people to unleash terror on the society, including the abduction of perceived opponents considered to be obstacles to such people's success. Hardly any day passes without a newspaper report on one daring escapade of one of the bandits. The parade of members of such bandits by the Police, when caught, has become a regular show on the television during evening newscast.

It is not difficult to conclude that these problems will continue to escalate if nothing is done to empower these restless youth legitimately through effective poverty alleviation programmes and job creation schemes. So far, it does not seem that what has been undertaken to this end is achieving the desired goals. There is a need to take a hard look at what has been programmed for poverty alleviation, particularly how it has been implemented, with a view to coming up with a viable policy on the matter.

Objectives of the Chapter

The objectives of this Chapter are as follows:
(a) To review the poverty alleviation and related programmes currently in place in Nigeria, particularly NAPEP and NEEDS, highlighting their successes and failures;
(b) From the results in (a) to assess their performance vis-à-vis the set objectives and identify why the performance is what it is; and

(c) To suggest policy options that could correct errors identified and achieve the desired goals.

Methods

The methods adopted for this study consist of literature review and content analysis, laced with personal experiences and observations as well as inter-personal discussions and communication. The literature reviewed covered both local and international endeavors towards poverty alleviation, job creation and gender equal opportunities.

Review of Contemporary Poverty Alleviation Programmes and Strategies in Nigeria

As hinted above, a number of programmes and strategies came on board in the past aimed at poverty reduction. Some of these were anchored on agriculture, some on financial arrangements and others on economic empowerment. However, only the contemporary programmes are of interest in this study, particularly because it is believed that the contemporary programmes/strategies have taken the past efforts into consideration. A glance at the contemporary strategies such as the banking reforms, diversification of the economic base through emphasis on agriculture, solid mineral extraction, and tourism would reveal that they are sub-sets of two important and all embracing programmes – National Poverty Eradication Programme (NAPEP) and National Economic Empowerment Development Strategies (NEEDS) and their state and local variants. NAPEP (where 'alleviation' has virtually replaced 'eradication') provides the general policy programme while NEEDS is a set of strategies towards achieving the objectives of NAPEP. Both are aimed at enabling Nigeria to achieve the United Nations declared Millennium Development Goals (MDGs), if possible before the United Nations deadline of 2015. Consequently, only NAPEP and NEEDS are reviewed in this study.

A Brief Review of NAPEP

A World Bank report around 1999 indicated that the Nigerian Human Development Index (HDI) was 0.416 and that about 70% of the populace lived below the bread line, often considered to be below US$1.00 a day. Thus, it showed that Nigeria, though a country blessed with a lot of resources, is inhabited by very poor people. That prompted the democratizing Federal Government to set up three committees/panels charged with the harmonization of existing poverty alleviation agencies and the review of poverty alleviation programmes, including youth empowerment strategies and design a blueprint for a new poverty 'eradication' programme. One of the results of the works of these bodies is the National Poverty Eradication Programme (NAPEP) which emerged in January 2001.

NAPEP was structured to integrate four sub-programmes as follows:

- Youth Empowerment Scheme (YES) which was designed to tackle youth Capacity Acquisition Programme (CAP) through training, mandatory attachment programme (MAP) and credit delivery programme (CDP) aimed at providing micro-credit for the youth;
- Rural Infrastructure Development Scheme (RIDS) aimed at transforming the rural areas through the provision of basic amenities to curtail rural-urban migration;
- Social Welfare Services Schemes (SOWESS) geared towards the provision of social services through qualitative education programme, primary health care programme and general social services programme; and
- National Resources Development and Conservation Scheme (NRDCS) aimed at achieving participatory sustainable development through agricultural resources programme, water resources programme, solid minerals resources programme and environmental protection programme.

To harmonize and coordinate these programmes three organs of administration were set in place. The apex organ for policy formulation, supervision and coordination, monitoring and review is the National Poverty Eradication Council (NAPEC) which is placed completely within the Presidency with the President as the Chairman, the Vice President as the Vice Chairman and the Secretary to the Federal Government as the secretary. Other members include those directly in charge of coordination, monitoring and evaluation. The second organ is the National Assessment and Evaluation Committee whose chairman is the Vice president. The third organ is the National Coordination Committee with the National Coordinator as the chairman.

The main objective of NAPEP is to wipe off poverty from Nigeria by year 2010 in three stages which are specified as:

- The restoration of hope through the provision of basic necessities to particularly the rural areas;
- The restoration of economic independence and confidence;
- The creation of wealth by the citizenry.

NAPEP is funded through the Poverty Eradication Fund which is separately budgeted by the Federal Government from the Federation Account. Additionally, there are budgetary allocation by federal participating ministries and agencies, provisions by state governments, financial commitments by the private sector and donations from international donors such as the World Bank, the UNDP, European Union, German Technical Assistance, British Department of International Development, and the Japanese International Cooperation Agency.

A Brief Review of NEEDS

NEEDS is an off-shoot of NAPEP and may be considered as the instrument or strategy to direct involvement in poverty alleviation. It was launched in April 2003. Its objectives are as expected very similar to those of NAPEP. Specifically, it was aimed at value re-orientation, poverty reduction, wealth creation and employment generation. Thus, the only modification to the objectives of NAPEP is the value re-orientation because two years of NAPEP must have taught the implementers that the general attitude of Nigerians was not helpful. The foci are therefore the same as that of NAPEP. These are education, health (primary health care, HIV/AIDS eradication, malaria removal, etc), agriculture, protection of the environment, gender development, security and rule of law, infrastructure development and services and SME development. These are to be achieved through a number or reforms including public sector reform which, according to Ogheme-Omoru (2005), involved privatization and commercialization, adoption of due process and transparency in procurement, budget and planning process, service delivery and expenditure reforms. Others include financing strategies and improved tax/revenue administration.

Indeed, FGN (2005) indicates that the achievement of the national goals would depend on a sound macroeconomic framework and that NEEDS has fashioned a reform agenda that addresses such a framework with emphasis on "strengthening the macroeconomic environment and strengthening the growth agents within the system". The government's institutional (public sector) reforms embedded in NEEDS are:

- Privatization and liberalization strategies;
- Reforms and strategies to ensure good governance;
- Strategies and reforms to ensure transparency and corruption-free nation, as well as;
- Strategies to improve service delivery by government agencies, such as SERVI-COM.

Other reforms were undertaken to ensure the success of NAPEP through NEEDS/ The most spectacular are those in the Financial Sector of the economy. These include:

- Global banking strategy which eliminated the dichotomy between merchant and commercial banks;
- Bank Capital Consolidation reform that mandated banks to increase their shareholders' fund to a minimum of N25 billion by December 2005;
- The institutionalized support for a number of special banks, including the Agricultural and Rural Development Bank, the Bank of Industry, Mortgage Bank, the reactivated Community Bank and other mortgage institutions; and
- The mandated increase in the capital of insurance companies.

These reforms and others were expected to address some of the objectives and foci of NAPEP and NEEDS. Particularly, the financial reforms were expected to assist micro financing, job creation, wealth creation and a conducive macro-economic environment. The government was satisfied with itself that enough has been done to bring Nigeria out of the woods of poverty, even before the Millennium Development Goals' target of 2015. Thus, in its website, FGN (2005) indicated that:

> NEEDS also specifies private sector reforms which will address issues such as security and rule of law; infrastructure; finance; sectored strategies; privatisation and liberalisation; and trade and regional integration. It also entails a Human Development Agenda or Social Charter, which will focus on health, education, integrated rural development, housing development, employment and youth development, safety nets, as well as geopolitical balance.

> Finally, NEEDS specifies its financial and plan implementation strategies. Of course, whatever funds are spent on this programme would be money well spent. Though, NEEDS is a medium-term economic reform programme, its formulation has been made consistent with both short-term realities and long-term imperatives, that derive from the country's long-term goals of poverty reduction, wealth creation, employment generation and value reorientation.

The question now is how successful is NAPEP after six years and NEEDS after four years? This is the focus of the next section

Assessment of NAPEP, NEEDS and their Supporting Strategies

It is reported by Oghene-Omoru (2005) that NAPEP kicked off in 2001 with N6 billion which was expended as follows:

- The establishment of offices and structures in Abuja, the 36 states as well as at the 774 Local Government Areas;
- The training of 100,000 youth in skill acquisition;
- The employment of 50,000 unemployed graduates in various places of work
- The training of over 5,000 people in tailoring, fashion designing,
- The establishment of telephone in 125 local government areas;
- The delivery of 2000 units of Keke-NAPEP to some states;
- The establishment of 147 youth information centers in senatorial districts, and
- The granting of between N10, 000 and N50, 000 micro-credit to 10,000 beneficiaries, mostly women.

A search through literature has not produced a viable up-date on these figures. Indeed, the latest up date found on the FGN website (FGN 2005) on these programmes was reported to be 2005 as of May 07 2007. However, the NAPEP

(2007) updated its website up to December 2006. In that website, flurries of activities are reported at both the state and national levels in 2006 geared towards increasing the effectiveness of the NAPEP and NEEDS. At the state level, the launching of micro financing aspect of NAPEP was conducted in some states including Rivers State's N2 billion multi-partner micro-finance funds in June 2006 and the N440 million counterparts financing in Katsina State scheduled for March 31, 2007. When it is realized that micro-financing is meant to empower local entrepreneurs, a vital strategy in village-level poverty alleviation, these activities would seem to be coming too late.

At the national level, the Community Economic Sensitization Scheme (COMESS), another vital community level strategy of poverty alleviation, was receiving attention at the FCT on September 26, 2006 with a declared aim of establishing 37 Model Millennium Villages in the 36 states of the country and the FCT. The objective of the Millennium Village strategy is to provide integrated infrastructure and micro-credit support in the communities "to ensure sustainable economic activity and improved wellbeing". There is also the report of the activating of the GIVEBACK Programme with its launching in London in December 2006. The overall objective of the programme is to forge "a fruitful partnership between Nigerians in Nigeria through NAPEP and Nigerians in the Diaspora which will reduce poverty levels in the country". These are important moves, but they could have come on board much earlier.

However, the FGN operatives have claimed some other successes besides the initial take off. Such claimed successes include the improvement in communication, particularly mobile communication at various gatherings. For example, Soludo (2007) indicated that in 1999 the number of telephone lines in the country stood at 400,000; whereas there were 38 million lines by the end of 2006. The success of the banking sector and insurance companies' reforms are also usually cited. Others are the movement towards economic independence indexed by the foreign debt cancellation and settlement; the relative stability of the Naira for up to four years; the achievements of the EFCC and ICPC in exposing corrupt officials; the improved stock-exchange operations, the improvement in the agricultural sector, particularly the success of the cassava presidential initiative; the heightened investors interest in 'the Nigerian economy and a host of other claimed successes that have done the macro economy a lot of good.

Indeed, at the Economic Development Forum in May 2007 hosted by the FGN, Prof. Soludo (the Governor of the Central Bank of Nigeria) rolled out a number of economic achievements, traceable to NAPEP and NEEDS, illustrated with eye-catching graphics. Apart from the data on telephoning, he indicated that the percentage of people living below the breadline has decreased from 70% in 1999 to 54%; industrial capacity utilization has increased from 30% in 1999 to 53%; adult literacy has improved from 52% to 64% and inflation has come down considerably. Using 1985 as the base, he indicated that real minimum wage per month has increased from N464.00 in 1999 to N1, 633.00 while deficit budgeting has reduced from 6% of the GDP in 1999 to less than 1% in 2006 while the foreign reserves has jumped from just over $3 billion in 1999 through $5.9 billion in 2003 to $43 billion by the end of 2006. He also mentioned tremendous achievement in the recovery of stolen money by corrupt officials. All in all, there has been a great improvement in the macro economy. His conclusion indicated that the operators knew where the economy is and where it should be. Some progress has been made on the way to where it should be, but it is not there yet.

As if taking a cue from that concluding statement, the critics are quick to point out that these "successes", even if they are such, constitute a drop of water in the ocean of poverty that enslaves the country. At the level of inflation in the country, the workers' take-home pays are still insufficient to take them home. The macro economy may be responding well, but the micro economy is yet to pick up. Nigerian still ranks as one of the twenty poorest countries in the world and has just crawled out of the three most corrupt nations. Critics also doubt the reduction of poverty incidence to 54%, judged by the reality on the ground. Unemployment is soaring every day as more graduates and school drop outs roam the streets in search of a job that is not there.

Infrastructure development seems to have suffered the most. Power generation and distribution has taken a definite nose-drive rather than improve. Standby generators have become the main source of power supply to industries and other enterprises. Transportation, except some improvement in local air transport, has worsened. "There are no roads in this country", cried some motorists on what are expected to be priority trunk roads. And many rural areas are still cut off from communication, roads, water supply and power supply. Also the acclaimed success of the fight against corruption has only scratched the surface of that menace since corruption is still deep-rooted in the country. Indeed, the situation in Nigeria today reflects what was reported of Indonesia before the crisis that brought the country finally out of the woods thus:

> Indonesia was praised for its miraculous economic growth rates during the pre crisis period. This economic growth however, was not evenly distributed, and did not result in a full integration of the poorer members of society. Before the crisis, massive differentials still existed between the richer and poorer members of society not only in direct income terms, but also in their access to education, health-care, drinking water, transport, markets and many other basic goods and services. The crisis drastically changed the pattern of income and expenditure for many households in our country.

In summary, both NAPEP and NEEDS have failed to put expected food on the tables of the common Nigeria who are more than 70% of the over 140 million inhabitants. Even if it is only 54% that still lives from hand to mouth, this is about 76 million people living below the breadline. It is conceded that NAPEP and

NEEDS have great potentials to enable the country achieve the Millennium Development Goals, thereby reducing poverty to an acceptable level. Indeed, on paper, NAPEP driven by NEEDS seems very appropriate to tackle the problem of poverty in Nigeria. The supporting structures are also hanging well. The main problem appears to be the poor implementation of the noble ideas and technically sound strategies. There is the fear that the measures being implemented are not reaching the real targets in time and in sufficient doses due to the bottleneck created by the attitude of Nigerians and the persistent corruption that still bedevil transparency, honesty and accountability. This situation has resulted in the haves having more and the have-nots even losing the little they have. Consequently, some policy modifications are required before NAPEP and NEEDS can achieve the desired goals in Nigeria.

Suggestions Towards a Viable Alleviation Policy in Nigeria

Certain factors have been identified as militating against a successful implementation of NAPEP and NEEDS above. One of these factors has been identified as the attitude of Nigerians. This attitude affects development, even self-improvement, in a number of ways. An average Nigerian still sees any thing been handled by government as a "no-man's" matter, or at best "their thing". The fact that government is at the driving seats of NAPEP and NEEDS is unacceptable to, or unpopular with a number of people. It is this same attitude which makes any stand against the government of the day popular in Nigeria, even among the enlightened. Thus, good or bad, anything government does is wrong. There is a great need to be more vigorous in changing this attitude of Nigerians through properly focused re-orientation programmes. The problem is how to make Nigerian to believe in their government, how to inculcate the feeling of patriotism, how to make them help the country achieve greatness. It is often said that Nigerians are the worst critics of their country, and many relish this negativism. There is a need for an educational programme to start the process from the nursery through the other steps of the formal education ladder as well as informal education at the places of work.

Another attitude that needs to be corrected is the penchant of Nigerians to consider certain jobs a "no-go area". For example, once a Nigerian knows how to recite his ABC, he has nothing to do with farming anymore. This is why some of those trained as tailors, carpenters, etc, soon abandon such vocations shortly after passing out. They only value the time of training for the care and support they enjoy then. It is this attitude that aids and abets the syndrome of get-rich-quick that makes banditry a preferred alternative to honest menial job to the Nigerian youth. Yet, these Nigerian usually go out of the country to other places where they undertake to perform less attractive tasks. Proper education about this aspect is also required. Nigerians should be exposed to PhD. holders who are farmers in other countries and be shown that educated people are needed to develop the agricultural sector to its full potentiality.

Meanwhile, the private involvement in the implementation of NAPEP and NEEDS should be stepped up. Viable and trustworthy NGOs should be identified and funded for implementing the supporting strategies. For one thing, it is common complaint that the implementation of policies on poverty alleviation under government agencies have been turned into political patronage and money meant for loans to implement the micro financing strategy is often doled out as monthly allowances to party faithful (personal communication). Reliance on genuine NGOs would eliminate this type of abuse and clean the programmes of their present colour of political patronage. Indeed, poverty alleviation should be participatory and bottom-up in planning and execution. Government should be satisfied with the provision of the enabling environment.

The other factor that deserves serious frontal attack is corruption that manifests itself in many forms. The financial corruption that the EFCC is tackling is just of the many forms of corruption in the country. The introduction of SERVICOM is an attempt to correct official attitude to work. Dishonesty seems to have replaced honesty in dealings, even in such things as granting scholarships and the like. The author of this chapter was once very embarrassed as recently as 2006 when on being invited for a PDF trainees interview, his daughter wanted to know if he knew anybody who knew somebody in the presidency. Her source of worry was the information, judged reliable, that unless you had such a connection you were just going to the interview to swell the number of candidates and give the interview a stamp of transparency! Nepotism, ethnicity and other such "values" still replace merit in many transactions in the country. The re-orientation programme should address corruption in all its ramifications.

One believes that until these factors are successfully resolved, NEPEP and NEEDS would remain good programmes on paper, but would not be translated to proper poverty alleviation instruments in practice. It has been agued that poverty alleviation should be anchored on job creation. ILO (2000) asserts that:

> The four pillars of ILO's work, namely, rights to work, employment, social protection and social dialogue, are mutually enforcing in addressing poverty reduction and ILO (2000) is working to ensure that employment and decent work issues are addressed as an integral part of the economic and social analyses and policies comprised in the Poverty Reduction Strategies programme initiatives at the country level.

However, the creation of jobs that no one is really willing to take up will be counter-productive. Yet, there is a limit to the number of jobs government can create. The types of jobs government usually create are blue-collar jobs and the number that can be created is finite. Of course, with the proper orientation, sabotage-free infrastructure and economic development would be achievable all round. Industries would grow, agriculture would expand and mechanized, investment would flow in and millions of jobs would be created. Nigeria has a lot of room for such development. Too many things are imported to Nigeria today that can be produced within the country if there is the right attitude to work and the proper infrastructural support. With a less choosy attitude to types of jobs every employable hand would have something to do, and poverty would be drastically reduced if not eradicated.

Finally, since one of the important anchors of poverty alleviation in Nigeria is rural infrastructural development, in the pursuit of an appropriate strategy for effective poverty alleviation based on rural infrastructural development and job creation, the country can take some lessons from the Indonesian experience. The Indonesian government realized that:

> Different alternative options to attack poverty exist and could complement each other. One option, emphasized in this strategy paper, is to ensure that the existing and future capital investments in rural infrastructure development, investments to improve accessibility, will maximize the impact on employment creation and poverty alleviation by optimizing the use of local resources including labour in the planning, design, implementation and maintenance of the rural infrastructure works (MPAS, undated).

Indonesian's experience in different parts of the country confirmed that the provision of the infrastructure itself is necessary but not sufficient to achieve the goal of reducing poverty. It was discovered that making use of the resources or assets that rural communities have-physical, capital, institutional, technical-coupled with a process that gives them some ownership of the facilities provided resulted in a high potential for success. The country also found that the decentralization of responsibilities and authority was essential for local decision making and the development of good governance. Consequently, it planned to decentralize responsibilities for rural infrastructure development to the local governments, a strategy it believed presented an excellent opportunity to increasingly rely on local resources in its efforts to attack poverty and create jobs. To this end, the country, in mainstreaming its poverty alleviation through sustainable rural infrastructure development, opted for four strategic instruments as follows:

- *Labour-based technology* in which the use of labour, supported by light equipment, is equally or more efficient and socially desirable than the use of machines alone and which was believed would increase the flow of money through rural economies, often a pre-condition for diversifying their livelihood activities. Indeed, using labour-based technology was seen as capable of creating additional jobs and generate income as well as increasing demand for locally made products which in turn could create more indirect employment.
- *Small contracting development* that concentrated on the production of appropriate contract documentation, the training of local contractors, and establishing an effi-

cient contract administration capacity in local government agencies, while the government provided an enabling environment.

- *Rural Infrastructure Maintenance Systems* which is partly based on local participation during planning and implementation, using local resources for maintaining local infrastructure as a key factor in providing sustainable access in rural areas.
- *Rural Access Planning* which is concerned with improving levels of accessibility in rural areas and comprises a set of planning procedures that look at access, transport and mobility from a broader perspective. And promotes community participation and the optimum use of local resources including labour.

From this review, it is clear that the Indonesian poverty alleviation approach is participatory in formulation, planning and execution. The most important contribution of government is the provision of enabling environment and the facilitation of appropriate funds. The same experience has also been discussed in the alleviation of poverty among the urban dwellers in India in its Basic Urban Services for the Poor (UBSP) where: "the community organizational system is what makes UBSP a unique government effort for facilitating people's participation, beginning in urban poor neighborhoods".

The day-to-day development and maintenance of impacting schemes and programmes are largely left in the hands of the private sector, particularly the rural populace in the Indonesian case. This underlines the point made earlier on a deliberate participatory approach to the implementation of NAPEP and NEEDS if they are to achieve the desired goals.

Conclusion

The provisions of NAPEP and NEEDS are believed to be appropriate for a successful fight against poverty in Nigeria. The supporting instruments and reforms are also believed to be steps in the right direction. However, a review of the performance of these programmes and strategies indicates that not much success has been achieved in the alleviation of poverty in the country. The problem has been traced to faulty implementation of the programmes and strategies which in itself is the result of some faults in the Nigerian society such as the negative attitude of Nigerians to government-sponsored projects and their choosy disposition to jobs. The other factor is corruption in all its ramifications that still plagues the country. These negative factors must be attacked squarely and put at rest before NAPEP and NEEDS can make any headway in the alleviation of poverty in this country. Meanwhile, it is recommended that government should be seen less in the implementation of poverty alleviation strategies while focused education should be geared towards the re-orientation of Nigerians. The private sector should be involved in a clear bottom-up approach, taking a deep lesson from the Indonesian and Indian experiences.

References

Federal Government of Nigeria – FGN (2005), NEEDS, http://www.nigeria.gov.ng/NR/exeres/176145DB-FAE6-4231-AA6D-473ED89D611A.htm

NAPEP (2007), NAPEP News, http://napep.gov.ng/news.php?id=2

Oghene-Omoru, O. L. (2005), Recent National Economic Reforms and their Relevance to the Delta State Civil Service, paper delivered at the Year 2005 Civil Service Lecture Day, Government House, Asaba, July 2005.

International Labour Organization, ILO (2000), **The ILO and Poverty Reduction Strategies (PRSPs),** http://www.ilo.org/public/english/comp/poverty/mandate.htm

Mainstreaming Poverty Alleviation Strategies through Sustainable Rural InfrastructureDevelopment, http://www.iloasist.org/Downloads/INDONESIA%20STRATEGY.PDF.

Poverty Alleviation through Community Participation – UBSP India, http://www.unesco.org/most/asia12.htm

Soludo, C. (2007), Brief on the Economy, PowerPoint Presentation at the May National Economic Development Forum, NTA Live Coverage

Thapa, G. (2004), Rural Poverty Reduction Strategy for South Asia, Paper Presented at an International Conference on 10 Years of Australian South Asia Research Centre, http://rspas.anu.edu.au/papers/asarc/2004_06.pdf

SELECTED BIBLIOGRAPHY

Abba, A. et al. (1985), *The Nigerian Economic Crisis: Causes and Solutions,* ASSU, Zaria: Gaskiya Corporation Ltd.

Abdulkadir, A. (2001), "Government and Food Distribution in Zaria: 1902-1966" in *FAISJournal of Humanities.* Vol. 1, No. 4

Abdulkadir, M.S. (2005), "Changing World Economy, Economic/Religious Problems and Immigration in Nigeria" in Rimmington, G (ed.) *Empire and Inter-Dependence: AMulti-Disciplinary Conference on the Post-Cold War World ,* Wichita – Kansas: Friends University.

Abdulkadir, M.S.(2004), *Structuring, Struggling and Surviving Economic Depression in Northern Nigeria: The 1930s as Preview of the Present* (Kano: Bayero University) Inaugural Lecture Series. No. 9.

Abubakar, G.A.(2002), "Poverty Alleviation and Direct Job Creation in Nigeria" in Jega, A.M and Wakili, H (eds.) *The Poverty Eradication in Nigeria: Problems and Prospects,* Kano: Mambayya House.

Abubakar, M.M. (1989), *A Neglected Nigerian Export Crop, The Growth of Ginger Production and Trade in Kachia District of Southern Zaria: c.1900-1953.* M.A.History, History Department, Ahmadu Bello University, Zaria.

Achor, U. (2001), "Managing the Environment in Popular Neighborhoods" A Manual for Action, Lagos: Shelter Right Initiative.

Adi, A.B.C (2006), "The Moral Economy and the Possibility of Accumulation in Africa: How the IFIS can help to West Africa", in *Review,* Vol.5.

Agbebiyi, H.A. (2000), "Poverty Alleviation: Channel NYSC into Food Production", *The Nigerian Accountant,* Official Journal of the Institute of Chartered Accountants of Nigeria (ICAN), Vol.33, No.3

Aigbokhan, B.E. (2000), "Poverty, Growth and Inequality in Nigeria: A Case Study", in *African Economic Research Consortium (AERC)* Publication,

Ajakaiye, O. (2002), "An Overview of the Current Poverty Eradication Programme in Nigeria", in A.M. Jega and H. Wakili (eds.), *The Poverty Eradication Programme in Nigeria: Problems and Prospects,* Kano Benchmark publishers Limited

Albert,I.O. (1999), "Ethnic and Religious Conflicts in Kano" in Otite, O. and Albert, I.O.(eds.) *Community Conflicts In Nigeria: Management, Resolution and Transformation* Ibadan, Spectrum Books Limited

Alayande, B. and Alayande, O. (2004), "A Quantitative and Qualitative Vulnerability of Poverty in Nigeria." *Paper* presented on CSAE Poverty Reduction Conference, Growth and Human Development in Africa, March, 2004.

Ali-Akpajiak and Pyke (2005), *Measuring Poverty in Nigeria:* Oxfam Report 2005

Aliu, A. (2001), (NAPEP), "Conception, Implementation, Coordination and Monitoring" NAPEP Secretariat, Abuja, April.

Aliu, A.(2001),"National Poverty Eradication Programme: Completion, Implementation, Coordination and Monitoring" NAPEP Abuja.

Alkali, R.A. (1993), "Nigeria: Federation and Wage Differentials in a Mono-Cultural Economy", *Journal for Political and Economic Studies,* Vol. 1, No-3.

Al-Sawy, S. (2002), *Post September 11 American's Questions about Islam* Egypt: Umm Al-Qura

Anyanwu, E. (1997), "Poverty in Nigeria: Concepts and Measurement and Determinants", In *Poverty Alleviation in Nigeria*. Proceedings of the 1997 Annual Conference of the Nigerian Economic Society.

Amaeshi, K. et. al (2006), "Corporate Social Responsibility in Nigeria: Western Mimicry or indigenous practice", @ http://www.nottingham.ac.uk/business/ICCSR

Amale, S. (1991), "The Impact of the Structural Adjustment Programme on Nigerian Workers, in Olukoshi, A. (ed.), *Crisis and Adjustment in the Nigerian Economy*, Lagos: JAD Publishers

Aremu, I. (1990), "The Structural Adjustment Programme and Nigerian Labour", in Olaniyan, C.O. et.al (eds.), *Structural Adjustment in Nigeria: The Impact of SFEM on the Economy*, Lagos: NIIA Press

Arinze, A.I. (1995), "Review of the 1994 Human Development Report: UNDP" in CBN EFR, Vol. 33, No. 1, MARCH.

Aston-Jones, N. (1998), *The Human Ecosystems of the Niger-Delta:* ERA Handbook, Benin City: ERA, 1998

Ayeni, F. (2002),"Stimulating Economic Growth Through Entrepreneurship", paper presented at the 34th Annual Accountants Conference of ICAN, Sheraton Hotel & Towers, Abuja, October.

Bangura, Y. (1987), "Crisis and Adjustment: The Experience of Nigerian Workers", *Paper* Presented to the Conference on Africa: The IMF and the World Bank, Organized by the Institute of African Alternatives, London, September 7-10.

Bangura, Y. and Beckman, B.(1991), "African Workers and Structural Adjustment: The Nigerian case", in Ghai, D. (ed.), *The IMF and the South: The Social Impact of Crisis and Adjustment.* London: Zed Books Ltd.

Bashir, I. (2005), In Search of Peace in the Heart of Nigeria: A Political Economy Analysis in Bobboyi, H. and Yakubu, A.M. (eds, *Peace Building and Conflict Resolution in Northern Nigeria*, Kaduna, Arewa House

Butler, K. (2007), "Portraying Poverty in the News" a paper on http://mainstream Journalism.suite 101.com/article.cfm/

Beckman, B. (1991), "The Politics of Labour and Adjustment: The Experience of the Nigerian Labour Congress". *Paper* presented to conference on the politics of adjustment, organized by CODESRIA, Dakar, Senegal, September 9-12.

Bellu, L. G. (2005), " Impacts of Policies on Poverty – The Definition of Poverty", in On-line Resource Material for Policy making, *EASYPol* , Italy: Policy Assistance Division, FA.

Boserup, E. (1981), *Population and Technology:* Oxford: Blackwell.

Boserup, E. (1995), *The Conditions of Agricultural Growth.* London: Allen and Unwin.

Bradshaw, T.K. (2006), "Theories of Poverty and Anti- Poverty Programs in Community Development" http//:www.rprconline.org/

Butler, K. (2007), "Portraying Poverty in the News" a paper on http://mainstream Journalism.suite 101.com/article.cfm/

Bureau of African Affairs [BAA] (2007), Background Note: Nigeria, U.S. State Department,　　　Bureau of Public Affairs, Electronic Information and Publications Office,http://www.state.gov/

Blackwood, D.L. and R.G. Lynch (1994), "The Measurement of Inequality and Poverty: A Policymaker's Guide to the Literature", *World Development*, 2 (5).

Bradshaw, T.K. (2006), "Theories of Poverty and Anti- Poverty Programs in Community Development" http//:www.rprconline.org/

Blomstrom, Magnus, and Ari Kokko (1996) "The Impact of Foreign Investment on Host Countries: A Review of the Empirical Evidence." *Policy Research Working Paper 1745.* Washington DC: World Bank.

Borenzstein, Eduardo, Jose De Gregorio, and Jong-Wha Lee (1998) "How Does Foreign Direct Investment Affect Economic Growth?", *Journal of International Economics.* 45

Baron D.P (1995), " Integrated Strategy: Market and non Market Components", in *California Management Review*, 37(2)

Brautigam, D. (1997), "Substituting for the State; Institutions and Industrial Development in Eastern Nigeria", in *World Development,* 25(7).

Canagarajah, S. (undated), Poverty and Welfare in Nigeria, Washington, D.C: American　　　Writing Corporation,

Centre for African Settlement Studies and Development (CASSAD, (undated), "Poverty Eradication Programmes in Nigeria", Being A Conference paper Presented at The Third Conference of the International Forum on Urban Poverty Yamoussoukro, Cote D'Ivoire Cassad@infoweb.abs.net

Christiaensen, L., L. Demery, and S. Paternostro (2003), "Macro and Micro Perspectives of Growth and Poverty in Africa", *World Bank Economic Review,* 17.

Cornia, G. and Danziger, S. (1997a) *Child Poverty and Deprivation in the Industrialized Countries, 1945–1995,* Clarendon Press, Oxford.

Committee for the Defense of Human Rights (CDHR) (1991), *Annual Report on Human Rights in Nigeria*

Civil Liberties Organization (CLO) (1996), *Annual Report on Human rights in Nigeria.*

Christian Aid (2004), "Behind the Mask: The Real Face of Corporate Social Responsibility"@ id.org.uk/indepth/040.csr/index.ltm.

Chambers, R. and Conway, G.R. (1992), "Sustainable Rural Livelihoods: Practical Concepts for the 21st Century", *Institute of Development Studies (IDS) Discussion Paper* No. 296, University of Sussex, Brighton: IDS.

Crocker, W.R. (1936), *Nigeria: A Critique of British Colonial Administration,* London: George Allen and Unwin.

Crowder, M.(1968) *West Africa Under Colonial Rule,* London: Hutchinson

DFID, (2006), *Nigeria Competitiveness and Growth, Poverty Reduction and Economic Management 3*, Country Department 12, Africa Region, *Report* No. 36483 – NG.

Dobmeyer, D. (1995) "20 Steps to Improving Media Coverage of Poverty Issues", A Paper developed for Chicago Community, USA

Dollar, D., and A. Kraay, (2002), "Growth is Good for the Poor"; *Journal of Economic Growth,* Vol. 7,

Dudley, B. J. (1975), "Power and Poverty" in *Poverty in Nigeria*. Proceedings of the 1975 Annual Conference of the Nigerian Economic Society.

Dobmeyer, D. (1995) "20 Steps to Improving Media Coverage of Poverty Issues", Paper developed for Chicago Community, US

D'Silva, E. and Bysouth, K. (1992), "Poverty Alleviation Through Agricultural Projects", in *Economic Development Institute of the World Bank*, Policy Seminar Report, No. 30.

Echemeri, R. N. (1997), "The Structure of income, inequality and poverty in Rural Southeastern Nigeria." Proceedings of the 1997 Annual Conference of the Nigerian Economic Society.

Ehrlich, P. (1968), *The Population Bomb*, New York: Ballantine.

Egwuatu, B. (2002), "Strategies Towards Strengthening the Poverty Eradication Programme in Nigeria", in A.M. Jega and H. Wakili (eds.) *The Poverty Eradication Programme in Nigeria: Problems and Prospects,* Kano: Benchmark publishers limited.

Elumilade, D.O. et al (2006), "The Institutional Framework for Poverty Alleviation Programmes in Nigeria", in *International Research Journal of Finance and Economics,* ISSN 1450-2887 Issue 3.

Evbuomwan, G.O. (1997), "Poverty Alleviation Through Agricultural Project: A Review of the Concept of the World Bank Assisted Agricultural Development Projects in Nigeria", in *Bullion*, a publication of CBN Vol. 21, No. 3, July/Sept,

Federal Republic of Nigeria., (2001). *A Blueprint for the Schema of National Poverty Eradication Program* (NAPEP), Abuja.

Federal Office of Statistics, (2005), *The Nigerian Statistical Fact Sheets on Economic and Social Development,* Abuja and Lagos.

Federal Office of Statistics, (2005), *Draft Poverty Profile for Nigeria*, Abuja and Lagos.

Federal Office of Statistics (2006), *"Core Welfare Indicators Questionnaire , A survey:"* www.nigerianstat.gov.ng/index.php

Friedman, T.L. (2005), The *World is Flat,* New York: Farrar, Straus & Giroux.

Fwatshak, S. U. (2003), "Globalization and Economic Development in Nigeria: the Challenges of poverty reduction through E-commerce", in Maduagu, M.O & Onu, V.C.(eds.), *Globalisation and National Development in Nigeria,* a publication   of Fulbright Association of Nigeria

FGN (2000), *Draft National Policy on Poverty Eradication,* ABUJA: Federal Government of Nigeria.

FGN (2001) *National Poverty Eradication Programme (NAPEP)* ABUJA: Federal Government of Nigeria (FGN).

Forsyth, J. (2000) *Letter to 'The Economist',* Oxfam Policy Director, June 20.

FOS (1999), *Poverty Profile for Nigeria 1986-1999*, FOS, Lagos

Foster, J. J. Greer and Thorbecke, E. (1984), "A Class of Decomposable Poverty Measures", *Econometrica,* 52(3)

Global Monitoring Report (2004), "Policies and Actions for Achieving the Millennium Development Goals (MDGs) and Related Outcomes", Washington, D.C: World Bank

Galbraith, J.K. (1969), "A Schema for Monitoring Poverty Alleviation", in *Journal of Economics and Finance* VOL 6 No2 Portland.

Green, R.H. & Faber, G.M. (1994), "The Structural Adjustment of Structural Sub-Saharan Africa, 1980-1993", *Editorial of International Development Studies (IDS)* Bulletin, Brighton: Institute of International Studies, Vol. 25, No. 3 July.

Harrison, G.W., Rutherford, T.F., Tarr, D.G. and Gurgel, A. (2004), 'Trade Policy and Poverty Reduction in Brazil', *the World Bank Economic Review*, Vol. 18, No.3

Harris, L. (1986), "Conceptions of the IMF's Role in Africa", in P. Lawrence (ed.) *World Recession and the Food Crisis in Africa*. London: James Curry.

Havnevik, J.K. (1987), "Introduction" to Seminar Proceedings No.18 Havnevik, K.J. (ed.). *The IMF and the World Bank in Africa*. Uppsala: Scandinavian Institute of African Alternatives.

Howard White, H., L. Jennifer and Andrew, M. (2003),"Comparative Perspectives on Child Poverty: A Review of Poverty Measures", *Journal of Human Development*, Vol. 4, No. 3, November.

Hirsch, A. (2005), *Season of Hope: Economic Reform Under Mandele and Mbaki*, Scottsville: University of Kwazulu –Natal press.

Ibrahim, F.O. (2003), "Poverty and Local Government Performance in Nigeria" in Dalhatu, S. and Umar M.A. (eds.), *Towards Improved Local Government Management*, Kano Munawar Books.

Ibrahim, F.O. (2004), "State, Religion and Federalism within the context of Nigeria: A case study of the 2001 ethno-religious crisis in Kano State", Msc. *Thesis* Submitted to The Department of Political Science, Bayero University, Kano

IMF, (2005), *Nigeria: 2005 Article IV Consultation* – Staff report; Staff Supplement; and Public Information Notice on the Executive Board Discussion, IMF Country Report No. 05/302.

Ihonvbere, J.O. (1991), "Structural Adjustment in Nigeria", in Turok, B (ed.), *Debt and Democracy: Alternative Strategies for Africa*, London: Institute of African Alternatives (IFAA).

Jalingo,U A (2001) ,"Poverty And Poverty Alleviation in Kano State: Some Preliminary Observations", in *ECPER Journal of Political and Economic Studies*, Kaduna: Emwai Centre For Political and Economic Research

Jega, A. (2004), "Democracy, Economic Crisis and Conflicts: A Review of the Nigerian Situation", in *The Quarterly Journal of Administration* Vol. XXXII, No.1 March 2004 Ile-Ife; Obafemi Awolowo University

Jones, D. R. (2004) "How the News Media Covers Poverty", *Urban Agenda Index*

Jung, Hong-Sang, and Erik Thorbecke (2001), The Impact of Public Education Expenditure on Human Capital, Growth, and Poverty in Tanzania and Zambia: A General Equilibrium Approach. Working Paper No. 01/106, International Monetary Fund (September).

Joshua, S. (2007), "Nigeria's Many Fight Against Poverty", in *Empowerment News*, a publication of LEEMP, Vol. 1, No. 1, May.

Kanbur, R. (2003), *Q-squared: Qualitative and Quantitative Methods of Poverty Appraisal*. New Delhi: Permanent Black

Kapteyn, A., P. Kooreman and Willemse, R. (1988), "Some Methodological Issues in the

Implementation of Subjective Poverty Definitions." *Journal of Human Resources*,

Khan, H. A. (1999), "Sectoral Growth and Poverty: a multiplier decomposition analysis

for South Africa, *World Development*, March.

Khan, H. A. (2004), Using Macroeconomic Computable General Equilibrium Models for Assessing Poverty Impact of Structural Adjustment Policies, ADB Institute Discussion, July, Paper No.12.

Loxley, J. (1986), "IMF and World Bank Conditionality and Sub-Saharan Africa", in T. Lawrence (ed), *World Recession and the Food Crisis in Africa*. London: James Curry.

Maduagwu, A. (Undated), "Alleviating Poverty in Nigeria", in Anthony Maduagwu's Forthcoming book: *Growing Up in Oguta: The Economics of Rural Poverty in Nigeria* "Please send comments to amaduagwu@hotmail.com"

Maduagwu, A. (2000), 'Alleviating poverty in Nigeria', *Africa Economic   Analysis*.

Malthus, T. R. (1798), "Essay on the Principles of Population, As It Affects the Future Improvement of Society with Remarks on the Speculation of Mr. Godwin, M.Conduced, and Other Writers, Penguin Classics (ed). (Hammondsport, 1982).

Mujeri, M. K. and Khandaker, B. H. (1998), Impact of Macroeconomic Policy Reforms in Bangladesh: A General Equilibrium Framework for Analysis. Paper presented at the Micro Impacts of Macroeconomic and Adjustment Policies (MIMAP), Third Annual Meeting, November 2-6, Kathmandu, Nepal.

Mbanefoh, G.F. (1992), "The Public Sector and the SAP", in O.P. Adeotun & E.C. Nigeria. Ibadan: *Nigerian Institute of Social and Economic Research.*

Mohammed, H. (1998), "The SAP and Workers in the Public Sector: A case Study of Kano civil Servants, 1986-1994". Unpublished M.Sc. Dissertation, Department of Political Science, Bayero University, Kano.

Mustapha, A.R. (1991), "Adjustment and Multiple Modes of Social Livelihood in Nigeria", in United Nations Research Institute for Social Development (UNRISD), Discussion Paper, No 26.

Myrdal, G. (1957), *Economic Theory and Underdeveloped Regions,* London: Gerald Duckworth & Co.

NEEDS, (2005), National Economic Empowerment and Development Strategy, Abuja: Central Bank of Nigeria CBN).

Nnoli, O. (1993), "Nigeria: The Failure of a Neo-colonial Society", in Nnoli, O. (ed.), *Dead-End to Nigerian Development: An Investigation on the Social, Economic and Political Crisis in Nigeria*, Oxford: CODESRIA

Nigerian Labour Congress (NLC), (1987), "Wage Freeze, freezing Workers to Death", in NLC *Bulletin* III, April 10,

Nissanke and Thorbecke (2007), "Linking Globalization to Poverty", *Policy Brief,* United Nations University-World Institute for Development Economic Research No.2,

Nwaobi , G. C. (Undated), "Solving the Poverty Crisis in Nigeria: An Applied General Equilibrium Approach", Department Of Economics, University Of Abuja, Nigeria

Obadan, M.I. (1997),"Analytical Framework for Poverty Reduction: Issues of Economic Growth Versus Other Strategies," NES Annual Conference.

Obadan, M.I. (2001), "Poverty Reduction in Nigeria: The way Forward" *CBN Economic and Financial Review* Vol. 39 No. 4

Odah, J.E. (1993), " Labour Response to Structural Adjustment Programme in Nigeria", Paper presented at a *Workshop* on Structural Adjustment Programme and Workers' Health in Nigeria, Organized by the Department of Sociology, University of Jos, Jos April 22-24

Odusola, F. A. (1997) Poverty in Nigeria, An Eclectic Appraisal, in National *Conference Proceedings* Organized by the Nigerian Economic Society (NES) on Poverty Alleviation in Nigeria, Chapter 7.

Ogwumike, F. O. (1991), "A Basic Needs Oriented Approach to the Measurement of Poverty in Nigeria", in *Nigerian Journal of Social and Economic Studies (NJESS)*, Vol. 33 No. 2.

Ogwumike, F. O. & D. B. Ekpenyong, (1996), "Impact of Structural Adjustment Programme on Policies on Poverty in Nigeria", *Research Report* Submitted to Africa Economic Research Consortium (AERC), Nairobi

Olukoshi, A. (1989), "The Impact of IMF-World Bank Programme on Nigeria", in Onimode (ed.), *The IMF, The World Bank and the African Debt: The Economic Impact*, London: Zed Books and IFAA

Olukoshi, A. (1991), "The Origins, Dimension and Consequences of the Nigerian Economic Crisis, 1982-1985", in Olukoshi, A. (ed.) *Crisis and Adjustment in the Nigerian Economy*, Lagos: JAD Publishers

Olukoshi, A. and Nwoke, C.N. (1994), "The theoretical and Conceptual Underpinnings of Structural Adjustment Programmes", in Olukoshi, A.O, Olaniyan, R.O. and Aribisala, F (eds.), *Structural Adjustment in West Africa*, Lagos: Punmark Nigeria Ltd.

Onimode, B. (1988), *A Political Economy of the African Crisis*, London: Zed Books Ltd.

Osadchaya, I. (1987), "Keynesianism Today", *A Critique of Theory and Economic Policy*, Moscow: Progress Publishers

Ogwumike, F.O. (1995), "The Effect of Micro level Government Policies on Rural Development and Poverty Alleviation in Nigeria", in *Journal Of Social Sciences*, Vol. 1 No 1

Ogwumike, F.O. (1998), "Poverty Alleviation Strategies in Nigeria", Proceedings of the 7th Annual Conference of the Zonal Research Unit of CBN

Ogwumike, F.O. (2001), "An appraisal of Poverty and Poverty Reduction Strategies in Nigeria", *CBN Economic and Financial Review* Vol. 39 No. 4

Oladeji, S.I. & Abiola, A.G. (1998), "Poverty Alleviation with Growth Strategy : Prospects and Challenges in Contemporary Nigeria", in *Nigerian Journal of Economic and Social Sciences NJESS* Vol. 40 No. 1

Oyiza, M.(2003),"Poverty Alleviation Programs and Rural Development: Which Way?" Unpublished Seminar paper UNIBEN, Nigeria.

Olaniyan, O. (2000), *The Role of Household Endowments in Determining Poverty in Nigeria, Department of Economics,* University of Ibadan, Nigeria

Onah, F. E. (1996), Post Adjustment Policies Towards Poverty Alleviation in Nigeria, *Nigerian Journal of Social and Economic Studies (NJESS)*, Vol. 38 No. 1, 2, 3.

Osunubi, T.S (2003): "Urban Poverty in Nigeria: A case of Agege Area of Lagos State", Nigeria, Unpublished field Work

Putman, R.D. (2000), *Bowling Alone*. New York: Simon Schuster.

Paudel, L. (2004), "Analysis of the Relationship Between Poverty and Income Inequality", An Unpublished M.Sc. Thesis Submitted in partial fulfillment of the requirements for the Degree of Master of Science in the Department of Agribusiness, School of Graduate Studies Alabama A & M University.

Perotti, R. (1993). "Political Equilibrium, Income Distribution and Growth," *Review of Economic Studies*, 60,

Rogers, E.M. (1998), *Social Change in Rural Societies: An Introduction To Rural Sociology*. Prentice Hall, New Jersey

Ravallion, M. (1994), "Poverty Comparisons Chur, Switzerland", in *Fundamentals of Pure Applied Economic*, Hardwood Academic Press. Volume 56

Rein, M. (1970), "Problems in the Definition and Measurement of Poverty", in Romer, P. (ed.) *Advanced Macroeconomics.*, New York: McGraw-Hill.

Rodrik, D. (1998), "Where did all the Growth Go? External Shocks, Social Conflict, and Growth Collapse." John F. Kennedy School of Government, Harvard University, Memo.

Rowntree, P. B. S. (1901), *Poverty-A Study of Town Life*. London: Macmillan.

Ross, M.L. (2003), "Nigeria's Oil Sector and the Poor", in a paper Prepared for the U.K. Department for International Development, May 23

Sachs, J.D. (2005), *The End of Poverty: How can we make it Happen in our Life time,* London: Penguin Books

Sala-i-Martin, X. (2001), "The Disturbing "Rise" of Global Income Inequality", Retrieved from http://www.columbia.edu/

Sala-i-Martin, X. (2002), 'The World Distribution of Income (Estimated from Individual Country Distributions)". NBER Working Paper 8933, Cambridge MA (May).

Sala-i-Martin, X. (2007), "Global Inequality Fades as the Global Economy Growth", in *Index of Economic Freedom*.

Scitovsky, T. (1978), *The Joyless Economy*. Oxford: Oxford University Press.

Shane, M. and Roe, T. (2004), *Overcoming Food Insecurity: A CGE Analysis*, Economic Research Service and University of Minnesota, Washington, DC and St. Paul, Minnesota.

Sirageldin, I. (2000), *Elimination of Poverty: Challenges and Islamic Strategies,* The John Hopkins University.

Sen, A. (1985), *Commodities and Capabilities* Amsterdam: North-Holland.

Sen, A. (1987), *The Standard of Living*. Cambridge University Press.

Sen, A. (1990), More than 100 Million Women are Missing, *New York Review of Books,* December 20, 1990. vol. 37, number 20.

Steeten, P. and S.J. Burki. (1978). "Basic Needs: Some Issues" *World Development Report* 6 (3).

Sofo C. A. et al. (2003), *Measuring Poverty in Nigeria, Oxfam Programme Team,* Abuja, Nigeria.

Townsend, P. (ed.) (1974, *The Concept of Poverty*, London: Heinemann Educational Books.

Toyo, E. (1990), The Impact of SFEM on the Economic Development of the Population in Town and Country", in Olaniyan, et.al (eds.), *Structural Adjustment in Nigeria: The Impact of SFEM on the Economy*, Lagos: NIIA Press

UN Population Division, (2006) World Population Prospects: The 2004 Revision: Volume III: *Analytical Report;* www.un.org.

UNESCO (1995), *Basic Indicators on Young Children* [www.unesco.org/education/educprog/ ecf/html/chart/stats.htm].

UNICEF (1999), *The State of the World's Children 1999* [www.unicef.orf/sowc99].

UNICEF (2000), *The State of the World's Children 2000* [www.unicef.orf/sowc00].

U.S Department of State (1998), " Nigeria: Country Report on Human Rights Practices for 1998", Released by the Bureau of Democracy, Human Rights, and Labor, January, February 26, 1999

World Bank (1990), *World Development Report 1990: Poverty.* New York: Oxford University Press.

World Development Report (1990), "Mechanism for Poverty Reduction", the United Nations Impact Assessment.

World Bank (1993), Poverty Reduction Handbook, WB, Washington, D. C.

World Bank, (1994), *Adjustment in Africa: Reforms, Results and the Road Ahead*, A World bank Policy Research, New York: University Press

World Bank (1994), *World Development Report: Infrastructure for Development,* World Development Indicators, Oxford: Oxford University Press.

World Bank (1996), Nigeria: Poverty in the Midst of Plenty, The Challenge of Growth With Inclusion, WB, Washington, D. C.

World Bank (1998), "Poverty and Welfare in Nigeria", Washington, DC: American Writing Corporation.

World Bank (1999), "Nigeria: Poverty in the Midst of Plenty: The Challenge of Growth Inclusion", *World Bank Poverty Assessment Report,* May.

World Bank (1999), *Human Development Index,* New York: World Bank HDI Reports

World Bank (2000), *World Development Report,* Washington, D.C.: World Bank.Worldbank.org reference (2007).

ABOUT THE CONTRIBUTORS

Sani Lawal Malumfashi is a Senior Lecturer in the Department of Sociology, Bayero University, Kano, Nigeria and Sub Dean, Faculty of Social and Management Sciences in the same University. He specializes in Environmental and Industrial Sociology with research interest on Waste Management and Public health.

Shehu Usman Rano Aliyu,PhD, is an Associate Professor of Economics in the Department of Economics, Bayero University, Kano, Nigeria and Deputy Dean, Faculty of Social and Management Sciences in the same University. His research interest is in trade liberalization and international economic analysis.

Mohammed Sanni Abdulkadir, PhD, is a Professor of History at Bayero University, Kano, Nigeria and currently the Head, Department of History. His research interest is mainly in the area of economic and political history.

Kabiru Isa Dandago, PhD, ACA, is an Associate Professor of Accounting in the Department of Accounting, Bayero University, Kano, Nigeria. He is currently the Dean, Faculty of Social and Management Sciences in the same university. His research interest is in the areas of management accounting, auditing and taxation.

Murtala Sabo Sagagi, PhD, is a Senior Lecturer in Business Administration. He is currently the Head, Department of Business Administration, Bayero University, Kano, Nigeria. His research interest is in economic globalization, corporate strategies, strategic thinking and entrepreneurship.

Ahmed Audu Maiyaki is a Lecturer in the Department of Business Administration, Bayero University, Kano, Nigeria. Currently, he is the examination officer of the department. His research interest is in corporate marketing and strategic thinking.

Shehu Dalhatu, PhD, is an Associate Professor of Political Science in the Department of Political Science, Bayero University, Kano, Nigeria. He is currently the Dean, Students Affairs Division of the University. His research interest is in public administration, especially local government administration.

Garba Bala Bello, PhD, is a Senior Lecturer in the Department of Business Administration, Bayero University, Kano, Nigeria. He was a former Head of that Department. His research interest is Islamic Banking and Finance as well as Industrial Relations.

Balarabe Maikaba is a Senior Lecturer in Mass Communication Department, Bayero University, Kano, Nigeria. He specializes in Political Communication, Media Research, Electronic Media, Media Law and Documentary Production.

Fatima Oyine Ibrahim is a Senior Lecturer, Department of Political Science, Bayero University, Kano, Nigeria. She is a female students counselor in the university. Her research interest is in Gender and Women Empowerment, Peace Studies and Conflict resolution.

Mahmoud Mohammed Lawal is a Senior Lecturer, Department of Political Science, Bayero University, Kano, Nigeria. He is a Senate member representing the university congregation. He specializes in political economy, democratic process and whistle blowing.

Adamu Idris Tanko,PhD, FRGS, is an Associate Professor of Geography in the Department of Geography, Bayero University, Kano, Nigeria. He is a Senate member representing the university congregation. He specializes in soil analysis, environmental management and climate analysis. His research interest is in Development Geography and Environmental Management.

Kabiru Ahmed is a Professor of Geography at Bayero University, Kano, Nigeria. Currently, Professor Ahmed is the Deputy Vice Chancellor in charge of academic matters in the university. He was a Dean of the Faculty of Social and Management Sciences of the university. He specializes in water quality study and environmental management. His research interest is in water management and hydrology.

Habu Mohammed, PhD, is a Senior Lecturer in the Department of Political Sciences, Bayero University, Kano, Nigeria. He is the coordinator of the research project on poverty in the Faculty of Social and Management Sciences, Bayero University, Kano. His areas of specialization are Political Economy and Comparative Politics. His research interest is in Democracy and Civil Society.

Sadiq Isa Radda, PhD, is a Senior Lecturer and Head, Department of Sociology, Bayero University, Kano, Nigeria. His area of specialization is Criminology with specific interest in Human Right, Criminal Justice Agencies, Corporate Crime, and Youth Delinquent Behaviors.

Mustapha Muktar is a Lecturer in the Department of Economics, Bayero University, Kano, Nigeria. He is the coordinator of the research project on quantitative techniques in the Faculty of Social and Management Sciences, Bayero University, Kano. His research interest is in poverty reduction strategies and waste management.

Emmanuel Ajayi Olofin, PhD, is a Professor of Geography at Bayero University, Kano, Nigeria. He was a Dean of the Faculty of Social and Management Sciences of the university. He specializes in land administration and environmental management. His research interest is in Fluvial Geomorphology and Environmental Management.

INDEX

www.ingramcontent.com/pod-product-compliance
Lightning Source LLC
Chambersburg PA
CBHW080235270326
41926CB00020B/4245